Breaking the Cycle of
Educational Alienation

Breaking the Cycle of Educational Alienation

A multi-professional approach

Richard Williams and Colin Pritchard

Open University Press
Maidenhead   New York

Open University Press
McGraw-Hill Education
McGraw-Hill House
Shoppenhangers Road
Maidenhead
Berkshire
England
SL6 2QL

email: enquiries@openup.co.uk
world wide web: www.openup.co.uk

and Two Penn Plaza, New York, NY 10121-2289, USA

First published 2006

A catalogue record of this book is available from the British Library

ISBN-10: 0 335 21917 9 (pb)   0 335 21918 7 (hb)
ISBN-13: 978 0 335 21917 9 (pb)   978 0 335 21918 6 (hb)

Library of Congress Cataloguing-in-Publication Data
CIP data applied for

Typeset by BookEns Ltd, Royston, Herts.
Printed in Poland by OZGraf. S.A.
www.polskabook.pl

Contents

Preface   vi
Acknowledgements   ix

Part 1   Setting the scene   1

1   Social exclusion   3
2   The cycle of educational alienation: the evidence   13
3   'Drink, drugs and sex': media perception versus objective reality   23
4   A school-based solution: reaching the 'disaffected'   34
5   Becoming part of the solution: the family context. Outcomes   46
6   Comparing the project and control schools   57
7   Teachers as 'consumers'   62

Part 2   Meeting the needs   79

8   Maintaining/reaching disaffected pupils in mainstream schools   81
9   Special vulnerable groups: education and social inclusion   96
10   Attendance and truancy   116
11   All our children   138
12   Practical development for mainstream schools   152
13   Interagency liaison   180
14   A vision for children   186

Bibliography: A Resource   191
Index   209

Preface

I speak of a race of real children.
Not too good or wise, but bounded up and down by love and hate.
Oh may their early joys be nature and of books
And Knowledge, rightly honoured by that word,
Not purchased by the loss of power.

(Wordsworth, *The Prelude*)

Wordsworth's vision of children enjoying nature and completing an education that fulfils mind, body and spirit is an ideal worth pursuing. Yet practice and research teaches that a substantial minority are chained to a cycle of educational deprivation that is a barrier to the joys of education. Joys of education, you may exclaim? Are the authors serious about education being a joy when all we hear from the mass media are the inadequacies of education? Yet, there is evidence that the *majority* of children *do* like school (Rutter *et al.* 1979; Pritchard *et al.* 1986b; Pritchard 2001; Pritchard and Cox 2005) and for those of us who go on to higher education, a moment's reflection tells us that we have been given keys to the joys of nature and of books for a lifetime. Moreover, teaching is less of an occupation than a vocation because of the way in which it often touches the lives of children. Most of us can recall a teacher who touched our lives: opening the mysteries of mathematics; the marvel of the heavens and physics; the thrill at grasping the eternal humanity of Shakespeare. Teaching is a noble profession, and we leave a mark upon our pupils that can affect their lives as much as medicine can.

However, children and fellow citizens who remain educationally alienated have been left under achieving and with undeveloped talents. The authors were involved in a project that broke into this cycle and created a school–family alliance, which reduced truancy, delinquency and school exclusion in schools that suffered from chronic socioeconomic disadvantage. This was an innovative collaboration between an academic with strong practice links (Colin Pritchard) and a practitioner (Richard Williams) with an interest in evaluating what works. For whilst truancy, school exclusion, fighting, vandalism, drug and solvent misuse, bullying, theft, criminality, classroom disruption and teacher stress is predominantly associated with pupils who did not like school, when these youngsters began to enjoy school, much of this behaviour was substantially reduced. Moreover, liking school is as good a definition of breaking the cycle of educational alienation as one could wish.

The book adopts a practical approach and shows what can be achieved. The first third of the book (written by Colin) will tell this story, warts and all, and then moves on to Richard's contribution to the development of the project and the lessons learned. The principles discussed here are applicable for every school and teacher taking on the exciting challenge of making *Every Child Matters* (DfES 2003b) a reality, so that their new Ofsted responsibility to 'promote emotional health and well-being' will contribute to the education and development of 'healthy minds' (Ofsted 2005).

Teachers in the schools we work with still confront the challenges associated with inner-city disadvantage, with no advantage of selection, with serious funding problems and a significant minority of educationally alienated pupils, a situation familiar to many teachers. Nevertheless, the schools' practice seeks to include all children in the educational process and relies upon a progressive 'Social Inclusion Unit', led by Richard, who works directly with children with problems, ranging from the mildly disaffected to those with clear special educational needs.

This book offers a practical model for any mainstream school and is ahead of the field in that it is practising 'joined-up government', recommended in *Every Child Matters* (DfES 2003b). This report recognised the importance of the education–child protection continuum, which is at the heart of the Education Act 2005, and although it focused on school inspection it includes all forms of child care and how well schools promote the 'Healthy Minds' initiative (Ofsted 2005). It is therefore believed that the authors are almost uniquely placed to offer evidence-based material to enable classroom teachers to respond to their new responsibilities inherent in the education–child protection interface, which is at the core of social exclusion and potential inclusion.

We are realistic, and whilst the 'big politics' needed to deal with structural socio-economic disadvantage is outside the scope of this book, the 'small politics' of improving individuals and their areas via the school-in-the-community is practicable as it reaches out to individual children and families, empowering them to make life choices which can free them from the chain of intergenerational psychosocial disadvantage.

Rather than produce a homogenised text, we have written in our own style to provide the reader with a sense of the immediacy of day-to-day practice, shorn of the usual academic gloss, so that Richard can 'tell it as it is', since so many 'experts' and commentators have been away from the classroom too long.

Acknowledgements

Our intellectual indebtedness will become clear in the text. But, as will be shown, an effective educational and community-orientated school to meet the challenges facing teachers must involve different agencies and disciplines relevant to services for children, and we must express our indebtedness to many colleagues who have guided and developed our thinking in how to get children to enjoy school.

We are very grateful for the generous help of Nigel Bowes, Mark Whitby, M. J. Patterson, Tim Watts, Sylvia Whitaker, Lyn Clarke, Brian Traves, Philip Mullings, Tara Civil, Dana Leake, Hayley Carney, Terry Scragg, Chris Deshpande, Pratap Deshpande, Amanda Jarvis, Andrew Whelen, Carolyn Godfrey, Dawn Gibbs, Jill Davey, Pam Small, Hilary Evans, Chris Harvey, Sanjay Sunak, Tess Mariner, Graham Davies, Phil Corbin, Becky Brookwell.

Acknowledgements can be formulaic but without the tolerance, professionalism, understanding, humour, love and support of our partners, Beryl Pritchard and Fiona O'Regan, this text would have been considerably poorer. Finally we dedicate this text to 'Joe' Williamson who was committed to 'giving every child a chance'.

Part 1
Setting the scene

1   Social exclusion

Background

The book lies within the debate about social exclusion and inclusion and offers education professionals a model that can bring about change, facilitating the teacher's primary goal of educating children and improving their chances of appropriate social inclusion. We recognise that the school seeks to reach all children: the average, the gifted, or the potential/actually disaffected child. The text outlines the initial creation of a school-based 'healthy alliance' that linked the main 'inclusion' stakeholders of education, health, police and social services. This approach was a forerunner of *Every Child Matters* (DfES 2003b), and argued for greater awareness of the indivisibility of the education–child protection continuum.

Government has increasingly recognised that the pursuit of social justice demands that we seek to be an inclusive rather than an excluding society, exemplified by the Social Inclusion Unit of the Cabinet Office. This reflects a growing consensus in Western societies that no child should be left behind, and though it is easy to be cynical about such aspirations, which if inadequately funded are just so much spin, nonetheless it has echoes with the very greatest educational ideals, as Saint Ignatius Loyola knew: 'Give me the child until seven and I will give you the man'. Whilst this dictum can carry dark overtones of indoctrination, it contains a crucial truth. Inculcate a self-belief in children, provide them with opportunities to test out and expand their capacities and curiosities, encourage them to think for themselves, and you will have provided the maximum opportunity for those individuals to achieve their full potential. Conversely it is possible to bring children up in a society that infers that they are of little worth, and to suppress their natural curiosity; to 'teach' them that as their parents barely identified with education, they do not need to do so either. They may only be exposed to the sort of limited reading material provided by tabloid newspapers. The result at best will be compliant, docile, limited adults, whose potential was strangled almost from birth, or at worst angry, frustrated individuals who feel excluded from a society that blames them for not achieving the outcome it expects.

Realistically, apart from the remote chance of becoming a 'celebrity' as a result of an exceptional talent, such as on the football pitch, the media fame they dream about is a chimera and the most likely outcome for educational under achievers is that they are chronically marginalised by society for being virtually unemployable. Without an occupation in Western society, you are a non-person. Educational underachievers can expect at best a poorly paid job, with few opportunities to exercise their minds, few prospects, chronic threat of unemployment or, at worst, taking an 'alternative market economic response' via crime, drugs and/or sex working, which compounds their situation, exposing them to a range of health risks and further social exclusion. Yet if 'every child matters' then we would ensure that all children have an education enabling them to optimise their potential. This is not a utopian pipe dream, but is achievable for the vast majority. Moreover, in society's own interests, we cannot afford to leave a substantial minority of children under-educated to be the continued victims of the cycle of deprivation (Audit Commission 1998). An inadequate education means a further twist to the vicious circle, adding yet another victim who, inadequately equipped for our complex and technological world, perpetuates the sorry chain. And since the teacher is at the front line of the battle to reach such children, he or she must successfully contribute to the protection of the next generation of children.

Successive governments are seeking 'joined-up government', and education is central to providing future citizens with the opportunity to maximise their talents and be capable of responding positively to the ever-changing world we live in. Indeed, within the National Curriculum there are principles for social inclusion, which are now a clear responsibility for teacher and school. The debate around social inclusion and social exclusion, however, is complex, not least because of the ambiguity of the term, which for different actors have very different meanings, epitomised by this quotation from the Scottish Office:

> Social exclusion is shorthand for what happens when individuals or areas suffer from a combination of linked problems such as unemployment, poor skills, low incomes, poor housing, high crime environment, bad health and family breakdown.
>
> (1998: 2)

Such a graphic picture is familiar to the authors as more than 40 per cent of the pupils in the schools and project within which they work live in such socially excluded families, in a relatively chronic disadvantaged area, where local fathers still have an unemployment rate more than twice that of the regional average. From research projects, which crossed the education, health, social services and criminal justice boundaries, it emerged that the various 'client' groups of the different agencies all had linked educational problems (Farringdon 1995; Pritchard 2001). For example, the child of a father with a criminal record, on probation, will typically be an educational underachiever, alienated from education at the start of his own disruptive behaviour, who was also a victim of the intergenerational cycle of psychosocial disadvantage, resulting in another troubled and troublesome young boy. Our disaffected youngster will already be stealing, smoking from an early age and truanting. He will be a nuisance to himself and others and, of course, without any model at home, will have little aspiration to realise his potential.

Another typical example is the overwhelmed single parent, whose own drug habit, in part an attempt to self-medicate against her continued feelings of low self-worth, is now part of her dependent personality. She has little emotional energy to give her own daughter, resulting in another confused, angry, out-of-control, troubled and disturbing pupil. Looking at her background one often finds she comes from an equally disrupted and chaotic home, with little or no parental involvement, leading to desultory engagement with education, early truancy, smoking, early sexual experience, and an early 'attachment' with another young, often equally unstable, adult. She leaves her unhappy home and, having children early, finds not the love and affection she craved but her children's overwhelming emotional demands, which compounds her situation. Her daughter is in danger of repeating her mother's lifestyle, often ganging up with equally disaffected young people, adding to the school's burden, and resulting in a range of anti-social disruptive behaviour.

Then there are the aggressive parents, who call upon the school and, even before you have met them, accuse you and the school of being prejudiced, in part because their own alienated experience was little more than a form of state 'childminding'. Their encounter with education was that it was not for them; they perceived school as being the preserve of the 'posh', the middle-classes. The trouble with this type of parent is they can so easily irritate the people who can best help them, because much of their anger is fuelled by the half-realisation that education is important and they want the best for their child. But they do not know how to go about it. Paradoxically, such parents are potential allies, if teachers can reach across the barriers and engage them in a meaningful dialogue about their child.

These typical examples are what the criminologists, sociologists and politicians really mean about people who are socially excluded and whose children are often reluctant to go to school. Our common aim is, where possible, to ensure that our reluctant children join the majority of their peers and learn to enjoy school. And the good news should be declared at the outset: over the years we have found that the *majority* of primary and secondary school children from 'ordinary' homes generally like school (Rutter *et al.* 1979; Pritchard *et al.* 1986a, 1997; Pritchard 2001; Pritchard and Cox 2005), and this majority can be extended.

Social inclusion, not exclusion

The incoming slogan of the 1997 Blair government was 'Education, Education, Education.' It meant many different things to many people and we would not be human if some of us in education did not assume that there would a rectification of salary shortfalls, and the need to improve social respect for teachers (Rhodes *et al.* 2004). Underlying the slogan is the belated recognition of the centrality of education as a means of resolving a range of social and economic problems. Mr Blair had come to public prominence with his catchy slogan 'Tough on crime and tough on the causes of crime', an approach which could unite the left and right and made a broad appeal to the public who have, at best, a somewhat vague appreciation that not all criminals are simply evil but sometimes simply caught up in crime as a result of circumstances that reduce their choice (Audit Commission 1998). What Mr Blair realised was that 8 per cent of all offenders are responsible for more than 85 per cent of recorded crime and that the association with educational underachievement is beyond question (Barr and Pearce 1992; Audit Commission 1996; Cox 2003; Brooks-Gunn and Leventhal 2004; Smith and Farrington 2004).

It was appreciated that the school is the one universal provision that reaches every child, and it is where the state meets 'normal' children and their families. Consequently, the Blair government must be given credit for acknowledging that some crime and ill-health problems have social origins that can and need to be addressed (DoH 1998; Audit Commission 1998). The creation of the Social Inclusion Unit attached to the Cabinet Office was the clearest manifestation that government intended to deal with something of the 'causes of crime' in order to be 'tough on crime' and, in a number of key reports on socially excluded children and young people, the school was central to changing their exclusion into social inclusion (Social Inclusion Unit 1998a, b, c).

The philosophy and the politics of social inclusion

There are few subjects today more likely to put off the student than 'politics'. But in truth, politics should be the practical means of implementing a vision, or ideology, or philosophy of the nature of the society in which we would live; as the poet says, 'Where there is no vision, the people perish' (*Proverbs*, 29:18). There are real benefits in understanding how policies emerge, which is the practical process that evolves from a philosophy of a 'vision of society'. And if one agrees with the philosophy, the practicalities of that policy – in this case education – are recognised as beneficial.

One policy the overwhelming majority of British people support is that of the National Health Service (NHS). Today the NHS is claimed to be central to the thinking of the main political parties, Conservative, Labour and Liberal Democrats. Indeed, even the minor parties, for example the Scottish and Welsh Nationalists, Sinn Fein and Democratic Unionist Party in Northern Ireland, agree that the NHS is a good thing. The only arguments that arise are about how the NHS should be funded. Moreover, contrary to the media perception, our NHS is doing better than many other countries in reducing mortality: for example England and Wales has reduced cancer deaths over the past quarter-century even more than the USA (Pritchard and Galvin 2006). In the case of education, though some might argue for a greater degree of 'freedom' for private education, as with health, the majority are committed to a national form of education for most children, and we do better than the media portrays, although we could do even better.

This practical consensus in British politics has long been recognised, as even at a time of the divisive ideologies rampant in the 1960s and 1970s, the political arguments on issues like education and health overlapped (Pritchard and Taylor 1978, 1981). Hence the 'governmental' agency, in our case the school, was part of the ideological objective to shape society along the lines of a particular political philosophy, creating a degree of consensus because it appeared to achieve common goals.

More recently, Levitas (1998) in a brilliant analysis explored the underlying philosophies of social inclusion, which is generally perceived to be 'a good thing': are any of our party leaders likely to argue against social inclusion? Indeed as Farrell and Ainsow (2002: 1) point out, all policy makers recognise the 'need to move in a more inclusive direction'. The problem is that social inclusion means different things to those with different ideological perspectives and varied objectives, as Levitas outlined succinctly.

Her simple mnemonic helps us remember the three underlying 'ideologies', of Left, Centre and Right. It is RED for the left, which Ruth Levitas calls the *Red*istributionalists, SID for the *Social Integration Discourse* of the centrists, and the MUD commentators reflecting the right-wing philosophy of Charles Murray (2000), who suggested that most social problems were due to a 'social underclass', the *Moral*

Underclass Discourse. The work of Charles Murray recalls the contro-versies of the 1960s when psychologists such as Eysenck suggested that there were innate differences in intelligence amongst the ethnic groups (Eysenck 1971). Now it is appreciated that IQ tests, while useful, are limited, not least by their cultural specificity, so that the average 'outback' aboriginal teenager, who might stumble on confronting the Western 'Wechler's Verbal Intelligence Test', would survive in the Australian outback, while the majority of computer-technocratic competent Western youths would be dead within twenty-four hours. Indeed, the 'street wisdom' of some of the most disadvantaged children is remarkably culturally specific – one can only wonder if the average well-adjusted middle-class child would continue to appear competent if he or she changed places with his/her disadvantaged peer (Barnes 2000)?

The MUD position is essentially conservative in the classic sense of the word. In effect it accepts society as it is but seeks to correct any deviant members and positively ameliorate any imperfections in society, not wishing to leave members without remedy.

Murray's position is to infer an intrinsic moral turpitude of dysfunctional people and argue that society needs to be protected from them (Murray 2000; see also David 2000). Whilst the MUDs do not propose a 'war' on such people, they do not ask the question: how did they come to be so dysfunctional in the first place? In short, while keen on being 'tough on crime', they are less concerned with the 'causes of crime', taking an almost Kantian position that the mature human being has a right to punishment, otherwise we treat the offender as less than a fully responsible human being (Barnes 2000; Green 2001). However, to be fair to a number of successive Conservative governments, their rhetoric is somewhat more punitive than their practice in specific situations. And, of course, the MUD position is totally congruent with the objective of social inclusion. If individuals can learn to see the error of their ways, then they can resume the rights of full citizenship. Again, in terms of equity, the traditional MUD position accepts that a minority of people, due to severe illness, incapacity, physical or mental disability, will need state aid to maintain themselves in the bare necessities of life. Whilst initially Winston Churchill fought the advent of the NHS, on returning to power he accepted that it was the 'will of the people' and, as Margaret Thatcher once famously said, 'The NHS is safe in our hands.' Incidentally, under Edward Heath's 1970s Conservative government, proportionately more of Gross Domestic Product (GDP) was spent on education than any by other government before or since (Pritchard and Cunliffe 1983).

The *Social Integration Discourse* (SID) reflects the classic 'liberal' tradition, arguing for involving the citizen, and recognising some imperfections in society, seeking to improve individuals' chances, to enable them to rejoin society and, on the way, improve their position in society. For the SID commentator, getting people into employment is a key objective, for the benefit of all. More recently, the Liberal Democrats, recognising the accumulative shortfalls of successive governments in resources for education, famously said they would increase income tax by a penny in every pound, for education. They realised that to improve our educational system, and to give every child a chance, and to improve society, we need adequate resources. What few political commentators ever mention is that Britain does extremely well in terms of educational outcomes relative to educational inputs, which we believe is due to the quality and commitment of frontline teachers, who do not get the credit they deserve. Nonetheless the SID position seeks to improve society through assisting the individual to enter the market/workplace, appreciating that without a job one is a non-person in our society.

The RED philosophical position (*Redistributionalist*) basically differs from the other two in that it starts from the premise that society needs to be changed. To do that there has to be a greater degree of equitable distribution of national wealth, to enable people to grasp an equality of opportunity, which means policies should not only be aimed at reducing poverty, but at restructuring society on a fairer basis, to ensure equal opportunity in the market/workplace. Bearing in mind that the UK had the highest rate of relative child poverty in the 15 European Union member states, which the present government are committed to reducing, there is much to do. Although there is no absolute poverty in Britain compared to that of the street people in India, or those living in shanty towns in Africa or Peru, for example, if children and their families do not have sufficient for what are seen as the basics in their society then they suffer in comparison with their peers, and their morale is significantly lowered. As George Bernard Shaw says, 'As with Poverty it is easy, terribly easy to shake a man's faith in himself', and as is long known from educational research, it is children's expectations, as much their natural ability, which leads to their achievement. This is relevant not just to children from ethnic minorities, as discussed in Ofsted (1989), but to all children (DfEE 2003a). Which in part goes some way to explain the tirade of anger heard from Barnes (2000a), who claims that 'educational reforms are a fraud', as they ignore the 'social class' issues. Certainly there is evidence that youths who are 'excluded' quickly find themselves part of the 'underclass' (McDonald 1997; Pritchard and Butler 2000a; Lindjord 2001). Therefore children from families that have few or low expectations of education are unlikely to benefit, whereas parents who have already benefited from education will go to the greatest lengths to ensure that their children have every chance to maximise their potential.

Every year one of us gives an introductory lecture to two hundred or more second-year medical students, in a large lecture theatre but using a seminar-type presentation, with questions, answers and discussion. There are no pedagogic difficulties and it is relatively easy because the students have high expectations and commitment, whereas the same author struggled to hold a class of 4D school leavers together when trying to introduce the topic of equal opportunities. Thus the RED commentators would essentially wish to change, rather than improve or ameliorate society, and this is where the ideological debate lies. Where the three orientations converge is in the desire for social inclusion for all but, as Levitas showed, politicians will interpret social inclusion differently.

One problem for the SID and the RED orientations is the concern expressed by Zunz *et al.* (2000) that the 'social contract' around 'social inclusion' is under stress by a 'middle class' in the USA, Japan and Europe, who are increasingly reluctant to support the necessary changes and resources. It seems to us that for the majority of taxpayers, only with an evidence-based approach, will justify their financial contribution, but, as we shall see, such evidence exists.

Practicalities

What are the practical outcomes of this debate so far? The creation of the Social Inclusion Units was an early initiative of the Blair government and the then Department for Education and Employment (DfEE), which issued draft guidelines concerning social inclusion and how to support vulnerable pupils (DfEE 1999). Incidentally, it should be noted that the notion that the Department for Education is crucially concerned with employment indicates a serious commitment to the SID position, especially as it is now the Department for Education and Skills (DfES).

The DfEE (1999) recognised that there were specific groups of pupils at risk: the non-attender, the classic truant, which we discuss later; children from families under stress, including physical and psychological 'poverty'; youngsters who are showing emotional and behavioural difficulties; African–Caribbean boys, and Travellers' children, who are identified as being at potential risk, in part because they reflect the clash of cultures. Last, but equally important, are young people in transition and/or in the care of the local authority, now described as 'looked-after children' of the local authority.

This has had a considerable impact on the concerns of policy makers, head teachers and their colleagues. It has in effect extended the concept of children with special educational needs (SEN), which in the past were seen as rather special in the sense of being unusual minorities, almost along the MUD and SID approach, whereas the new emphasis of the DfES is much more SID and RED in that they are seeing the SEN sector as also being concerned with inclusion (O'Brien 2001) and the SEN framework has in effect been expanded to involve inclusion issues. Self-evidently, while numerically Travellers' children are not numerous, their peripatetic lifestyle poses particular educational problems of continuity. African–Caribbean youngsters, on the other hand, as well as children from other minorities such as the Hindu and Islamic tradition, have to battle with competing cultures and sometimes overt racial prejudice in many parts of our major cities. The new emphasis for schools and teachers will be on providing an 'effective learning opportunity for all pupils' (DfEE 2003), so the frontline teacher will need to be aware of these competing pressures and sensitive to them. Bearing in mind the range of pupils considered at risk, this promises to be a formidable responsibility for the teacher, and one which is perhaps as yet not fully understood by the profession. Indeed, one of the purposes of this text is to bring together some common themes that can assist the teacher in dealing with children whose families are in crisis, be it legal, psychological, financial or psychiatric. This is irrespective of whether or not it involves child protection issues, or children from minority cultures whose family first language is not English, while from another perspective, those children recently or currently being looked after by the local authority, which currently stands at around 50,000 per annum (DfES 2003c), will pose another set of demands for the school – overall a formidable list indeed.

The implications of 'social inclusion' to provide 'effective learning opportunities for all pupils' will be different from the recent past, as previously the child was seen as being at the centre of the educational process; now, by implication, the school and its results will have an equal claim in terms of outcomes. The teacher not only has responsibilities to the child but also wider responsibilities to the class and, to a lesser extent, the school. Certainly the head teacher's role was to attempt to merge these tripartite responsibilities, but as the wider good of the class and the school begins to take precedence, it is a classic example of a clash of rights. Hence, albeit reluctantly, for the 'good of the school', 'tearaway Johnny' would have been excluded from mainstream education as he was thought to be unmanageable in an ordinary educational setting. Under the new regulations and orientation, this may well prove more contentious, and aggrieved parents might well be within their rights to argue that the school did not meet their child's particular needs appropriately. So in practical terms, the teacher will no longer primarily be a manager of a class, a group worker, but potentially more of a counsellor, as the focus turns more upon the individual child whose situation and background is less typical. Not that this will be a 'bad thing' providing resources and appropriate training are available. The following chapters will show that, unless we meet the child's needs, the result may be, as the poet says, that 'The villainy that you teach me will I execute and it shall go hard but I will better the instruction' (Shakespeare, *The Merchant of Venice*).

In terms of human rights and fiscal probity, education is expensive but ignorance is more so, and we cannot afford to leave any child behind.

2 The cycle of educational alienation: the evidence

The most exciting aspect of the green paper *Every Child Matters* (DfEE 2003b) is that it reflects the accumulative research wisdom of the past thirty years, that neither man nor child is an island and that every child's lack of optimal fulfilment diminishes everyone. This has been found in many studies across the disciplines. For example, the Audit Commission (1996) rediscovered, as it were, the 'cycle of deprivation', which had long been out of 'political favour' as the 'MUD' orientation was the dominant paradigm during the previous ten years. The Audit Commission, with its economic and fiscal orientation, saw that children and youths who ended up in the courts and prisons very often came from families with a history of clashes with the law. At another end of the spectrum Dr Jack Oliver, a paediatrician from 'leafy, sleepy Wiltshire', noted that he was dealing with the children or grandchildren of former patients whom the hospital had treated for a range of accidents or frequent serious illnesses well above the statistical average, often inadequately dealt with by failing parents (Oliver 1983, 1985, 1988). His study, 'Five generations of mishandled children', epitomised intergenerational problems. Associated with such difficulties was school attendance, or lack of it, and in a classic longitudinal study of working-class children born in 1958, these Wiltshire children still had an above-average incidence of educational alienation (West and Farrington 1973; Ingoldsby and Shaw 2002; Andersen and Cheung 2003; Hill 2003; Thornberry *et al.* 2003; Flouri and Buchanan 2004; Hogland and Leadbeater 2004; Phillips *et al.* 2004; Bennett *et al.* 2005; Smith and Farrington 2004).

Yet life is not so simple, as even with three or four risk factors some are not involved in anti-social behaviour (Farrington 1995). Positive life events can be a mediating feature; as Pitts (2005) reminds us, we deal with individuals, not statistical tables. Hence the individual teacher, social worker or involved person can and does make a difference even when the odds seem stacked against the youngster.

We explore, albeit in a schematic way, research from the educational, psychosocial and medical fields, factors which lead to children's educational alienation, which are so often a repetition of their families' negative experience of education.

The family

A brilliant study by Flouri and Buchanan (2004) brings to life longitudinal data from the National Child Development Study of children born in 1958. They looked at 7-year-olds in their families and highlighted the importance of parental involvement with the child, not only with regard to physical, psychological and social development but also how this involvement *impacted upon the child's education*. They were able to show that active parental involvement could predicate educational outcome at 20, although it was not as strong for boys as it was for girls. More involvement generally corresponded with a better outcome at 20. Interestingly, however, they found that not growing up in intact families did not weaken the association of parental involvement with education, providing the now separate parents continued to take an interest in the child.

A key feature is that family factors interact with the others, influencing educational and delinquent outcomes (Farrington 1995), while Knapp *et al.* (2002) found that the costs of the breakdown in child–family relations to the child and the community were extensive in terms of social disruption and often caused other psychosocial problems to be carried into adulthood.

Moreover, family influence and parenting styles last over genera-tions (Smith and Farrington 2004), confirming the general findings of Wiltshire paediatrician Dr Jack Oliver (1985,1988). Children 'inherit' poverty as they might do wealth and genetic predispositions from their parents. Sadly, this is not just socio-economic poverty but poverty of mind and spirit, while negative parenting styles are associated with a lack of engagement in the classroom (Glasgow *et al.* 1997). Thus, if parents have been alienated from education, often their children are too. Nonetheless, as Thornberry *et al.* (2003) have shown, while anti-social behaviour and poor educational achievement spans the generations, it is parenting styles and financial income that can play an important mediating role. Cole *et al.* (2004) show the importance of parents in particularly poor outcomes when children have to be removed from their parents, and are looked after by the local authority. While there have been improved outcomes in children needing to be looked-after, they still tend to lag behind their age and ability peers (Pritchard and Butler 2000a; Weyts 2004). However, Richman *et al.* (2003) showed that support from peers, neighbourhood and teachers can ameliorate matters to a degree, though the gap remains.

The 'traditional' family of children and two parents has changed rapidly over the past 30 years. For example, in 1985 81 per-cent of 14- to 16-year-olds lived in 'intact' families; by 2005 this figure was 74 per-cent

(Pritchard and Cox 2005). In effect we are living at a time of 'social revolution' as child-rearing patterns are changing. However, what matters is the degree of commitment the child receives in terms of education; in female-headed households, the mother's attitude and expectations of education were the key to the children's educational response, and it was this commitment that compensated for the absence of a father (Sherraden and Zhan 2003). Crucially, the difficulties of teenage mothers can be eased somewhat if they are supported by the child's father (Roye and Balk 1996). Nonetheless, few of us are fully equipped for modern life in our teens and the *ability* of a mother who is little more than a child herself to meet a child's needs is severely limited. Sadly, Britain faces a significantly bigger problem of teenage pregnancies than the rest of the European Union (Social Exclusion Unit 1998a), an outcome that is more common among teenagers who did not like school (Bonnell *et al.* 2005). Recently it was found that as many as 29 per cent of year 10 and 11 girls report having had sexual intercourse (Pritchard and Cox 2005), often unplanned and associated with 'binge' drinking (Bellis *et al.* 2002), while the 'family' link with undesirable behaviour, truancy, theft, early sex, drugs and so on, was more prevalent in children whose parents smoked (Pritchard and Cox 2005).

Socio-economic/social class and ethnicity

Families operate within their particular socio-economic and social class situation, which impacts upon their life chances and their children's educational opportunities (Farrington 1995; Smith and Farrington 2004). Socio-economic poverty *per se* is a burden upon mind and spirit. As George Bernard Shaw wrote, 'Poverty blights all who come within its purview', and even in the USA, the world's richest country, poverty has a devastating impact upon children's educational achievement, which perpetuates a negative economic 'ecological' chain (Jozefowicz-Simbeni and Allen-Meares 2002). Some from the MUD persuasion suggest or infer a 'natural' selectivity, arguing that the 'poor will always be with us', but a brief historical reflection demonstrates the absurdity of the position. A hundred years ago the author's ancestors would have been described as 'the lower orders', and perhaps you or your parents were the first of your families to have attained university education. Conversely, even belonging to the 'royal ruling classes' does not guarantee educational achievement, as one struggled to meet minimum requirements to become an army officer. In societies throughout the world there is a clear link with economic inequality, social capital and educational achievement being inversely correlated (Muntaner *et al.* 2002). Indeed, it has been shown that lowering the risk of infant deaths associated with low birth weight is more successful in countries which have more politically Liberal women in government, which in turn is linked to stronger welfare systems (Muntaner *et al.* 2002). Low birth weight and poor antenatal care are almost surrogate measures for low social class. This is associated with a raft of negative psycho-health outcomes, described as the 'foetal origin of disease' in adulthood (Barker 2003), while poor health outcomes in both Britain and the USA have long been associated with relative socio-economic poverty (Heyderman *et al.* 2004; Levi *et al.* 2004; Mensah *et al.* 2005). Andersen and Cheung (2003) showed that though social class and family income were less important for *young* children's early educational prowess, they were strongly linked to *eventual* university graduation. Thus, bright youngsters in the 'wrong' social class deteriorate relative to their middle-class peers in educational achievement.

These features overlap with issues of ethnicity. Compared with twenty or thirty years ago, Britain, as a multicultural society, is now far less overtly prejudiced, although the way people see themselves and are seen by others with regard to their ethnicity still impact upon their self-worth (Thompson and Pritchard 1987; Killen *et al.* 2002). But today, ethnicity is less important than the socio-economic status of the family. It has been shown that the achievement of children in African–American families with two parents depends more upon their social class than their ethnic origin. The autobiography of the first black American Secretary of State, Colin Powell (1995), is a fascinating study of how ability and the key influences of family and school overcame traditional barriers. Nonetheless, if we compare Powell's experience with the British situation, one wonders how many black British generals we have, leading us to question how far we still have to go before 'every child matters' and their potential is maximised?

Housing/neighbourhood

The neighbourhood in which a child lives is strongly associated with educational adjustment, for better or worse, as economically poorer neighbourhoods have poorer educational results. Ainsworth (2002) demonstrated that the school–family and neighbourhood link ac-counted for up to 40 per cent of the child's eventual educational outcome. In effect, neighbourhood is more than just 'housing' but is vitally concerned with social inclusion (Stewart and Rhoden 2003). The mechanisms are interrelated not only with socio-economic but also psychological factors: Targosz *et al.* (2003) showed an important link with depression in isolated lone mothers, which in turn impacts upon their children's psychosocial development (Pritchard 2006). Boys in particular are more vulnerable to the 'wrong' ambience, especially if exposed to domestic and community violence and a high rate of background crime (Ingoldsby and Shaw 2002). Inevitably this affects their educational engagement. However, it is not all negative; Brooks-Gunn and Leventhal (2004) found that while neighbourhood affects low-income children, moving out of a poor area is associated with improved educational outcomes (though girls appear to benefit more than boys). The most extreme manifestation of this is when young people become homeless. Rebecca Pritchard of Centre Point, the largest charity for homeless teenagers, graphically describes the problems facing homeless youngsters. A common theme for many of these young people was educational alienation, which was a key contributor to their current situation (Pritchard 2006). Efforts to reintegrate these young people focus upon trying to engage them in the educational/vocational process to improve their life chances (Pritchard 2006).

Personality (psycho-biological)

'No man is an island' said John Donne, and family and socio-economic environment obviously influence personal psychological development, while relationships between parents and children are crucial (Flouri and Buchanan 2004). The power of personal relationships cannot be overstated as those of us know who are fortunate enough to have had parents who loved us, and who demonstrated that essential parental attribute of 'altruism', no matter how imperfect it seemed to us as adolescents. Equally, many can recall a particular teacher whose relationship with us made such a difference to the way we saw their subject. Indeed, in a classic but under-appreciated study, Rutter and Quinton (1984) looked at the life outcomes of some of the most socially excluded children of their day – girls from orphanages of the 1960s. As parents approximately 30 per cent of these women proved to be equally competent mothers as their social class peers, which was associated with their having a key stable personal relationship with a 'significant other'. Another third of the women, while having some problems, were coping and this was associated with having a significant other in their lives as adolescents, often a school teacher, sometimes a social worker. Sadly, the remaining women repeated the disasters that had led them to be taken into care in the first place, and they lacked any significant sustaining personal relationship in their lives.

One area of development is that of the influence of the child's genetic endowment. This has been controversial since the days of

Eysenck (1972) and his crude, crypto-racist presentation of the contribution that the bio-physiological makes to the development of the person. The use of cultural specific 'IQ' tests, which spuriously suggested that different ethnic groups were more or less intelligent, brought the whole area of study into disrepute. Conversely, there was the 'nurture' orientation that denied any 'nature' influence, though for us the 'nurture versus nature' debate is redundant as more and more research shows that we are a product of the constant interaction of both (Pinker 1997; Wilson 1998). Wilson's work in particular brings together the social and biological sciences, reflecting the philosopher Karl Popper's great synthesis of the 'self and its brain' (Eccles and Popper 1974). A key element in the contribution of genetic factors is seen in a small minority of children who have behavioural problems from a very young age, rather than, say, from age 8 or 9, when they appear to be responding to the interaction of lack of poor parenting and/or psychosocial pressures (Hill 2003). This is seen in studies where early hyperactivity is associated with later anti-social behaviour in adolescence, which often continues into adulthood (Simonoff *et al.* 2004). Interestingly, the 'other' side of the interaction of environment on genetic endowment is the ideas put forward by MacDonald and Leary (2005). They found that when the youngster experienced 'social exclusion/isolation', either from peers or from adults around them, the centre of the brain which reacted to the 'social embarrassment' was close to the brain's pain centres. This may account for the often extreme overreaction and aggression to what to most would be thought of as a minor social threat so that a 'social hurt' is felt as a 'physical hurt'; the person is thus more inclined to respond with flight or, sadly, more often a fight reaction.

The strength of twin studies cannot be ignored. Taylor *et al.* (2000) presented evidence of early onset of delinquency; if it occurred in one twin, it more often occurred in the 'identical' (monozygotic) twin, who shared the same genetic inheritance, rather than dizygotic twins, who are genetically only as alike as siblings. Yet a genetic endowment does not mean unchangeable attributes. Indeed, as any physiological textbook shows, there is seldom more than an 80 per cent physiological concordance between monozygotic twins, and when it comes to issues of personality, the figure is often well below 50 per cent (Wilson 1998; Kendler *et al.* 2000; Hay 2001; Holmes *et al.* 2001). Yet, at the other extreme, even twins who were adopted early both experienced premature deaths as adults, showing the inherited disadvantage persisting, albeit in the physical area (Petersen *et al.* 2004).

When it comes to educational achievement Walker *et al.* (2004) acknowledged the interaction of 'nurture and nature' but found that among a set of 1189 pairs of twins the monozygotic genetic contribution to their maths and English results accounted for almost twice the level found in dizygotic twins. Plomin and Walker (2003) argue that educational psychology is just beginning to take note of the link between genetics and learning disabilities, including reading disability. For us the implications are practical. If a youngster is truanting, it is rather like the patient who goes to see the doctor with a headache. Is the headache due to too much drink the night before, or a mild viral infection, or is it meningitis? So too for the 'symptom' of truancy: is it an isolated incident, or is there an acute but temporary problem with the pupil, the class, or the pupil's family? Or could it be more profound and long-lasting, possibly with a heavier genetic weighting which was demonstrated from the earliest days? If so, then we need to do much more intensive work with such children in order to compensate them for their 'double jeopardy'. After all, the example of the young prince showed what intensive individualised care could achieve: he overcame any innate or/ and family disadvantage, to reach the level of an Army officer.

One particular problem facing teachers is that of attention difficulties and hyperactivity in children, designated as Attention Deficit Hyperactivity Disorder (ADHD).

How big a problem is this in British schools? Pasteror and Reuban (2002) report that 3 per cent of all US children have been designated as suffering from ADHD, which is itself associated with learning disorder/ disability. Thapar *et al.* (2001) have argued that ADHD is slightly different from what child psychiatrists call 'conduct disorder', suggesting that ADHD has a stronger genetic link or is caused by an underlying physiological problem.

Merrell and Tymms (2001) showed that a child with ADHD had significantly lower reading and maths achievement compared to children with low or virtually zero ADHD scores. Taking a wider perspective, Danckaerts *et al.* (2000) found that ADHD children's social adjustment was worse than non-ADHD children but, interestingly, they did not find any link with drug misuse in adolescence or lowered self-esteem.

Kristensen and Smith (2003) ask whether the syndrome could be linked to 'institutional' deprivation, as they found marked differences when comparing Romanian and UK disadvantaged adoptees with non-disadvantaged adoptees in the UK when tested at 6 years. Moreover, they found that over-activity and inattention was *not* always linked to low birth but rather correlated with attachment disturbances. Thus a physical factor influences and is influenced by the environmental. Nothing is more dangerous than for professionals to misunderstand their experience or anecdotal evidence. Notwithstanding, one of us practised in child psychiatry in the 1960s where about 1 per cent of clients were diagnosed as having 'minimal cerebral dysfunction'. This meant that their behaviour was erratic, with a poor attention span and hyperactivity, but was apparently of an organic rather than a psychological nature. Today ADHD is the 'minimal cerebral dysfunction' of yesterday and accounts for one of the largest number of referrals to the caseload of many child mental health teams. Another 'rare' condition was the apathetic, listless patient with symptoms that were considered as possible psychological concomitants of glandular fever; today we have a substantial minority of youngsters with 'chronic fatigue syndrome'. Both of these former rare conditions raise the question of whether these are the end product of multiple environmental pollutants, which at the extreme have been found to be correlated with (though not necessarily caused by) changing patterns of the incidence of malignant neoplasms and brain disease (Pritchard and Evans 2000; Pritchard *et al.* 2004; Pritchard and Sunak 2005). It is reiterated that anecdotal evidence should always be viewed extremely cautiously, but the marked changes in young people's behaviour noted over the past 20 years (Pritchard and Cox 2005) may have other causes than social change.

Peers and bullying

After parents, as any parent of over-5s will tell you, the child's peers are crucially important to them. One consequence of this is an association with anti-social behaviour in adolescents who are rejected by their peers, either because of being a bully or being bullied (Laird *et al.* 2001). This bullying–bullied dyad is complex and the profile of victims and non-victims of bullying show diverse interactions. Continuing victims were often more isolated children, who disliked others and had more time off school but were likely to cross over and bully others (Smith *et al.* 2004). An interesting gender variation is in the way young people deal with bullying. Girls' bullying strategies appear to be internalised but boys externalise their reaction, with girls being much more willing to seek help of their peers and others, whereas boys 'stick it out' (Kristensen and Smith 2003). One approach is the development of 'laddish' behaviour', which Jackson (2003) found to be linked with the fear of failure and fear of the feminine, as boys were scared of losing face with peers, and for some the message was 'it's not cool' to achieve.

However, bullying can have very serious consequences, resulting in a 'shattered childhood'; for many young adults who become addicted to drugs and engage in suicidal behaviour, bullying was a major childhood event (Rossow and Lauritzen 2001). The 'source' or 'rationale' for being bullied can vary, ranging from being overweight (Eisenberg *et al.* 2003) to having a gay or lesbian orientation (Rivers 2004; Warner *et al.* 2004), and is later associated not only with poor self-esteem, depression, poor psychosocial health (Eisenberg *et al.* 2003; Van de Wal *et al.* 2003; Wild *et al.* 2004) but also suicidal behaviour either in adolescence or in young adulthood (Rossow and Lauritzen 2001; Rivers 2004; Warner *et al.* 2004).

The school

After family and peers nothing is more important or influential to children than their school. It is the context for their peers, their neighbourhood, and not only where, hopefully, they can maximise their potential, but where society meets the child in trouble and can go some way to compensating them for any disadvantage. Indeed, irrespective of socio-economic and family structure, if a child likes school, this is a formidable barrier against being involved in many problematic behaviours (Pritchard 2001; Pritchard and Williams 2001). O'Donnell *et al.* (2002) showed that in children who were exposed to violence, if they could be helped to identify with the school, this proved to be a barrier against typically anti-social behaviour associated with the disadvantaged neighbourhood in which they lived.

One issue that continues to bedevil schools, however, is that of class size. Bennett (1998) found that while research results are ambiguous, American work shows that smaller class size, especially in early years, is extremely important *if* teachers can utilise the advantage, that is individualise and engage the child. Research by Arum (1998) also showed that schools with better resources per pupil had better higher education outcomes i.e. more went on to college. Indeed, the 'comprehensive' model, which latterly has been derided, nevertheless continues to thrive in such schools as Eton, Harrow, Marlborough and so on, for *de facto* they are comprehensive, inclusive, and focus upon encouraging a child's potential strengths. So, with optimal educational resources, ordinary pupils go on and achieve great things. As will be seen, children with a range of accumulative problems can be helped, and Webb and Vulliamy's (2003) study of the role of a School Support Worker brought about positive change. However, the school has to appreciate that behavioural problems and their solutions are linked to educational outcomes, and to reach the child we have to deal with the behavioural issues first.

Schools, of course, are vitally important to parents and, paradoxically, especially so if they were alienated as children. It is our practice experience that the vast majority of parents, irrespective of their backgrounds, want the best for their children. Indeed, we have never met a parent who wanted to be a failing parent. Hence if the school can engage and recognise common aspirations, much can be achieved. Conversely, it has been found that there is considerable pain and distress felt by parents of children who are either excluded or admitted into an Educational Behaviour Disturbed Unit (EBDU) (Crawford and Simonoff 2003; Bloomfield *et al.* 2005).

School exclusion has become an over-simplistic political football. Yet, on reflection, to be excluded from your peers is a psychosocial disaster. It goes without saying that a few children, a desperate few, are not capable of being educated in an ordinary school. But such a decision needs to appreciate the often lifelong serious consequence of such action. Former 'excluded-from-school' adolescents go on to be the most socially excluded people of all, having worse psychosocial and criminal outcomes than even looked-after children (Pritchard and Butler 2000a, b). Sociologists speak about labelling and stigmatising (Goffman 1961), whereas in *Macbeth*, Shakespeare writes: 'I am one, my liege, whom the vile blows and buffets of the world hath so incensed I am reckless what I do to spite the world.' Such exclusion can have bitter outcomes, not only for the pupil but for wider society. This is seen in the criminal statistics of extreme violence, where it is the accumulation of socio-economic deficits and educational alienation allied with harsh parenting that are associated with homicide (Hill-Smith *et al.* 2002).

Thus, parents, family, peers and neighbourhood, as well as the socio-economic and genetic endowment and the school contribute to what makes the fully autonomous citizen or a persistent psychosocial casualty. However, the 'ordinary' as well as the problematic child is of concern to the teacher. Hence in the following chapter we explore how he/she behaves in a society in which social norms are changing rapidly.

3 'Drink, drugs and sex': media perception versus objective reality

Media images of young people's behaviour trot out the cliché 'drugs, sex and rock 'n roll', which is an easy stereotype. Yet, as an eminent public commentator complained, 'Today's young men are obsessed by foreign fashion, loud music and long hair', which was Aristotle complaining of Athenian youth, so perhaps little changes? While the experienced teacher probably has as good an idea of their pupils' behaviour as any, we briefly explore in an objective way how Year 10 and Year 11 pupils actually behave.

Over a twenty-year period we have been measuring young people's behaviour, focusing upon 'ordinary' comprehensive schools, and have found our results very similar to national patterns (Pritchard et al. 1986a, b, 1987, 1993, 1997, 1998; Diamond et al. 1988; Pritchard and Cox 1990, 1998, 2001; Balding 2004). This recent research, carried out in August 2005, utilised earlier standardised self-report questionnaires, enabling us to contrast the behaviour and attitudes of young people from the mid-1980s and 2005.

Table 1 shows the behaviour of adolescents across the period 1985–2005. Mid-1990s results are not shown, though the changes then were moving in the same direction as those arrived at in 2005.

The good news is that smoking is down in males and in adults but the bad news is that it is up in females and so too is consumption of alcohol for both genders. The marked feature might be described as '2005 girls behaving badly' compared with the mid-1980s when boys significantly fought, stole, truanted and 'drugged' more than girls. In 2005 the only things boys did more than their female peers was to continue to vandalise more, though cannabis and hard drugs experimentation is up slightly on the 1985 figures. Interestingly, in both periods the 'problematic behaviour' was most often done with others, an indication of the persistent power of peer pressure. Conversely, there is clear evidence that schools, despite the picture portrayed in the media, are engaging boys more effectively.

Table 1: Changing patterns of adolescent behaviour by gender, 1985–2005 (aged 14–16), %

Item	1985 [n = 807]		2005 [n = 854]		1985 v 2005	
	M	F	M	F	M	F
	n = 460	n = 347	n = 498	n = 356	P value (2005 worse: –, better: +)	
Both parents at home	77	78	76	72	0.06–	
Unemployed father	21	18	16	15	0.05+	
Mother in full-time work	39	38	54	55	0.0001–0.0001	
Large family 4+ children	14	16	6	9	0.0001–0.005	
Ethnicity – white	98	97	91	93	n.sig	
Ever smoked	52*	44	28	45	0.0001+	n.sig
Smoke 5+ a day	15	12	4	9	0.0001+	n.sig
Father smokes	47	45	18	26	0.0001	0.0001+
Mother smokes	37	39	14	19	0.0001	0.0001+
Drinks alcohol	52	56	68	85	0.0001–	0.0001–
Drinks in pubs	18***	27	16	22	n.sig	
Sniffs glue	5	7	7	9	n.sig	
Truants	52****	28	26	30	0.0001+	n.sig
Truants often	31****	11	11	14	0.0001+	0.9t–
Fights	42****	10	19	16	0.0001+	0.02–
Fight often	33	3	11	10	0.001+	0.0001–
Smokes cannabis	15****	5	16	19	n.sig	0.0001–
Smokes cannabis often	10	2	10	13	n.sig	0.07t–
Smokes cannabis with others	11	4	15	18	n.sig	
'Hard'	6***	2	8	7	n.sig	
Hard drugs often	3	1	3	4	n.sig	
Vandalises	38	18****	28	18	0.01+	n.sig
Vandalises school	4	2	3	3	n.sig	
Vandalises often	22	6****	18	7	n.sig	
Steals	23	20	10	18	0.001+	n.sig
Steals from local shop	23	t 18	6	11	0.001+	0.05+
Steals from school	17****	6	4	6	0.001+	n.sig

Note: Levels of statistical probability refer to incidence of the result occurring by chance, i.e. p<0.05 = less than 1 in 20, p<0.01 = less than 1 in 100 times.

*	=	<0.05
**	=	<0.02
***	=	<0.01
****	=	<0.001

As might be expected youngsters across the years who experiment with drugs are also more likely to truant significantly, steal, vandalise and so on than those who do not. It should be noted that now as then such behaviour is *still a minority activity*.

We also explored 'binge drinking' and sexual behaviour, as there is evidence that bingeing is associated with 'unplanned' sexual behaviour (Bellis *et al.* 2002). Again, binge drinking was a minority activity of only 21 per cent but, as Table 2 shows, bingers were significantly more likely to be involved in other problem behaviours.

Table 2: Binge drinkers (n = 180, 21%) versus non-binge drinkers (n = 674), significant only results, %

Item	Bingers	Non-bingers	P value
Males–Females	15–29	85–71	<0.001
Years 10–11 [n = 409 n = 445]	30–70	54–46	<0.001
Home both parents	67	75	<0.05
Father employed	79	88	<0.01
Smokes	73	33	<0.0001
Father smokes	33	21	<0.01
Mother smokes	26	17	<0.01
Drinks at home	81	89	<0.05
Drinks in pubs	39	19	<0.0001
Drink from parents	54	76	<0.001
Drink from off-licence	37	9	<0.0001
Drink from supermarket	52	29	<0.001
Sniffs solvents	17	7	<0.001
Solvents often (>3 times)	8	1	<0.001
Truants	52	24	<0.0001
Truants often	28	10	<0.01
Truants with others	50	34	<0.001
Fighting	32	15	<0.0001
Fights often (>3 times)	23	9	<0.05
Bullies	17	9	<0.05
Vandalises	39	21	<0.001
Steals	26	10	<0.001
Tried cannabis	44	14	<0.0001
Cannabis often (>3 times)	36	8	<0.001
'Hard' drugs	19	3	<0.001
'Hard drugs' often	11	1	<0.01
Had protected sex	41	14	<0.0001
Had unprotected sex	20	8	<0.001
Had sex last week	22	3	<0.0001
Had sex last month	27	9	<0.01

Table 2 (contd)

Item	Bingers	Non-bingers	P value
Been offered drugs	49	24	<0.0001
You know drug taker	73	53	<0.001
You know cannabis supplier	67	36	<0.0001
You know heroin supplier	20	6	<0.001
You know cocaine supplier	33	11	<0.0001

As expected the 'bingers' were more often into drugs, and crucially were more often involved in underage sex. It needs to be remembered that our respondents were still at school in Years 10 and 11.

Sexual behaviour

As to be expected it is the sexually active who are more often involved in more of the other problematic behaviours but of especial concern was their greater involvement in drugs and alcohol. Bearing in mind that Britain has one of the highest teenager rates of pregnancy in the European Union (Social Exclusion Unit 1998a) it should be noted that 29 per cent of our female respondents and only 19% per cent of our male respondents reported that they had been involved in early sexual behaviour. It must be assumed that these predominately 13- to 15-year-old girls often had partners older than themselves. Table 3 shows the significantly different behaviour compared with the non-sexually active (only significant results are shown).

Table 3: Behaviour and attitudes of 'protected sex' v the rest of respondents, %

Item	Protected sex n = 141	The rest n = 713	P value
School year 10 v 11	32 v 67	51 v 49	<0.001
Males–Females	41–59	61–49	<0.001
Home both parents	67	75	<0.05
Father employed	77	86	<0.01
Smoked	77	27	<0.0001
Father smokes	35	19	<0.001
Mother smokes	33	13	<0.0001
Drinks alcohol	95	71	<0.0001
Drinks in pubs	44	14	<0.0001

Drink within last week	71	36	<0.0001
Friends buy you drink	69	27	<0.0001
Drink from parents	49	63	<0.05
Drink from off-licence	36	8	<0.0001
Drink-knock-down-places	14	6	<0.01
Drink from supermarket	50	23	<0.001
Goes binge drinking	52	15	<0.0001
Binge monthly	21	6	<0.01
Sniffed solvents	18	6	<0.001
Solvents often (>3 times)	10	2	<0.07t
Truants	63	21	<0.0001
Truants often (>3 times)	33	8	<0.05
Fighting	43	13	<0.0001
Fights often (>3 times)	29	7	<0.01
Bullied	21	8	<0.001
Bullied often (>3 times)	17	6	<0.05
Vandalises	45	20	<0.0001
Steals	30	10	<0.0001
Steals from school	33	15	<0.001
Tried cannabis	57	10	<0.0001
Cannabis often (>3 times)	43	6	<0.001
'Hard' drugs	19	5	<0.01
'Hard drugs' often	11	2	<0.05
Had unprotected sex	45 (55% haven't)	0	<0.0001
Had sex last week	39	0	<0.001
Had sex last month	60	0	<0.0001
Had sex often (>3 times)	56	0	<0.0001

The teacher, however, needs to know something of young people's attitudes to psycho social health and Table 4 shows the sexually active's group's knowledge compared to the majority and provides some rationale of their behaviour.

Table 4: Protected sex v non-sexual behaviour, attitudes respondents, %

Item	Protected sex n = 141	The rest n = 713	P value
Been offered drugs	50	22	<0.0001
You know drug taker	82	46	<0.0001
You know cannabis supplier	71	32	<0.0001
You know heroin supplier	23	5	<0.001
You know cocaine supplier	35	10	<0.001
Likely to take drugs because:			
Mates do	49	30	<0.001

Table 4 (contd)

Item	Protected sex n = 141	The rest n = 713	P value
To see what it's like	71	46	<0.001
To wind up parents	14	4	<0.001
Help solve problem	18	11	<0.05
To lose weight	12	5	<0.01
Like the feeling it gives	45	16	<0.001
Likely to drink because:			
Have good time	89	69	<0.0148
Like the feeling it gives	65	33	<0.001
Help solve a problem	27	10	<0.0018
Seeing celebs drinking	8	3	<0.05
Attitudes and health knowledge			
Majority of athletes don't smoke	72	80	<0.06t
Taking drugs – serious	77	91	<0.001
Getting legless – serious	32	52	<0.001
Tobacco – serious	29	56	<0.0001
Drug lifestyle and HIV/AIDS	90	80	<0.05–
Most of time **enjoy school**	52	66	<0.002
School helps you get on with people	76	83	<0.01
Been bullied coming and going	16	10	<0.001
Been bullied in playground	24	16	<0.001
Staff try to deal with bullying	29	45	<0.001
Bullying a big problem my school	35	39	<0.09t
Usually get home <10pm	**55**	**76**	**<0.0001**
Ever stay out >12pm	70	32	<0.0001
Go sports/leisure centre	22	30	<0.1t
Often go to sports/leisure centre	39	52	<0.01
Mainly hang around street/shopping	**60**	**33**	**<0.0001**
Evenings out a week 1–2	7	25	
3–4	32	51	
5–6	41	15	
7+	20	9	<0.0001

In brief it can be seen that the sexually active are significantly less 'on the ball' about a range of attitudes and knowledge about drugs, drink and sex. There were similar findings for those youngsters who try cannabis, go binge drinking and truanting. It might well be part of the bravado behaviour of adolescence that if adults place restrictions on their behaviour, adolescents will seek to test or extend the boundaries. For example, while the vast majority of the sexually active were concerned about the dangers of HIV/AIDS, their behaviour did not follow through. Moreover, they stayed out later and were less involved in organised youth activities, all reflecting less effective parental supervision. One important feature to be noted, however, is that only 7 per cent of the sample reported having had sex more than three or four times, emphasising that for this age group sexual behaviour was still a minority activity.

On the plus side we should highlight that the majority of our teenagers actually liked school (52 per cent and 66 per cent respectively), a theme to which we shall return.

Interaction of behaviours

Undoubtedly today's young people are physically more developed than 20 years ago and sexual mores for adults have changed; for example, in 2005 for the first time in 600 years an heir apparent married his mistress! Our concern is with the combination of behaviours, that is, the interaction of binge drinking and drug experimentation with increased likelihood of unprotected sex, and greater likelihood of unplanned, unwanted pregnancy (Hingson et al. 2003; Kuntscher et al. 2004).

Without being moralistic, and of course adults envy adolescents' vibrant vitality and their relative freedoms, adolescence is a time of poor judgements, and in the presence of a sexualised media it has never been harder to be an adolescent. Indeed, it is also very difficult to be a parent as even recent social boundaries disappear in a world of increasingly relative social mores.

Parent mentors – pupils' behaviour and smoking parents

The vast majority of parents, irrespective of their backgrounds, want the best for their children. While we are concerned not to condemn parents who have a different lifestyle, parents as mentors for their children can pose the educationalist and the adolescent with the dilemma of 'do as I say, not do as I do'.

We found that if the child's parent smoked, that child is far more likely to be involved in more problematic behaviour than children of non-smoking parents. It is appreciated that to some extent smoking is a surrogate category of 'working-class' (though not always), but proportionately fewer 'middle-class' people smoke than 'working-class' people.

We found that children of smoking mothers significantly more often smoked themselves, and more often engaged in binge drinking, drugs, sexual activity and fighting. Moreover, they were significantly less likely to like school (63 per cent to 19 per cent), which, as we know is a barrier to children becoming entrenched in problematic behaviour (Pritchard and Williams 2001; Bonnell *et al.* 2005). The question is, therefore, how can we best reach out to these youngsters and improve their engagement with the school?

Think positive

It is easy inadvertently to reinforce negative behaviour by concentrating upon problematic youngsters and parents with problems. Thinking positively can highlight the fact that for the majority of Year 10 and Year 11 secondary school students 82 per cent of their parents do not smoke, and 64 per cent of the young people did not smoke, 85 per cent did not steal, 82 per cent did not have sex, did not fight or truant, 79 per cent did not binge and 74 per cent did not vandalise. In other words, the majority of our young people are not trapped into self-defeating behaviour, and we should avoid giving them the impression that it is cool and normal for them to do so. Conversely, are some of these behaviours nothing more than adolescent experimentation which should not overly concern us?

Although illegal, are the 'soft' drugs dangerous?

How dangerous is cannabis? Youngsters could rightly assert that it is less associated with fatal outcomes than either tobacco or alcohol and that we are hypocrites. Therefore is it really only illegal rather than dangerous? It is acknowledged that for many of the post-1970s generation the 'social use' of cannabis has gained a degree of acceptability, as a casual alternative to the delights of alcohol in moderation. However, we have long known that cannabis has been associated with psychotic attacks, and we should be alert to the fact that psychedelic drugs do carry a serious risk. Based upon a five-year study of all Swedish national services men in the 1980s, Andreasson *et al.* (1990) were able to show that fifteen years on, there were two identifiable groups of people who developed schizophrenia. The first were those who had a first- or second-degree relative with schizophrenia and the second were young men who had started using cannabis early and continued to do so. Indeed, in one author's practice caseload, there were about ten students each year who developed psychotic symptoms following cannabis use.

The link between early onset schizophrenia and cannabis is now well confirmed in more recent studies (Kalant 2004; Rey *et al.* 2004), as well as being linked to increased accidents, lower employability, increased oral cancer and so on (Gruber *et al.* 2003; Verdejo *et al.* 2004; Hall *et al.* 2005; Llewellyn *et al.* 2004).

There is also a myth that 'ecstasy' is really a safe drug and that the occasional deaths highlighted in the media are because the victim went 'over the top'. An important British study explored the outcome in 430 regular MDMA 'ecstasy' users, looked at the acute, sub-acute and long-terms effects of frequent users of ecstasy and it was not cheerful reading, especially as 59 per cent showed increased tolerance of the drug.

Linked to this question of dangerousness, should we worry about youngsters trying alcohol? Certainly Britain and McPherson's study (2001) sounded sweet to the brewers as 'drinkers' have a 2 per cent better life expectancy than total non-drinkers. However, they also found considerable morbidity and mortality toll from alcohol in young people and adults, with an association of deaths from drug overdoses, suicide, road and other accidents and increased liver disease. Invariably, the presence of either drugs or alcohol exacerbates any fraught situation and compounds long-standing psychosocial difficulties (Farrington and Loeber 2000; Loeber *et al.* 2001; Bellis *et al.* 2002; Foxcroft *et al.* 2002; Bonnell *et al.* 2003; Stallard *et al.* 2003; Stanistreet and Jeffrey 2003; Williams *et al.* 2005).

Moreover, it should be remembered that more people die in Britain from road accidents every year than died in the tragedy of 11 September 2001, and a significant proportion of these deaths were alcohol-related (Pritchard and Wallace 2006).

Multi-social dimensions are associated with adolescent substance abuse, as the above factors overlap and interact. Sutherland and Shepherd (2001) in a national study on 4500 11- to 16-year-olds, identified the interaction of family situations, socio-economic factors and attitudes and perceptions of academic achievement, plus subsequent delinquent police-involving behaviour. They conclude that none of these psycho social factors can be considered in isolation.

Sexually transmitted diseases (STDs)

Bellis *et al.* (2002, 2004) highlight the dangers of drug and alcohol consumption among young people and young adults in the current 'youth culture' of clubbing and overseas nightlife. In the presence of drugs and alcohol there is a considerable lessening of sensible sexual hygiene and an increase in casual and unprotected sex with 'strangers', which is also linked to the inevitable rise in sexually transmitted diseases. (See also Pritchard and Cox 1990; Pritchard *et al.* 1993; Apostolopoulos *et al.* 2002; Coniglario *et al.* 2003; Seeman *et al.* 2003; Williams *et al.* 2005).

One particular feature is the relatively new phenomenon of 'binge drinking'. Over the past twenty years there have been marked changes in young people's response to alcohol. Crucially, more girls are drinking than ever before but both genders are consuming drinks with a higher alcohol content, such as wine and spirits. Even the popular 'alcopops' contain higher levels of alcohol than most beers. One result of this trend towards increased alcohol consumption from an earlier age is the striking increase in liver disease, which results from alcohol abuse. Table 5 makes the point. Based upon WHO data (2005) we compare liver deaths in young adults. While all rates are up over the last twenty years, the young adults' age groups increased significantly more.

Liver deaths among young men aged 25–34 quadrupled, and as it usually take 10 to 15 years to kill a person from alcohol this is clear evidence of early starts; while the 35–44 age group increased substantially, they did not start as early as the younger age group. Moreover, compared with the general increase in liver deaths, the younger age adults had significantly worse outcomes, and this does not bode well for today's adolescents, exposed to earlier and stronger alcohol.

Table 5: Average three years chronic liver disease deaths (1979–81 v 2000–02*) in young UK adults (rates per million p.m) by gender

Years	All ages (15–75+) M F	25–34 M F	35–44 M F	All ages V 25–34 Ratio of ratios	All ages V 35–44 Ratio of ratios
1979–81	53 44	7 6	45 30	0.13–0.14	0.85–0.68
2000–02	153 89	30 16	147 72	0.20–0.18	0.96–0.81
Index of change	2.89 2.02	4.29 2.67	3.27 2.40	**1.54–1.29**	**1.13–1.19**

Ratio of ratios in **bold**

Deliberate self-harm and suicidal behaviour

There is little that is more distressing than the threat of a young person taking their life and its link with misuse of drugs and/or alcohol crosses all the age bands (Pritchard 1999). Ayton *et al.* (2003) explored the 'attempted suicide' or 'deliberate self-harm' (DSH), the preferred term, in a cohort of 730 children and adolescents. Key findings were the cluster of family problems and poverty and part of the 'symptomatolgy' was their early involvement in drug and alcohol, which undermined their educational achievement and was later linked with unemployment, which itself is a factor in the ultimate suicide of young people (Pritchard 1999; Blakely *et al.* 2003). Unemployment frequently follows on from educational alienation and the youngster is virtually unemployable. However, the motives of young people with suicidal ideation are complex, as Rodham *et al.* (2000) found in a study of 6000 15- to 16-year-olds. Young women were predominantly engaged in 'self-harm' cutting, and were impulsively responding to an acutely felt distress, whereas the males were more 'testing' out to see whether they could create a reaction in key personal relationships; bullying was often also a contributory factor (Rivers 2004; Warner *et al.* 2004). School can be a place of real distress, precipitating DSH episodes. Hawton *et al.* (2003) found that amongst the psychosocial precipitants was 'stress at school', ranging from being a victim of bullying to social isolation, and anxiety about examination pressures. Consequently, there needs to be a broad interdisciplinary understanding about 'mental health' problems that includes consideration of drug and alcohol education and schools being more sensitive to the crises of adolescents (Hawton *et al.* 2003).

We now explore an innovative project that not only aimed to reach potential or actual disaffected pupils but, by improving their situation, to reduce class and school tensions, benefiting pupils and staff.

4 A school-based solution: reaching the 'disaffected'

Following a range of studies within health, education, probation and social services, a common theme emerged, namely the 'educational underachievement' of the clients/patients of all the agencies. This led to an 'alliance', which sought to make an impact upon health, education, crime and child protection problems by focusing on school to reach the potential or actually disaffected pupil in order to reduce truancy, exclusions from school and other linked behaviours.

The project started from the premise that child–parent conflict, irrespective of cause, impacts upon the child in school, which 'disrupts' or 'diverts' the teachers' energy, diminishing the education of the majority, with reverberations throughout the school and into the community. Hence if our three-year prospective project could break into this negative, mutually reinforcing cycle, we would benefit both problematic and 'ordinary' children (Farrell and Ainsow 2002; Webb and Vulliamy 2003). Moreover, as delinquency commences in the primary years and lasts into adulthood, any success would have cumulative benefits, including monetary ones, adding value to this preventive investment (Farrington 1995; Smith and Farrington 2004).

Project targets

A Chief Officers' steering committee of the four agencies developed the following objectives:

1 Provide an appropriate school-based social work service to children and families where necessary.
2 Provide easily accessible assistance to teachers to enhance their professional and pastoral inputs, enhancing the morale of the school.
3 Early identification of difficult pupils and appropriate referral.
4 Early identification of family difficulties likely to disrupt educational progress.
5 Enhance pupils' integration into school, with full attendance.

6   Maximise support wherever possible for families.
7   Empower parents, enhancing their involvement and commitment to the child's education.
8   Enhance health education awareness.
9   Enhance social and educational achievement, contributing to the community.
10   Contribute to the reduction of crime and delinquency in school and community.

To maintain the confidentiality of staff, pupils and schools, anonymised nomenclature was used – Attlee, Bevan, Churchill and Disraeli. A small project team to 'enhance' the work of the school was led by a Senior Education Social Worker, with two teacher–social workers based in the project schools and given the above tasks.

Project schools

To reach proportionately more vulnerable children 'Attlee' primary was chosen because the housing estate in which it was situated was one of the most disadvantaged in the county. As most Attlee children go to 'Bevan' comprehensive, this school was the obvious project secondary school.

Control schools

To ensure a rigorous evaluation of the project, 'standard' provision comparison schools were required. While seeking as close a socio-economic match as possible, it was more important that the 'standard' provision be known as relatively successful with children from less favoured backgrounds. Consequently the primary control school 'Churchill' was chosen as it had a slightly *less* disadvantaged pupilage, and fed into the secondary comparison 'Disraeli School', which was marginally *more* disadvantaged than 'Bevan'. Any demographic and socio-economic variations over the three years were controlled by school-wide surveys at the start and end of the project.

Project team roles

The coordinator, a social work-qualified senior educational welfare officer of Project Social Worker (PSW), worked intensively with families and their children and supported teachers in their work with difficult pupils, as well as ensuring effective interagency collaboration.

The Project Primary Teacher (PPT), a qualified teacher, was very 'community-orientated', working directly and intensively with troubled children in the school. Both she and the PSW were able to respond immediately to a crisis, aiming to reduce pressures on the teacher and other children. When appropriate she also worked with the PSW, hence her role was that of a teacher–social worker, but the emphasis was upon the teacher's role (NASWE 1996).

The Secondary Project Teacher (SPT) had health education expertise, and initially had similar responsibilities to the PPT, but direct work with troublesome children was not his area of expertise and after a year he concentrated upon specialist health education. It meant, however, that the primary school 'teacher–social worker' role was not replicated in Bevan. This was offset by the PSW's developing direct work with the pastoral year heads, encouraging them to be more proactive and enhancing their response to children with problems. This was exemplified by a Year Head's anonymous comments (see Chapter 6):

> Through the project we have been able to make additional efforts to reach these problem children in the development of a parent support group. This has eased the burden on the Head, and other Year Heads and the School Managers – and in an unthreatening manner, eased the pressure on others. I cannot rate too highly the availability and accessibility of the PSW before the crisis brews.

The whole project was independently evaluated for the Home Office and can be found on their website (Pritchard 2001).

At Attlee primary school (ages 5–11), specific aims were to improve the integration and identification of child and school; reduce disruptive behaviour and absenteeism; improve literacy and numeracy, improve staff morale; reduce the 'costs' to the schools and public services of disruptive children; improve family and school relationships; and facilitate the positive transfer of children to their secondary schools.

At Bevan secondary school (ages 11–16) the aims were to aid the integration and identification of new and older pupils; reduce truancy and delinquency; decrease drug taking; improve literacy and numeracy; increase the awareness of the dangers of HIV and other STDs; improve educational achievement and increase employment and training prospects; improve staff morale; and develop parent–school contact and improve community networks. Furthermore, in both Attlee and Bevan schools, the team aimed to reduce stress in teaching staff, thus contributing to improved family relationships and parent–school partnership.

The team's first task was to become an integral part of the school's social system. This was facilitated by the PSW and the PPT already being known to the schools, though the project still needed to gain the trust and cooperation of often pressurised class teachers. This was done in five simple, interconnected ways.

1   The PSW avoided 'competition' for scarce office space, maintaining a desk in the County office of the Education Welfare Department) instead.

2   He sought entrance into the 'staff room' by invitation and was able 'informally' to consult and be consulted about various children and families, as it was recognised that the teachers were often best placed to notice problems, and subsequently most referrals came from them.

3   This required a speedy and appropriate feedback, thus further enhancing trust, and avoiding the reduction of the teachers' responsibilities for one of their pupils, creating a sense of partnership.

4   The team offered direct and indirect support to the teachers in their professional and pastoral work. Easy access to the team was vital, and problems ranged from intra- and extra-school difficulties of the children and how they impacted on both class and teacher. This professional support outside a hierarchical structure was especially appreciated by staff.

5   Most dramatic was the team's initial invitation to each school to refer the ten most time-demanding children. This immediately put the team in the 'front line' and gave them an opportunity to demonstrate their professional worth.

Thus the PSW avoided the problem of differing orientations between social worker and teacher that concerned Webb and Vulliamy (2003), as home–school support workers need to have a strong sympathy with primary educational objectives so that their 'social work' type of intervention facilitates the school's primary educational role.

The project teachers, especially in the primary school, provided an extension of the caring practice of the schools, by being able to respond to a child in difficulties. Being educationally focused, any early professional integration problems were resolved, as the team were accepted by the school. Nonetheless, a less sensitive approach to the dangers of interdisciplinary rivalry could have been counter-productive.

Role of the head teachers

Negotiations were necessary with the school governors, to gain confidential access to potentially sensitive material. Head teachers' agreement was also vital, for without the head's active support there would have been no project. Following initial development the heads gave their wholehearted support to the project and were active in their support with other agencies and the LEA.

Ethos of the team

The team's ethos was that young people need clear and consistent limits and rules for behaviour, appropriate stimulation, care and consideration, all within a well-structured and well-managed environment, and the school should be a valued part of the local community, creating a partnership with parents and guardians.

The team had direct access to the heads, but because they gained the trust of the rest of the school, they avoided any jealousies that could have occurred.

Project intervention

There were a range of interventions, predominantly counselling led by the PSW and supported by the PPT. The team's initial contact with children and their families often confirmed earlier social and educational failure spanning generations, consequently major efforts were made to enhance parents' aspirations for their children by reinforcing parenting skills, and affirming the parents' personal self-worth.

An eclectic social work approach was used, based upon the establishment of a sustained enhancing rapport to maximise many parents' inherent desire to do their best for their children. The team recognised that many children and their parents have 'learned' behaviour based on very poor experiences of both education and authority and they needed to relearn and reframe negative experiences. Equally, disruptive and self-defeating behaviour had to be contained and reshaped. The necessity of ensuring that families received their welfare entitlements was never forgotten, nor was the importance of practical advice and guidance for the successful achievement of social and employment goals.

The PPT gave extra attention to the reception class years, recognising that early educational focus on the child laid the foundations for further developmental successes. She also took an individual counselling role with children, though would sometimes undertake specific educational remedial tasks with them in the class or in a room set aside. In addition, she often gained the cooperation of a parent to assist directly in his or her child's education. The team supported the parents' predominant wish for the child to be maintained within mainstream education whenever possible, reinforcing the parents' view that the team were 'on our side'.

Efforts were made to demonstrate to children that, although the focus of help was upon them, their integration into the school would improve their capacity to take better control of their lives; for example, one 15-year-old said of the PSW: 'He was straight with me and I knew where I stood.' This approach assisted the positive child/teacher/team relationships, demonstrated in later outcomes.

Parental support

This was a central activity of the team. It was feasible for the team to offer an almost optimal school-based service compared to the standard service, simply in terms of availability and the continuity brought about by being responsible only for two schools. In effect, the project staff 'potential' caseload was only a quarter of that of the average county EWO, which is one to 3500 pupils, compared to the project's approximately 1800 children (NASWE 1996), though all the families involved had above average psychosocial problems.

Apart from school and other agency referrals, self-referrals increased from families. Counselling was used to help these parents, not least reducing their frequent sense of isolation. The overall effect was to reduce the family–child stress levels, as evidenced in the consumer outcome results.

To reach the potential caseload the team adopted two simple but effective tactics. In the first few weeks the PSW would stand outside the gates of the school and introduce himself, and inform parents of the team's availability to respond to any problems. The second was to visit the estate in the early evening, informing parents who seldom or never came to school of a forthcoming event and asking whether they needed any assistance in attending. Initially, when they saw someone from the school parents expected problems, but on finding that it was a general invitation, this was greatly appreciated and improved the school–community link. Indeed, so successful was the school in reaching families that by the last year of the project, every parent in both schools had attended school at least once for a non-disciplinary meeting. This was unprecedented.

Child protection

The estate was one of the most disadvantaged in the county and proportionately had the highest level of 'child protection' cases, so knowledge of child protection procedures was essential. Here was a potential for misunderstanding but, supported by the coordinating child protection social worker, the team avoided clashes over areas of responsibilities, and complemented the local child protection team. It was specifically pointed out to the schools that the project was not an alternative service but, rather, fed into the local child protection team.

The nature of child protection problems usually means that families are wary of 'authority', but the team often became an important bridge between families and the local Social Service Departments (SSDs). This was so effective that by the end of the project child protection referrals from Attlee fell by 76 per cent (from 25 cases to 6) at a time when referrals rose by 33 per cent in the rest of the county (270 to 374). Equally important, half the referrals were self-referrals, which is half the battle when parents appreciate they need and can obtain help.

Transition to secondary school

One particular task of the project was to assist pupils in making a better adjustment on transferring to their secondary school, which can be quite traumatic. Indeed, if initially problematic it can set a disruptive pattern, which may last years. The Year 6 pupils at Attlee (about thirty), were given weekly group work discussion sessions to prepare them, and the team liaised with parents to facilitate the transfer, often by getting parents to recall memories of their own experience. It proved to be very effective, as in the final year Bevan teachers said that the Attlee children were amongst the best entries into school.

Bullying

To resolve bullying, it was necessary to communicate with peer groups, as much as with individual children. Bullying is a feature of all schools (Smith *et al.* 2004) and, late in the second year, group work was undertaken to deal with the problem. The PSW adapted the Norwegian system. This included perpetrator, victim and often the class and, not infrequently, the parents. A parental network was developed to assist children either to avoid or not to participate in bullying. This coming together of parents further enhanced the sense of community and identification with the school.

Truancy

A key object of the project was to reduce truancy and sustained efforts were made in this area. Parents of truanting pupils were contacted very speedily and were fully involved. *Each incident was treated seriously and dealt with thoroughly*, as team and school appreciated that frequent and/ or persistent truancy is a vital sign that something is wrong with the child, the family or the school, or is an interaction of all three (O'Keefe 1994; Smith and Farrington 2004; Pritchard and Cox 2005). Pupils received a loud, clear message: they would not be able to 'get away with it', and non-attendance was not tolerated. Yet the counselling skills of both PSW and PPT were such that both quickly became valued by potential truants, as many learned that non-attendance was against their own interests. Again, the teams' cooperative approach to parents further enhanced parents' links with schools.

Health and social education

The SPT undertook a full audit of the school's Health and Social Education Programme. This involved an assessment of each subject area's contribution to health-related issues, the identification of gaps and, in consultation with external advisers and most importantly, a series of parental discussions about their expectations, which crucially contributed to the final report. Most of the recommended changes were accepted and implemented.

Crisis team's process

A crucial element in teams' success was the total acceptance of the educational and social objectives of the school. The often 'sociological' critique of schools which scapegoats teachers was completely eschewed, as the team shared the professional aspiration of teachers to meet children's educational and development needs.

The team appreciated that teachers meet children in a personal and group relationship and are ideally placed to understand the normal range of children's behaviours. Equally, they understood the teacher's wider agenda i.e. how the teacher, his or her class, as well as individuals, fit into school. The team could give unfeigned respect to the frontline teacher who operates in four distinct areas: the child, the child-in-the-class, the class and the class-in-the-school.

The project's introduction into the schools established the team's credentials, while also providing them with a structure of work, and gave a framework for direct intervention. This avoided the dangers of interminable team meetings about 'what to do', which can sometimes become ends in themselves.

There was no limit placed on the number of pupils to be referred. The initial ten were the starting point to help cope with the pressures on the school's resources, though it was quickly seen just how disproportionately a number of severely disadvantaged children were being maintained in the schools.

As the children and families received intensive support from the team, this was often reflected in improved adjustment in school, freeing up teachers' time, including that of heads and year heads. As it happened, every one of the early cases had, at the core, child protection issues. Thus the opening period of activity was quite exhausting, but its impact was valued by teaching colleagues as well as the families.

Child protection procedures were checked, followed, monitored and communicated. Parents were contacted, listened to, brought into school and kept informed. Health professionals were contacted, given referrals, invited into school and engaged as partners in the 'Healthy Alliance'. Social workers from SSD were welcomed into the school, invited to use it as a resource and given every cooperation. During this time good professional relationships were formed, as were good relationships with parents, all creating a body of work that unpinned growing interagency trust and collaboration.

The following practical experience gives a taste of the team's activities, including practical issues, which could not have been anticipated.

In the case of 'Alan' (all names are pseudonyms) he had experienced the most severe, long-term physical, emotional and sexual abuse. His single parent made extensive efforts to keep his family together, following the disclosure of the abuse and the press coverage and the trial of the perpetrator, which was singularly unhelpful. Alan came into school to explain that he could not cope any longer. He was leaving; his washing machine had broken! It was the 'straw that had broken the camel's back'. Through a range of activities the team arranged for the laundry to be done, and a loan was obtained to tide him over the crisis, which was later was repaid. Every effort was made to avoid taking responsibility away from the parent, the team preferring to advise and to offer strategies to achieve agreed goals, such as behaviour modification programmes applicable to home and school. In brief, Alan's stresses were greatly reduced, and the crisis did not become an emergency leading to exclusion and/or the child being taken into care.

Community development and inter agency collaboration

The school is an ecologically defined community, not only for the children, but also for a range of agencies, which can deliver their services in a non-stigmatising way. Barriers to interagency collaboration could and did arise, but were overcome by calling upon the principles inherent in the Children Act 1989, i.e. the welfare of the child is paramount. This led to a number of innovations, such as a weekly 'surgery' which brought onto the Attlee estate advisers from the probation service, the police, SSDs, housing, community and school health. Liaison duties across the agencies and disciplines proved to be especially important so that often the PSW might represent the school.

The interdisciplinary origins of the project were useful, so that the Project Social Worker made contact with middle or sometimes senior management to resolve any difficulty or misunderstanding. Each successful resolution of a problem enhanced the team's ability and the mutual trust between school and other agencies.

As time progressed there were major benefits from the accumulation of positive work with individuals, which led to a change from negative to positive expectations – to the extent that the team had to guard against unrealistic expectations. Though initially the work focused upon 'emergencies', an active preventive role eventually became at least half the team's activities.

Some comments on the projects structure

The team enjoyed professional freedom but not licence by having minimal bureaucratic demands made upon them. This enabled them to respond to evolving needs of children, family, school and community more flexibly and speedily.

The programme heightened the team's sense of accountability, indeed they were energised as they recognised they were operating in an optimal professional situation, i.e. maximum professional freedom with appropriate professional supervision. This meant they exceeded the strict 'hours' guideline, thus enhancing each member's contribution to the whole project. In practice this often meant that families were visited at their convenience 'out of office hours', which re-emphasised the 'consumer' focus and the project's accessibility.

The importance of access and negotiation with the head teachers cannot be overstated, nor indeed the confidential relationships the team had with their teacher colleagues.

The team developed its own support system, partially through weekly supervision meetings with the evaluator, who initially undertook this social work role, which was later taken up by the coordinator. It must be admitted, however, that the need for team building had not been anticipated and it was recognised that interdisciplinary projects need from the inception to include team building and supervisory capacity.

All the above cost considerably more than the usual cost of one Educational Social Worker to the usual eight schools: a total of £73,700 p.a. (including all costs), raising two questions: did the project achieve its goals, and was the project 'worth the money' (Pritchard and Williams 2001)?

From the outset the evaluation of the project was an integral part of the programme. This required careful negotiation and a sympathy for what the team were trying to achieve. Nonetheless, independence was crucial. However, because of the close monitoring, this could not be a blind laboratory-type research, but rather an action research project. Consequently, where appropriate, the evaluator fed back to the team both positive and negative findings, and it is to the evaluation that we now turn.

The evaluation

James Baldwin once said, 'If you ain't part of the solution, then you're part of the problem', and to us this applies to teaching as much as to social work, medicine or any of the human services. Hence the project was thoroughly independently evaluated.

In brief we had privileged and confidential access to education, some health, police, probation and social service records which enabled us to examine a range of contextual features such as crime, children on the 'At Risk of Abuse' register, statutory referrals, prison rates in the areas of the schools, as well as family backgrounds and so on. We undertook 'consumer' surveys of the project's clientele and teachers in all four schools, looking at changes in stress levels over time. An annual survey of children's behaviour and attitudes (9- to 16-year-olds) before, during and after the project, provided opportunities to measure change over time and evaluate to what extent the 'enhanced' service was better than the 'standard' provision.

Each school was *measured against* itself over a time period, i.e. a baseline and final year, from which a ratio of change is calculated. An example best explains this. Initially Bevan secondary school had 41 per cent girls to 59 per cent boys i.e. 1.44:1; by its end this had changed to 36 per cent to 64 per cent respectively, a ratio of 1.78:1. By dividing the previous ratio by the latest yields a 'ratio of change' of 1.24. This means there was an extra 24 per cent of males at Bevan compared with the start of the project.

Paradoxically, because of local reorganisation, the gender balance in control secondary school Disraeli moved in the opposite direction, from 45 per cent girls to 55 per cent boys, 1.22:1, becoming 47 per cent to 53 per cent, 1.12:1, a ratio of change of 0.92. This was equivalent to a proportional fall of 8 per cent boys in Disraeli.

So, after three years how effective was a school-based social work service for children and families in reducing truancy and improving educational outcomes?

5 Becoming part of the solution: the family context. Outcomes

Context

Unemployment

An important contextual consideration was unemployment, as the region, while traditionally having one of the lowest male unemployment rates in the UK, was particularly affected by the last recession and experienced the third biggest rise in unemployment in the UK. This meant a significant gap between available jobs and the numbers of people seeking them. In better days the gap between jobs and the jobless was 1:2, i.e. there were two people seeking work for every job available, but during a large part of the project the job-to-vacancy ratio exploded to 1:10.2. It subsequently improved to 1:5.7, and is now 1:2.5.

However, it is the least skilled who are first made redundant, and they are re-employed at a slower rate than the average unemployed person (Bjarnason and Sigurdardotti 2003; Brugha *et al.* 2004). This may explain the fathers' unemployment rate: Attlee primary had almost four times the regional rate, Churchill more than double, and Bevan and Disraeli virtually treble the rate. Thus our children's families experienced an unprecedented increase in unemployment, coinciding with a sharp reduction in available jobs: all likely to exacerbate any tensions within family or community.

Crime, probation and contact with Social Services (SSD)

Table 6 shows the family's contact with the statutory services of our children, and former ex-Attlee pupils now aged 22–27. To place the project and control schools' children's family backgrounds in context we were able to identify the level of crime in the area in which the children lived. Furthermore, the percentage of their families' involvement with the probation and social services departments is shown at the start and end of the project.

Table 6: Children's family agency contact and ex-Attlee pupils' grown-up contact, %

SCHOOL	Start probation	After project	Start SSD	After project	% Change Probat'n SSD	
Project – Attlee	4*	0.5	8	5.1	−3.5	−2.9
Control – Churchill	0.2	1.2	1.9	2.5	+1.0	+0.6
Project – Bevan	0.4*	0.9	3.4	1.4	−0.5	−2
Control – Disraeli	0.6	1.3	1.6	2.6	+0.7	+1.6

* Families in contact with both agencies

The county average male crime rate was 6 per cent, but almost 24 per cent of Attlee estate men had a criminal conviction. However, by the end of the project numbers of known crimes on the estate fell from 11 per cent of households to 7.4 per cent. Notwithstanding, Attlee estate male offenders still had an average of nine indictable crimes, markedly higher than the average county rate.

The degree of Attlee family disruption is seen in that almost 24 per cent of its men have been involved with probation, and 3 per cent of its women, which is more than 8.5 times that of the average person.

However, by end of the project while Attlee families still had a significantly higher contact than the other schools, they had almost halved their rate. The negative changes in the control schools probably reflect the impact of the phase of recession as it hit ordinary families. Figures released by the SSD showed that before the project Attlee had 25 child protection referrals, the highest in the county. At the end of the project this was down to six, a fall of 76 per cent, coinciding with annual rises in the rest of the county, increasing from 270 to 360 – a 33 per cent rise over the lifetime of the project.

Attlee intergenerational problems

Of the 228 former Attlee pupils, now aged 22–27, 8.7 per cent of the men and 10.2 per cent of the women were currently known to the SSD, considerably more than the age-related average. Furthermore, a small pilot survey found that they had five times the age-related pregnancy rate of the county.

An in-depth analysis on 36 family case-records of children from Attlee showed amongst the multiplicity of problems that 40 per cent had serious child protection issues, 10+ per cent child sexual abuse, one in 10 had predominantly mental health problems and one in five had medical and chronic health disorders, with 7 per cent a physical disability.

Overall, children in all four schools, especially Attlee, came from more disadvantaged backgrounds than their average peers, with a significant minority of intergenerational difficulties. To illustrate these a brief case example is offered.

A 40 year old mother who herself had been in care as a child, a victim of particularly severe abuse, had a history of disruptive and drug-dependent behaviour, requiring long-term monitoring from community psychiatry and primary health. Next to her case file was her daughter 'Mary', now aged 18, who had been excluded from school six months before the project because of pregnancy. She has two children, is pregnant again, and is currently under the supervision of the SSD, having been involved with the EWO service, police, probation, SSD, primary health care, and paediatrics. This is an example of the speed of a further twist in the intergenerational cycle of vulnerability.

Counselling and community work outcomes

Over the first 12 months the team dealt with 94 cases, a number that continued into the third year. At the weekly team meeting the PSW assessed the cases' degree of severity: 'very severe', i.e. if unresolved would lead to exclusion, 'severe', and 'moderate or mild'. A degree of subjectivity in these judgements is acknowledged, but it is the reality for frontline staff – after all, statutory decisions are made like this. 'Very severe' constituted 27 per cent of the 94 cases, 33 per cent 'severe', with 39 per cent 'moderate' and 1 per cent 'mild'. Most were multi-problem but the main overlapping difficulties were: behavioural disorders 54 per cent; 'neurotic/anxiety' difficulties 29 per cent; reactive educational problems 11 per cent, and 9 per cent medical troubles contributing to the child's school adjustment, with 18 per cent being parental rather than the child's problems. Ten per cent of referrals were extra-school, 9 per cent and 22 per cent were child and parental self-referrals, and the remainder were school (teacher) referrals.

Over a quarter (28 per cent) of cases required continuous work by the PSW, 12 months plus, facilitating in-depth preventive and supportive work, which receive a much closer commitment than the usual standard service. Some, however, especially the 40 per cent of 'moderate' severity, only required short-term but intensive work, but provided an important 'preventive' dimension as such cases might not be allocated in a standard service until there was a breakdown.

Face-to-face work

Although some cases continued to require welfare payments, broadly 40 per cent of problems appeared to be totally resolved; 46 per cent were much improved, 9 per cent improved, 2 per cent showed no change, and 3 per cent became worse or much worse.

In regard to the 'resolved' cases, it was invariably emphasised to the children/families that they could always be seen again. Hence, while some cases were closed, a proportion were under tacit continued supervision, allowing a speedy response if necessary.

The outcomes of the severe and very severe cases was encouraging as 42 per cent were resolved, 52 per cent were much improved and only 5 per cent were worse or much worse. Overall, therefore, the evidence points to the benefit of an accessible resource, which can target those most at risk to prevent further deterioration and disruption in school or community.

Two brief examples of typical cases are illustrative of presenting problems and the team's activities.

Crisis indicative of long-term needs

'Alice', a 7-year-old girl in a temper tantrum attacked another child with a knife and the dinner lady alerted the project teacher. The PSW found a very chaotic background in a family new to the area, and overt rejection by a neglecting mother (whose cohabitee was aggressive to the mother, Alice and the other three younger children). Alice's school achievement was not high, considering her very high measured IQ, while her behaviour was judged to be reactive to the tribulations at home. The project teacher worked with her intensively in the first week, partly to resolve the reactions of staff and the parents of the attacked child, while the PSW began work with the parents. The psycho social problems included mother's suicidal behaviour, the criminal record of the 'stepfather', a risk of eviction for non-payment of rent, physical and emotional abuse of Alice and mother, who was often defended by Alice. The case was classified very severe. The PSW's intensive counselling and support work with the parents resulted in improvements in their relationship, and they gained more appropriate expectations of the children. The PSW who was asked to be the 'key worker' following a case conference initiated by the school and the SSD ensured a high degree of supervision in order to reduce the risk of violence. Crucially, the PSW recognised the parental emotional needs and helped to set boundaries and structure in the family, maximising the mother's inherent aspirations for Alice and helping her avoid a typical immature parental response. The project teacher's work with Alice led to a major improvement in her work and she delighted in her school success which was no longer just a refuge but a place to maximise her development. The PSW helped the stepfather in getting employment, which relieved much of the intra-family tension, while Alice's improvement eased mother's sense of inadequacy. The situation was clearly 'much improved', the intensive work lasting 11 months.

Short-term emergency intervention preventing long-term disruption

'Brian', a 13-year-old boy, arrived late in Bevan distressed and had a verbal outburst in class. Project teacher learned that Brian had first assisted two younger siblings to Attlee following emergency admission of mother to psychiatric hospital. PSW immediately dealt with the emergency as there was chaos at home. This was an example of stopping a crisis impacting negatively on all involved. In conjunction with father the PSW arranged support of neighbours for meals and for two nights' overnight stay as father's job entailed overnight absences two or three nights a week. SSD agreed to a short-term plan, avoiding the likely temporary admission into care, with all the associated disruption to children. Speedy action meant minimal disruption to children and the school. Involvement of neighbours who responded sympathetically to mother's plight; reinforced community networks; and began liaison with psychiatric services to improve mental health supervision of mother.

Table 7 gives a brief illustration of some representative cases.

Table 7: Brief details of direct work

Referred*	Age	Problem, outcome and time case lasted (months)
Mother	14	Single mother, relies on benefits, child's distress in response to new father and anxiety and aggression in new partnership. PSW helps mother resolve ambivalence in readjustment, child's anxieties reduced, follow-up shows problem resolved a year later. (4)
D/Head	15+	Bullying and disruption in class found linked to chronic family problem, the adolescent anxious about leaving school. Underachiever, counselled by PSW, improved self-esteem, assisted

		transfer into FE much improved relationships with peers and family. (5)
Self	15+	Out of school behaviour, parent pressures with poverty and welfare. Counselling to improve child/parent relations, enabling him to continue at home and assisted in gaining part-time employment – contact continues when required. Much improved. swn†
Teacher	14	Stress at home, educational under-achiever, disruptive in class. Resolved via direct counselling. (3)
Teacher	11	Learning difficulties, peer and adult relationships, family stress and disharmony quite severe. Needed long-term family counselling to assist home and school. Resolved. (13)
Teacher	15	Home conflicts with new parent figures, disruptive in class to self and others. Intensive counselling. Resolved. (3)
Teacher	14	Peer relationship problems, disruptive and disturbing and bullying. Engaged in group counselling, which 'diverted' him, later took lead role in school play, resolving problem. (3)
Outside	14	Severe family problems, mental health, poverty, cohabitee, acute crisis involved housing, with acute outburst in class, considered for exclusion. Counselling family and child, while threat to exclude gone, still 'has his moments' (4) swn
Outside	15	Family breakdown, temporary homelessness, intermittent disruption in school. Short work with boy, mainly intensive with mother, both acute family and housing problem resolved. (4) swn
Teacher	15	Every problem, school, peers, theft, community, sexual behaviour. Counselling and group to reintegrate into family, now at home, assisted into full-time job. (3)
Head	11	Numerous times in care in response to family breakdown and mental illness, encopresis, theft, but held in school as a place of continuity and avoided Pupil Referral Unit, some progress but still in care, needs long-term support. (20+)
Teacher	11	Parents over-protective, bullies and bullied, plus theft and disruption in class, started in junior school. Counselling for parents, more relaxed, positive transfer to secondary school. (14)
Teacher	13	Multi-problems with peers, adults, school, reaction to child neglect and abuse. School only refuge but after improvements parent left area, referred to new child psychiatrist and EWO for support. (13)
Mother	12	Educational difficulties, housing problems, peer relationships, as child borderline slow learner. Counselling for child, reassured parent has more confidence. (3) swn

* Referred by = e.g. mother
† swn = Team to 'see when needed'

'Consumer' study: the client speaks

What did the project mean to the *users* of the service? What follows are the written comments of project parents and children on their views of the PSW. This was part of a county-wide survey, thus avoiding the possibilities of stigmatising the families. Not surprisingly, as the PSW could give a more intensive service than the 'standard' control, project families' very positive response rate was better, 94 per cent (n = 49) to 72 per cent (n = 218) and he was viewed much more positively.

The quality of project–user interaction can be found in the remarks made in the open-ended responses. Only two of the 49 project respondents failed to add additional comments. Bearing in mind the backgrounds of the respondents this indicates that the survey had engaged their interest. Some clients commented extensively, welcoming the opportunity of making constructive criticisms.

The first example is given in some detail as it came from an initially hostile parent who described the conflict she and her child had before transfer to the project school. Their satisfaction with the PSW was in stark contrast with the disruption they had experienced earlier.

The mother wrote:

> The whole of my family and family relationships has been severely harmed. The most damaging aspect was the damage caused to my daughter. At the most crucial time of her life the opportunity of education has been denied her, and there is no way that she would have been able to obtain any educational standards, her whole future status and hence happiness has been denied by the gross incompetence of the aforementioned staff at X school. If there had been a legal way to obtain compensation from these members of staff I would have been willing to have taken the necessary action which may have helped in some way to save other children from the present and subsequent hardship that was caused to my daughter.

She complained of lack of support, lack of interest and failure to act, whereas now: 'He (the PSW) has been extremely helpful, sympathetic to the problems of my daughter and the problems caused in the family'.

Because this respondent gave her name, we know the outcome. This was very positive, with no further problems, and the child has begun to achieve some of her educational potential.

Some brief parental views

Asked to describe the three best and worst things about the PSW, the following comments illustrate the consumer's perception of the project.

'Practical help from someone who gave the impression he genuinely cared'.

'Being able to talk and feel he understood; knowing that everything said was in confidence; feeling this was a friend. I think the EWO has been a valuable asset to the school and hopefully will continue in this role'.

Always there when we needed help; very kind and understanding; very informative'.

'Very helpful and understanding; always there when I needed him for lifts or just a chat. Always listens and cares about everything about the family and school no matter what it involves. He puts himself out in every way; doesn't matter what he is dealing with, he treats you with respect. My family, me and three children, would be lost without our particular EWO; he has been very kind and very helpful to all of us, very friendly and cheerful'.

'He has been very helpful with the problems we have had with our child; he takes time to listen to you and to what you have to say; he will listen to the child's side of things as well. We are just very pleased with the way he has been so helpful and handled the problems we have had'.

'Above all he understands people, nothing is too much trouble, he can have a laugh'. The first open-ended *negative* was, 'Sometimes he is hard to contact'.

'The EWO in our area is very supportive; willing, friendly, gentle towards people, does his job well'. The child, a 14-year-old boy of this family said: 'The best thing really is you can talk to someone who listens to you, another thing, he helps you when you are in trouble at school; there isn't a bad thing about him.'

'Although my child has had no problems in school, he was there for myself when I lost my husband and for the months that followed; I shall always be grateful'.

'My son felt there was somebody on his side and was immediately less intimidated about being bullied. The social worker achieved everything he set out to do. The EWO worked closely with my son which gave my son the confidence to deal with the situation himself afterwards. We found the institution, and the Norwegian system to stop bullying very effective and left everyone involved feeling in a positive frame of mind. He was enthusiastic and dedicated. Keep up the good work and thank you'.

'He is always happy to listen to your point of view'.

'Helpful; reliable; sensible'.

'He was young [!] and so my son could relate to him. They met weekly for lunch and my son could open up to him. He was very supportive to me and telephoned regularly to check on the situation and to see how I was. He made my son feel important and worthy. He was having trouble with his father and needed to feel that his opinions were valued. He also helped P over the death of his grandmother. I can only speak very highly of him. P was going through a lot of emotional trauma, and I was not coping well. He took the pressure from me and helped my son through a very difficult time. We all felt that he cared about what happened to us. He helped P come to terms with the death of his Granny and the emotions attached to that, and his very mixed feelings towards his absent father. For the time being P is more settled and is happier within himself. I hope that should he become insecure again, that either I can be more help to him or the EWO would be able to fit him in again. He was sufficiently detached from the emotion and problem to see a way through. I was not'.

'He made me feel I'm not alone. Having him coming in my home makes me feel a lot better with the problems we have been having. Also it has helped our child a lot. Very pleased with our EWO, he has helped us a *lot*'.

'Support' – he was there when things went very wrong with my son. Patience – he really needed this at times. Calmness – his calmness really amazed me. Over the past few years I have had three children going through school, so I know, and my contact with the EWO, I found him to be very very helpful'.

Some children's views

A 16-year-old boy wrote: 'Helping me get through school. Helping me get a grant. He is a very useful and helpful person and a friend'.

A 12-year-old boy: 'He listens to you; he do something about it; he make sure the problem is done.' One of the rare negatives: 'Didn't always see him, sometimes it was hard to talk'.

A 12-year-old boy wrote: 'He was very nice'.

Girl aged 14 wrote: 'He always understood me and always

listened to what I had to say. He helped me by talking to my teachers. He was a very kind man. I am very glad I met him as he has helped me a lot'.

A 15-year-old boy stated: 'He helped me sort my life out. He got me back to school. He spent a lot of time on it, he didn't rush it. In the past he has helped me a lot to get back to school and is currently helping me find a school and is doing a good job'.

Another 12-year-old boy commented: 'Always listened and tried to understand my problems. Tries the easiest way for me to sort them out. If the first tactics did not work, tried different ways of approaching the trouble'.

A 13-year-old girl wrote: 'He has helped me sort my life, with people and family and problems. He has helped me get some confidence. He has been a great help, but the most important thinking I have learnt is that blokes are just as good at advice and listening as women are. [A rather unusual example of good equal opportunities practice!] On the negative side she mentioned, however, 'At first I did not like telling the truth to him first, because he was a bloke but I got used to it in the end'.

A 14-year-old girl, while generally very positive, said: 'Sorted out arguments, helped me talk to my parents about things they don't understand – always there to help.' On the negative side: 'Sometimes makes the world sound perfect and could go on a bit'.

A 14-year-old boy wrote: 'I would like to thank Mr Williams for being such a help and a friend, and for helping me through the past year. Helped me sort out my problem. Showed me how to deal with various situations. Gave me hope for the future'.

A 14-year-old girl wrote: 'You can talk about anything, they always listen to your problems. He don't do anything or say anything to parents if you ask them not to. I have good friends but I think I could talk more with the EWO. I like filling out this questionnaire, it made me realise just how much he has helped me'.

A 14-year-old girl wrote: 'No matter how bad I feel before I see the EWO, just knowing I am going there and talking makes me feel a lot better. I always make seeing him a positive thought and look forward to having someone to talk to and getting everything sorted in my mind – I feel as though he is the only person I can really trust'.

On the negative side the same girl said: 'Although my social worker makes it clear he would like to see me more, I fear he has more serious problems to deal with and he often has to be elsewhere – I feel the EWO is best and easiest to help, although my Mum knows nothing about my meetings, and as long as no one knows of my EWO in the school it is alright, because I don't want them to know I have got family problems'.

A 15-year-old boy having said nice things wrote: 'I am quite disappointed that there is only one officer at our school and it isn't easy to talk and not private. I'd would like to think they would have more officers at our school and it would be much easier to talk'.

Not untypically, from a 12-year-old girl: 'He has always been there for me when I have needed him and he listens to my Mum as well. My EWO was brill.'

The only negative comments were that sometimes the PSW was not easily available, while the secondary head teacher said a school his size could use a full-time officer. Nonetheless, bearing in mind that the large majority of clients had truancy and educational problems, this was a service that was valued by its consumers, demonstrating the benefits of strategic targeting of troubled children and families. The key themes were that they felt individualised, that personal interest was shown, with informed advice and guidance, trust, calmness and time and confidentiality given to deal with complex situations. We turn now to the general results of all the schools.

6 Comparing the project and control schools

The project assumed that its work would be cumulatively beneficial to the rest of the school in terms of improved attitudes and behaviour compared to the control schools over the three years.

The annual survey response rate was based upon numbers on the school roll. Junior schools' response rate never fell below 87 per cent and the rate for the secondary schools was 81–85 per cent. As average official 'absenteeism' was about 10 per cent, virtually every child in the schools completed the questionnaire.

Attlee v Churchill Primary before and after

Initially there were fifty 9- to 11-year-old Attlee and 183 Churchill school children at the start of the project and 55 and 171 children respectively at the end.

Social factors

In both surveys, Attlee children had a higher proportion of unemployed fathers than Churchill's (42 per cent and 40 per cent v 31 per cent and 20 per cent); more children belonged to single-parent families (32 per cent v 15 per cent); more had parents who smoked (50 per cent v 40 per cent) and a substantially larger proportion had free school dinners rate (33 per cent v 15 per cent). However, both schools had higher levels than the county average. Both schools had a greater number not living with both natural parents (non-intact families) than the national average, as Attlee deteriorated over the period, their rate rising from 34 per cent to 46 per cent, indicating an increase of family disruption during times of recession; new single-parent families also came onto the estate.

Problematic behaviour

Truancy is less of a problem in primary schools, since children are more easily missed. However, there was a virtual absence of truancy in both schools, confirmation that despite the socio-economic backgrounds they maintained pupil interest.

The child smoking rate had doubled in both schools over the three years, up to 27 per cent and 23 per cent respectively, a sad confirmation of the success of indirect advertising (Mindle 1995), while children drinking alcohol at home (51 per cent) reflected a new societal trend.

Compared with Churchill, Attlee pupils significantly reduced fighting, bullying, vandalism, theft and increased their enjoyment of school as Table 8 shows.

Table 8: Attlee v Churchill Primary School significant changes before and after (ratio of ratios indicate comparative change), %

Behaviour and attitude	Attlee n = 50–55		Churchill n = 183–177		Rate of change (ratio of ratios)
	Before	After	Before	After	
Fights often	48	29	29	38	2.17
Bullying	28	22	28	30	1.07
School vandalism	18	0	14	18	2.31
Likes school	54	75	69	72	1.33

Summary

In terms of the project's objectives the above are grounds to show that children from disadvantaged backgrounds benefited, but in addition the enhanced provision was associated with improved individual behaviour and greater integration into the school.

The secondary schools: comparison of middle school-aged children (11–13), Bevan v Disraeli

To avoid repetition we report only very briefly on 'middle school'-aged children (11–13) and focus upon the Years 10 and 11 pupils.

Problematic behaviour

Compared to control school Disraeli there were improvements in Bevan middle school pupils' truancy rates, theft, fighting and bullying. However, Bevan's out-of-school vandalism increased more than Disraeli's, which was one of only a few problematic behaviours where project children's behaviour worsened more than the control school.

Bevan v Disraeli 14- to 16-year-olds before and after

Initially Attlee and Disraeli 14- to 16-year-old respondents numbered 272 and 356; at the end of the project these figures were 365 and 503 respectively, reflecting the changed configuration of schools in the area.

Bevan contained proportionately more 14- to 16-year-old boys than Disraeli (65 per cent and 53 per cent), a ratio of ratios of 1.15 over the period. Unemployment of fathers in both schools was 2.5 and 2.8 times respectively the regional male jobless rate.

Problematic behaviour

There were major gains for Bevan over Disraeli over the three years, especially almost halving truancy, and reducing fighting, theft, and use of cannabis, solvents and hard drugs. There were, however, rises in general vandalism in Bevan, but this may have reflected the higher number of males in Bevan over the period. Table 9 shows the rate of change.

Table 9: Bevan v Disraeli behaviour before and after, % (rates of change)

Behaviour	Bevan n = 272–356		Disraeli n = 365–503		Ratio of ratios (ROR)
	Before	After	Before	After	
Truancy	28	16	40	37	1.62
Fighting	28	20	31	29	1.31
Theft	21	23	41	49	1.09
School theft	19	10	30	32	2.03
Vandalism	28	44	28	37	1.19*
In school	22	8	18	22	3.36
Cannabis	18	19	26	27	1.02*
Often	12	8	14	16	1.71
Solvents	18	5	8	9	4.05
Hard drugs	11	10	7	12	1.89
Often	7	4	3	9	5.25
Smoking	57	55	62	61	1.02
Drinking in pubs	22	18	35	38	1.32

* Bevan worse result than Disraeli

There are two points to note: all children involved in drug misuse and solvents smoked, and the influence of peers cannot be overstated as *all* problematic behaviour occurred more often in groups than alone.

Attitudes to school

Initially there was little difference between the students' views. Later, Bevan's attitudes were significantly more positive, with more Bevan pupils (67 per cent) liking school than Disraeli (58 per cent) with an ROR of 1.10 over the period, with increased scores for Bevan on their views of teachers and 'staff are fair' (ROR 1.22): 'staff listen to you' (ROR 1.12). Equally important was the improvement in Bevan's pupils' post-school aspirations e.g. 'Hope to go to university' moved from 33 per cent to 63 per cent v 38 per cent to 44 per cent for Disraeli (ROR 1.65).

Search for value added for core disadvantaged

Though both schools were relatively disadvantaged compared with the rest of the county, only a minority would be seriously disadvantaged. Therefore, how well did the project do in reaching a core group of the worst off children? We extrapolated all data on Y10 and Y11 pupils from the Attlee estate and compared them with Disraeli pupils from another comparable estate, 'Alpha Park'. Apart from ex-Attlee students having more unemployed fathers (56 per cent v 38 per cent), and almost double the statutory agency contact, they were the closest match obtainable. Former Attlee teenagers had a far better outcome, as shown by Table 10.

The project appears to have reached the potential core group of disaffected pupils. Of particular satisfaction was the decline in hard drugs, as initially the estate had a serious problem. This added an important compensatory 'socialising' element to these young people, a 'value-added' component indeed.

'Generally I like school': real value added

Further 'value added' was found when we asked which group behaved the least badly. Combining all Y10 and Y11 respondents, we found that the groups with the least troublesome behaviour were associated with belonging to a two-parent family, then having an employed father, then having non-smoking parents, but the group with the least troublesome behaviour were children who 'Liked school', even though 27 per cent of the group had an unemployed father and 28 per cent did not belong to

Table 10: Disraeli pupils from Attlee v Alpha Park estates, Years 10 and 11, %

Behaviour	Ex-Attlee n = 88 %	Ex-Alpha Park n = 180 %
Truancy	18	48
Fighting often	15	38
Theft	22	53
School theft	12	42
Vandalism	24	47
In school	9	26
Cannabis	21	25
Often	9	18
Solvents	2	10
Hard drugs	0	12
Often	0	10
Smoking	57	66
Drinking in pubs	20	43
Liking school	77	57

an intact family. Clearly, if we can engage young people in the educational process, they are well on the way to full citizenship.

Educational outcomes

Every school's objective is not just to enhance children's psychosocial integration but to maximise their educational potential. The schools under review, however, were not true 'mixed ability' as there were single-sex grammar schools, which 'cream off' many of the more able students. Indeed, initially Bevan and Disraeli had over 26 per cent of 'slow learners'. Nonetheless, while the percentage of Disraeli pupils that achieved five or more GCSEs at A–C went from 13 per cent to 20 per cent, Bevan's rose from 26 per cent to 37 per cent – their best ever result.

While no single finding should stand alone, but there are grounds to assert that the project schools met most of their aims and performed significantly better than the comparison schools. How helpful was it to the frontline classroom teachers?

7 Teachers as 'consumers'

The project sought to enhance the schools' ability to be inclusive, so what was its practical value to the teacher?

Teachers' concerns and morale

At the beginning and end of the project we measured levels of staff morale and stress in all four schools via an anonymous, self-administered questionnaire (Borg *et al.* 1991). Initially 74 teachers completed the questionnaire, a 73 per cent response rate, and at the end the figure was 84 – an 80 per cent response rate.

There were no significant differences in the teachers' backgrounds, with a female:male 3:1 ratio in the primary schools and more males in the secondary schools. Fewer than 10 per cent were aged under 30, with one in four having taught for more than twenty years, and 18 per cent had been in their current school for more than eleven years.

We asked about issues which concerned them and initially there were no significant differences between the schools; they tended to focus on issues such as poor public understanding; lack of interest and support from parents; the range and speed of change in schools; trying to teach 'children with poor attitudes'; and working with 'noisy pupils'. Interestingly, only half mentioned inadequate salary, but there was strong agreement that there was 'too much to do', and consequently a 'lack of time for individual pupils'.

While a broad consensus remained on 'issues of concern', over the period the project teachers were more positive, and sometimes significantly so, as shown in Table 11.

Included in the questionnaire were opportunities for open-ended responses and these are reflected below. Teachers were asked what gave them most professional 'satisfaction' and/or caused most 'dissatisfaction'. Some of the actual written comments will be presented later, but here we review the changes. The majority of experienced professionals gained satisfaction from a positive relationship with the development of the child, while their dissatisfaction was almost a mirror image of their job satisfaction. Afterwards there was a significant shift in the extent of satisfaction of project teachers, though both groups commented upon

Table 11: Matters that cause the teacher concern in project and control schools before and after project, %

Issue	Before n = 43–40		After n = 50–34	
	Project	Control	Project	Control
Lack of recognition of good teaching	80	90	62	66
Parents not responsible for child's bad behaviour	86	91	75	96**
Noisy pupils	93	92	46	80**
Pupils' poor attitude to work	93	90	70	76
Inadequate salary	82	80	86	75
Too much to do and not enough time to do it	100	98	84	95
Maintaining class discipline	81	93	40	63**
Poor relationships in staff room	12	17	4	21*
Lack of interest and support from parents	90	92	72	86*
Pressure from head teacher	48	38	24	48*
No recognition that we care about problem children	60	72	38	60*
Administration and form filling	98	96	76	86
Pressure from parents	61	63	25	41
Poor feedback about my work	66	62	25	51
Excluded from decisions about child in my class	52	46	23	47
Having large class size	100	100	89	91
Difficult class	92	96	59	84*

Significant * p<0.05 ** p<0.01

inadequate resources and a sense of the increasing 'politicalisation' of education.

The teacher's voice

All respondents had both positive and negative views, and it would be naive to ignore this ambivalence. Yet, on balance, what gave teachers most 'job satisfaction' centred upon positive outcomes concerning children's educational and psychosocial development, while the negative aspects concerned 'barriers' to their child focus.

Open-ended comments 'satisfaction v dissatisfaction'

Teacher with 20 years' experience

Positives: 'Knowing I am able to motivate, and stimulate children to do excellent work in a pleasant atmosphere despite the shortcomings of space, the numbers etc.'

Negatives: 'Paperwork which is not necessary to either me or the children – constantly having to write for and attend irrelevant meetings – behaviour at lunchtimes is bad and affects the performance of the children in the afternoons, this is due to lack of professional supervision, there is reliance upon poor quality dinner ladies, despite their efforts, it is terribly short sighted and demoralising'.

Teacher with 18 years' experience

Positives: 'Developing relationships with pupils and pupils responding in a situation within the school environment – some aspects of classroom teaching (when I'm allowed to) to try to put across the feeling I have for my subject unhindered by external constraints, still give me a buzz. If education is to be seen in a more positive light, it needs desperately a period of stability so that teachers can get to grips with all the rest of the changes, more money to be made available, staffing levels and the rest, and the DfE and Ofsted's many demands.

Specialist teacher

Negatives: 'Frustration from lack of progress in class is more stressful than any physical illness I have had. Sadly we have to accept far worse behaviour than I feel personally happy with'.

Teacher with 20 years' experience

'Having to put up with everyone that thinks they are experts on teaching, but don't actually have to do it (not a dig at you, dear Professor, but it does become a little wearing)'.

Teacher with 40 years' experience

Not all the respondents were 'progressives' by any means. One teacher felt that there was nothing positive to say: 'There is a lack of power to impose what cannot be obtained by civilised means – let us stop trying to fudge issues with money. Put discipline back into the classroom and the many difficulties (including most of the learning difficulties) will disappear'.

Teacher with 23 years' experience

'Education is about pupils and preparing them for life after school, not just examination results, truancy figures etc.' Negatives: 'Despite being reasonably intelligent, watching a pupil slowly switching off for reasons outside the school'.

Teacher with 11 years' experience

Had very strong satisfactions and gave good advice: 'I would like all the politicians to do a teacher's job for at least a term, so that they could understand our position a little better'.

Teacher with 22 years' experience

'We need extra time to give support where it is needed, time to talk to pupils, not just about work. Someone on the staff (non-teaching) to work with parents and outside agencies to see into social work files when absentees' and 'When EBDU pupils come back to school, they need continued support in class, and we need some way of getting them working and acting appropriately. We need to learn more social and study skills, lots of mentoring, which may be difficult to build up in the already hectic times'.

Change of career teacher

'It is frustrating to know that I work harder and longer than when I worked in industry and got paid more (even though I knew that when I changed careers' but 'the satisfaction that comes from seeing pupils able to understand and grasp issues, ... developing good relationships with pupils to feel that we are all approachable, ... despite everything it is the most satisfying job I have ever had'.

Anger about the politicisation of education is seen from a teacher with 19 years' experience: 'The arrogant and ill-informed decision makers – those who persist in telling us that pupils can be taught as mere statistics in terms of examination passes that schools can rise or fall because of the market place, and that education can be equated to a factory system. Some of us still do care about the individual.'

Teacher with 39 years' experience

'Job satisfaction is about helping pupils to achieve progress – sharing my own pleasure in the subject – warmth and spontaneity, and pupil/teacher relationships'. Finally, he said: 'I believe it is increasingly important to help pupils to respect language in the face of new speak'.

Teacher with 22 years' experience

'Small successes with children in work or socially – bringing some stability and humour into the lives of children whose previous experience has been so limited – good teacher – child–parent interaction'.

Teacher with 34 years' experience

'Seeing smiles on young faces after achieving and tackling assignments, and proving to themselves that they have done well – knowing one can always be approached within the class and school by child or parent; it is wonderful to be entrusted with this competence and to be part of their lives'.

'Here's to the future of our young people. More education and home care skills and future parenting are urgently needed'.

Teacher with 23 years' experience

Positives: 'Seeing children beginning to accept responsibility for their own learning and personal development – being part of a process whereby school and community develop mutual respect, genuine and functional and working with colleagues who share my aspirations'.

Negatives: 'Frustration of not having the time and energy to do all I would like to do – knowing that many children need attention and support but cannot demonstrate this clearly enough to get it through the bureaucratic system – being required to meet unrealistic and inappropriate demands in terms of curriculum and record keeping; the project has been a breath of fresh air'.

Here was the voice of the professional, balanced, realistic, but lamenting the oft underachieved potential of youngsters for whom school is the key in their education for adult citizenship.

Occupational stress

From the above there are indications that sometimes modern teaching can be stressful. We measured teachers' stress before and at the end of the project, defining it as 'dysfunctional' if the respondent felt 'more stressed than colleagues'.

Initially, there was little difference between project and control teachers' stress levels but there were significant differences after three years as Table 12 shows.

Table 12: Project v control teachers' stress levels – before and after, %

Type of stress	Project n = 34–39		Control n = 40–45	
	Before	After	Before	After
Little or no stress	9	23	10	11
Similar stress to colleagues	62	74	55	69
More stress than colleagues	29	3	35	20

X2+ 15.68 p = <0.02

Project teachers also benefited from the project as the 'More stress' category fell from nearly a third (29 per cent) to only 3 per cent, a significant improvement, indicating another 'value-added' element of the project. So how did teachers perceive the project? To counter any 'halo' effect, a number of 'negative' comments were included.

Table 13: Project teachers' structured views (n = 39), % (don't know responses excluded)

Comments about the project	Agree	Disagree
The project enhanced the pupils' integration in the school.	79	3
The project contributed to improving the children's school attendance.	85	3
The project was generally a waste of time.	0	95
The project helped to identify problem children earlier.	85	3
The project just encouraged feckless parents to continue being irresponsible.	3	67
The project worker/s were supportive to staff in difficult situations.	92	0
The project contributed to improved pupil's health education awareness.	72	0
The project was a real benefit to pupils' parents.	62	0
The project often helped to stop a crisis becoming an emergency.	64	0
The project did very little to contribute to improved teaching standards.	8	72
Having the project social worker was generally very helpful.	92	0

Table 13 (contd)

Comments about the project	Agree	Disagree
The project enhanced pupil/teacher relations.	69	0
A future project should not have even a modest priority for future funding.	80	87
The project often made excuses for undeserving pupils.	8	69
Having a project teacher was generally very helpful.	74	5
The project enhanced the school's ethos.	72	5
Improved work with disruptive pupils.	85	0
The project did little in reducing family tensions.	5	49
Enhanced interagency partnership/communication	56	0
Accessibility of social worker especially valuable.	79	0
Project generally irrelevant to work of the school.	3	90

Bold type indicates comment framed negatively

It can be seen that the vast majority of teachers found the project of practical help and strongly rejected the idea that the project was 'a waste of time, encouraged feckless parents, was irrelevant to work of the school', and so on.

In-depth interviews undertaken with a sample of teachers and the two heads yielded very rich and informative examples of how the project supported the educational task. The following are just a few illustrative examples.

Respondent one (R1) was initially hostile to the project and proudly subscribed to 'a very traditional approach to teaching, and I do not care who knows it'. He believed that 'society spends too much time trying to understand delinquents, and not enough condemnation of either them or their parents. You may think I'm hard; I'm not – I care tremendously about my children'. Yet he ended by saying 'I am happy that the project is here as it helps the children with their feckless parents, and I can get on and teach them'.

R2: 'Always available to deal with child and family ... gives important feedback to the teacher to help why kids may be off-colour, which is particularly important when you are feeling a bit fazed yourself'.

From 'inception it was an opportunity to develop the good quality of pastoral care we had into a major feature of school'. Additionally, it provided 'an extra academic interest in specific outcome of how it would affect our children – and – its relevance in a wider setting'. It gave us all 'an opportunity to celebrate good working practices in school – wonderful opportunity to enhance and, very important, provided vehicle where staff efforts and interest could be acknowledged'.

'The project has enabled the meeting of needs; meeting crises as they occurred; encouraged thinking further about how we can improve our service. It has limited the negative effects which often affected children and school. It has given us knowledge and experience so that, through proactive intervention, pupils do well at secondary level.

R3: It has had a 'direct effect upon the community, enabling common concerns to be aired ... standards to be raised in terms of ... social interaction and vandalism ... school has become involved in the direct support of these families, contributing to the education of the child, and at the same time, the community orientation of the school'.

R4: 'It has meant that teachers have been free to support the other children, with confidence that the needs of those causing concern are being addressed'.

R5: 'In class we have the support to allow identification of children with extra needs ... support staff in carrying out their heavy demands ... has given statistical evidence to actually argue for further funding for this school.'

R6: (Previous experience in Inner London.) 'Such an activity didn't occur, and you can see now that it would have helped immensely', because 'invariably there was an explosion before a child got any attention', and then was 'kicked out, to every-body's relief'. The respondent had always thought it was an integral part of the school.

R7: Enabled us to do 'things I have wanted to do for years', gave an example of 'social skills training with the older children, which is very, very good indeed', and 'working alongside the social worker, as matching and complementary skills to those of the teacher', to the benefit of the children.

HEAD A: 'Initially the project represented, at least in the early stages, an opportunity to become involved in that essential part of the school, the business of total pastoral care and student support. The project obviously intended to support the student from a holistic point of view, specifically relating school activities to those of other agencies and seeking to find methods of short circuiting the occasional hiatus between those agencies. Without wishing to be too "twee" about it, the better the students are developed as young people, the more they will be part of society and contribute to it, if not in a positive way, certainly not in a criminal way. The project is an extension because it enhances what we are trying to do, improves our ears, and eyes, and makes us think of how better to do it – it's an extension of the school approach, as the turbulence sometimes felt in school is almost invariably reflecting problems from home'.

HEAD B: 'Briefly the project has been both additional and an extension. Additional in the sense that it enhanced, developed and extended the activities that were going on within the school, and to some extent outside. Most certainly an extension in that it took the activities from within the school to the families, which matches many parents' intentions who desire to be part of something better for their children. The project took the school and extended it very much into the community as a whole. It has not, however, been a different thing in the sense that although some of the day-to-day and week-to-week activities by the case workers have obviously at times been different, in another sense, they provided a service which we could not otherwise have done in a meaningful way.'

Responses to the question 'What do you think the social worker–teacher actually does?' were as follows.'

    R1:   Closer contact with parents and therefore greater access to parents one to one, which is 'impossible for the teachers, because they can't control the parents, who in turn can't control the child', because many teachers 'are reluctant to have to deal with the parents'. The teacher 'is our link between family and my children; if I have got any difficulties I can speak to "Anne" (project teacher)'.

    R2:   The social worker identifies problems inside and outside the schools, as so often 'the behaviour in school is only the tip of the iceberg', but R2 stresses that it is very important 'to get the right kind of person', and with the time to 'be able to take on those emotionally stressful confrontational situations, yet maintain a calm'.

R3:   The social worker is a skilful bridge 'between difficult parents, the pupils and the school, and brings them together in a non-authoritative way' and provides 'an independent voice which makes us think'. 'Just a superb colleague', but he could be replaced, despite his exceptional personality, providing 'one employed another social worker who stood what he stood for, and has a sympathy with education'.

R4:   The project staff have been mainly involved at the crisis end, namely 'with the lower school and the exceptionally difficult 11th year'. The social worker has developed very good relationships with children, staff and head teacher, and has been accepted by all – it was important that he entered as a member of the staff room as soon as possible. Also it was 'important for the children to know that there is access to somebody who can help them immediately, without having to take the problems outside the school'.

R5:   Project teacher liaises direct with social services and family, often assists with administration, and can offer an immediate response to problems, and 'she is the bridging link person. Almost like a social worker'. This is partly 'due to personality, and her ability to cope with class and family, and partly from the support she gets from Richard (Williams)', so the two roles seem to be not repetitive, but complementary.

Gave an example of the problem of family feuding on the estate which affects children, and the speed of response time to deal with these problems, freeing up the staff and children's energy for education – 'can't be over-emphasised'.

R6:   'A great facilitator and bridge builder – he works at the "worm hole level" – gets inside structures which often are closed and helps people to come out and work together' – 'reminded us all by example and activity of indivisibility of classroom, child, family and community'. 'Made school and community a greater reality' – helps staff to give of their best and enjoy giving it'.

HEAD A: The social worker has actually given impartial advice and expertise, and his support work at the school has been fundamental in our increasing success. The social worker has also supported the project teacher and has helped to collate information, write reports and work directly with children, parents, agencies, to bring in other innovative projects within the umbrella of the Healthy Alliance.

I suppose the social worker has become an important member of the school team, which has been crucial, and to be supportive to me as head teacher, as well as the other teachers.

It has enabled instant responses to be given to problems which arise within or outside the school. In terms of the project teacher, again, it has been able to provide a critical analysis of the development of children within school and to enable us to target those children who are failing, so that early intervention can take place.

The project teacher has also been able to go out of school, to give an immediate response to any request, or to follow up the work of social services and other statutory agencies adding support, and at times acting as advocate on behalf of those parents and children. The teacher and social worker attendance at case conferences has meant there has been a reduction on my time also.

Yes, the project worker could be replaced. However, I do think that personality is crucial and that the person should be matched to the needs and make up of the school. It is vital that both school and any workers work in harmony together, and although there may be times when viewpoints are challenging, that there is a professional commitment to resolving those differences successfully. It is crucial therefore that personalities do fit in and that the social worker understands the school's agenda, while the school has to have an understanding about what the social worker can do and his role.'

HEAD B: 'I think, it would be difficult to sum up what he has done in the three years he has been here; he has tackled many cases, some in considerable depth. He has loosened up and facilitated communication between the school, its constituent staff and any number of external agencies, families, parents and guardians. He was generally successful in all that he did, and extremely hard working. This is borne out by the fact that the teaching colleagues, and support staff, *without exception*, see him as hard working and a very real benefit to the school.

Asked whether it was the personality or the role of the PSW that was important, while acknowledging the PSW's 'personality', all agreed it was the role and skill and the perspective the role brought that was important.

Responses to the question 'What are the weaknesses of the project?' were as follows.

> *R1*: 'Some families take advantage – "I want, I take, I do nothing", and sometimes frankly the support is too much, and you encourage them to dump their children on us – I've said it before, we are doing the social services' work for them'.
>
> *R2*: 'Bringing difficult children back into the school without adequate back-up and without resolving the original problem can be stressful'. Sometimes, 'listens too much to parents'. Main weakness is that 'there is not enough of the social worker – to represent the school where it matters'.
>
> *R3*: 'We have raised expectations of ourselves and certainly the social worker and teacher', and 'we sometimes find it difficult to share them with the other school – because there is just not enough time. Whilst we know he is doing other things, it is the sharpness of our problems we feel most'.
>
> *R4*: 'There aren't any weaknesses'.
>
> *R5*: 'Needs to run longer, we probably need another two years to get our parents viewing school differently; they are not convinced immediately, because they have a lot to overcome from previous bad experiences'.
>
> *R6*: 'You should be able to show that the costs of *not* excluding and having all that inadequate but costly home tuition can be saved. It would be good for kids, families, school'. [This idea was taken up later.]

The above are examples of how positive staff felt about the project, enhancing their sense of 'a job well done' and 'being just what our kids need'. The quote best summarising the effectiveness and spirit of the project was: 'When you first came, you were trying to stop the emergencies becoming crises. Now you are heading off the problems even before they become a crisis'.

Despite the obvious educational 'value added' to child, family and teachers, can such an initiative be afforded in other schools?

Costs and benefits

What follows is a cost – benefit analysis, based upon the costs to the education budget of making provision for special needs, and to the criminal justice system budget, of reducing delinquent behaviour.

Education costs were based upon the known expenditure of alternative education, i.e. home tuition and Emotional Behavioural Disturbed Units, which often follow exclusion from school. The criminal justice estimates came from Home Office calculations of the cost of offending and the administration of justice, reflecting the Audit Commission approach (1998) who were concerned at the wider financial cost of crime to society.

Education savings

These are linked to the costs of 'special education' following school exclusion. The project and control schools' 'exclusion and transfer-in of problematic children' numbers are compared. Such children being maintained in ordinary education are 'saving' the LEA considerable further costs.

Based on official LEA budgets at 2001 prices, figures are as follows. An ordinary pupil at a primary school cost £2,060 per place p.a. and a secondary school £2,210 p.a. but it costs £4,000 p.a. for a home tuition place and £17,000 p.a. for an 'Emotional Behavioural Disturbed Unit [EBDU] placement.

The argument here is that the project should have reduced school exclusions and enabled the schools, where appropriate, to transfer-in children at risk of exclusion, which is associated with future chaotic and disrupted lives (Smith and Farrington 2004).

Table 14 shows the numbers of 'excluded' and 'transferred-in' children of all the schools. In estimating costs the 'average' length of stay is used in the calculation, i.e. six months on home tuition, one year at an EBDU. The latter is longer because it is increasingly harder to get mainstream schools to reintroduce ex-EBDU pupils, especially the older adolescents.

The project schools significantly excluded fewer children and took in more, 78 per cent, of all 'transfers-in' than Churchilll and Disraeli over the three years. Such was the morale of the project schools that they were willing to accept the challenge of some of these transfers-in which inevitably meant further demands. Attlee had a net 'gain' of 28 extra pupils over the period, which in terms of costs 'saved' an estimated £470,800 over the three years, whereas Churchill had net 'losses' of approximately £117,600 at 2001 prices. While Disraeli demonstrated its commitment by having overall gains, saving £100,800, Bevan's 28 net gains yielded four times as much, at £470,400 over the period. Furthermore, Ofsted inspectors believed 25 Attlee children required

Table 14: 'Savings' by avoiding special education Project v control, exclude v transfer-in during the project

School	Children transferred-in	Children excluded	Gains +/−	Costs Home tuition 6 months £1,000's	Costs 1 Year EBDU £1000s
Attlee					
Year 1	8	0	8	23.5	134.4
Year 2	8	0	8	23.5	134.4
Year 3	12	0	12	35.2	202.0
Total +/− saving	28	0	28	81.2	470.8
Churchill					
Year 1	0	1	−1	−2.9	−16.8
Year 2	0	1	−1	−2.9	−16.8
Year 3	3	8	−5	−14.3	−84.0
Total +/− saving	3	10	−7	−18.1	−117.6
Bevan					
Year 1	10	4	6	17.2	100.8
Year 2	15	0	15	42.7	252.0
Year 3	12	5#	7	19.9	117.6
Total +/− saving	37	9	28	79.8	470.4
Disraeli					
Year 1	5	3	2	5.7	33.6
Year 2	4	2	2	5.7	33.6
Year 3	5	3	2	5.7	33.6
Total +/− saving	14	8	6	17.1	100.8

All exclusions and transfers project v control $X2 = 19.66$ 1 d/f $P = <.0001$

special education. If Attlee had followed the advice, the local provision would be overwhelmed, but they sought to meet parents' choice of keeping their children in mainstream education wherever possible.

What of the savings from reduced delinquency?

Criminal Justice savings

The Home Office and the Prince's Trust estimated that the average cost of any crime for the total criminal justice system was on average £3,250 (Audit Commission 1998). This sum does not include any subsequent adult prison costs, currently £28,800 p.a., or costs to the victim. These figures cannot be definitive, but they are indicative of the extent of the depredations of the rolling accumulative costs of an adolescent who moves into crime. The following calculations are based on Cooper and Lybrand estimates, adjusted for 2001 prices.

Middle and senior theft

Ignoring other behaviour, we concentrate only on the 95 Bevan students involved in theft. Far too many, perhaps, but if they had stolen at the rate of Disraeli students, there would have been 263 thieves, a 'saving' of 168 offenders. Using Cooper and Lybrand's rates only as an *indication* of potential saving, the figures become astronomic, i.e. in excess of £5,460,000, and this figure does not include possible costs to the victims! It is assumed, however, that most adolescent theft does not cost the same as 'adult' crime – therefore the above estimate will be ignored and only 'like-with-like' will be compared, i.e. those most at risk of 'criminality', the theft rates of the ex-Attlee and 'ex-Alpha' teenagers, at 22 per cent and 53 per cent respectively.

The differential in terms of numbers of offenders gives a 'saving' of 14 offenders, yielding a saving of £45,500. However, recent 16- to 17-year-old offenders in the county's biggest city, who are a year on from our 14- to 16-year-olds, cost £1,024,800 for the 183 young adults (16- to 23-year-olds) (Pritchard and Butler 2000a). If ex-Attlee had the same conviction rate this would be the equivalent of £222,000. Hence the suggested saving of £45,500 is a very, very modest estimate.

The limitations inherent in this cost – benefit analysis are acknowledged; nonetheless, set against the running costs of the project of £255,000, these leave a cautious net gain of £731,200, an equivalent of a 286 per cent return! This does not seem excessive, especially when remembering the potential intergenerational implications.

Cost of 'failure'?

These educational 'savings' are encouraging but what is the 'cost of failure', i.e. permanently excluding pupils, to the child and wider community? To answer this we examined a five-year consecutive cohort of 'excluded-from-school' (EFS) adolescents (n = 217) and followed them up for five years between the ages of 16 and 21 via police records. They were compared with a coterminous cohort of 'looked-after children' (LAC) (n = 837) on police records and a regional suicide register. In brief, the results were stark. Against expectations it was the EFS who had a far worse outcome in terms of crime, suicide and violence and, of course, this option 'cost' far more. While 32 per cent of the EFS had no subsequent police record, the remainder cost a minimum £4.9 million at 2001 prices, whereas only 37 per cent of the former LAC had subsequent criminal convictions, and 30 per cent of the EFS spent time in prison. Moreover, while there were no suicides amongst the LAC group, the EFS had a suicide rate 19 times that of the national rate for their age – a serious consequence indeed for the former pupil.

Moreover, the degree of alienation found within the EFS group was such that they had a murderer rate 18 times the national average for their age, including 15 per cent with convictions for 'offences against the person'.

We are not saying that one should never exclude a pupil, for sometimes they cannot be maintained in mainstream education. However, what we do assert is that this should be the last resort, for to exclude permanently means that these young people become virtually unemployable and the only alternative market response they can turn to is drugs, sex working or crime, leading to disturbed and disturbing lives.

However, the child–parent–teacher alliance, by actively seeking to enhance parental aspirations, broke into the cycle of educational alienation, and created a collaboration which reinforced parents' skills to provide more socially coherent and less coercive homes, to the undoubted benefit of both the disaffected and the 'ordinary' child. How this has been developed and could be developed in your school is explored in Part 2.

Part 2
Meeting the needs

8 Maintaining/reaching disaffected pupils in mainstream schools

The evaluation of the Healthy Alliance, with its access to education, social services, probation and health data, provided supporting evidence for continued educational and social inclusion and for the ongoing development of joined-up, interagency working practices. In Part 2, we explore how the original project developed and became an integral part of the school, and, we believe, offers a model to meet the new challenges ahead.

Clearly, understanding why children behave anti-socially and, more usefully, learning why children behave in a socially acceptable manner must be at the forefront of our research and development, to inform the Children's Educational Services as they shape policies to meet the needs of children and families effectively.

Behaviour was correlated with a variety of indices, e.g. whether parents and/or guardians smoked, whether they were in or out of employment, what sort of housing they occupied, their marital status etc., and all of the variables in combination with each other. The data brought out one piece of evidence above all others. It was that there exists one highly effective protective indicator against the four anti-social behaviours of theft, drug taking, vandalism and truancy.

For the young people, this protection was *liking school*, which brings together central educational and psychosocial objectives as, after the child's home, school is the most important developmental influence.

The Healthy Alliance highlighted the intergenerational cycle of families who experience educational failure and long-term social service and probation department intervention. This meant that in the drive for 'inclusion' we had to reach out to these families to support them in their aspiration that they should actually attain their potential and succeed as citizens. Crucially, any intergenerational failure represents the consumption of a significant proportion of the budgets of our public services. This single factor provides reasoned argument for these vulnerable citizens being a priority for the allocation of intervention resources. Clearly, early intervention is essential to break the cycle of psychosocial depravation and the school, as a universal, normative provision, is ideally placed within the community to act as a coordinating vehicle for the distribution of these resources.

The chapters that follow record efforts to translate the lessons of research, e.g. Healthy Alliance, into practice. They draw upon real, school-based experience of issues that confront teachers every day; progressive inclusion; strategies to raise attainment; dealing with behaviour; understanding the plethora of different learning needs; what it means to support looked-after children; working with parents; child protection; coping with Ofsted; improving pupils' attendance; how best to support pupils with special educational needs; working with external services e.g. the local authority, and so on.

Differing perspectives within the education system are appreciated. For example, the issue of behaviour in school and the impact of disruptive behaviour on teaching and learning is a dominant concern, and a discussion about behaviour and how to deal with it should recognise the impact that the differing layers of the educational hierarchy may have. For instance:

- An individual teacher: the quality of lesson preparation; the level of resources available; depth of subject knowledge.
- The whole school: the behaviour policy; opportunities for appropriate, accessible curriculum; implementation of effective retention policy to support a stable staff team.
- The local authority: policy on dealing with hard-to-place pupils; the level of funding delegated to schools.
- The DfES: the targets it sets for exclusions and attendance; changing funding levels it provides to LEAs and schools; its policy and funding for alternative provision.

As will become clear, despite the difficulties of meeting children and families with multiple and often long-standing problems, this part of the book is hopeful and pragmatic in outlook. Individual cases are used as illustrations and all names are anonymous. It reflects a fundamental belief that education in general and schools in particular can make a positive difference to the lives of young people and acknowledges the need to meet the needs of young people in order to help them to achieve their potential and to become effective citizens. Inclusive working practices are thereby understood as central to meeting the needs of young people and to their developing an enjoyment of school.

School as a normative context

The vast majority of the population leave school at either 16 or 18 and the next time they return is to attend their child's first day in school or their first parents' evening. This may explain why many people have such a strong opinion about schools; they have years of first-hand experience of the schools they attended. Crucially, their general knowledge of schools is dominated by this recollection, complemented by media coverage. Yet few people outside the teaching and social work professions know what really happens in school. Surely many teachers and social workers are left with a sense of frustration when they read what is written about their disciplines in the national press and when they watch television coverage of their work.

So, what's unique about teachers? It's simple: when we want to know whether someone is ill, then we ask a doctor; when we want to know whether someone is mad then we ask a psychiatrist. A teacher recognises who is 'normal' by asking: Is this youngster like most other youngsters, or is he or she very different, and dysfunctionally so? Teachers see just about everyone and they see them most days. They can tell when someone does not fit into the average range and, crucially, they can tell when a child changes in an abnormal manner, i.e. other than as a consequence of normal development. Teachers care and most enter the profession because they believe they can make a difference. They make enormous efforts to remain child-centred and, crucially, they are delighted and motivated by students' successes above all else, including school holidays.

Schools are as unique as the pupils who populate them. In the author's base school, there is a turbulence factor which means that some 50 per cent of the pupils who take their GCSEs here did not transfer from the primary school that usually feeds into our school, and the free school meals figure is slightly over 25 per cent. The profile of the school's intake is that 47 per cent have a reading (accuracy) age below 10 years and 42 per cent have a numeracy score below the 25th percentile. Pupils' countries of origin reflect a fabulous mix from across the globe: France, Spain, Canada, Turkey, Bangladesh, Eire, Holland, Afghanistan, Brazil, Germany, Macedonia, Iraq, Ethiopia, South Korea, China, Greece, South Africa, Slovakia, Eritrea, Libya, Russia, Syria. The main school building originates in the mid-1950s, which has one main advantage and one main disadvantage. The advantage is that, as with many public service buildings built after the Second World War, this one had a dual civil defence purpose: the emergency hospital. We have wide corridors to fulfil this purpose. On the down side, £5,000,000 could be lost in basic care of the building and still more would need to be spent to do the job properly. The hope is that the current Labour government will be able to fulfil its promise to renew all such schools in their ongoing programme of renewal.

Inclusion

Social policy development is heavily influenced by successive governments' agenda to improve social inclusion and education is at its forefront. Inclusion in education is a global concern and the UK has incorporated it within its legislative framework, its statutory guidance and its resource allocation. The drive to develop inclusion in education has been furthered by the support of groups representing both people with disabilities and communities where universal education continues to be an aspiration rather than a reality. The progress of the UK's inclusive policies in education can be understood alongside the development of international initiatives; for instance:

- 1989 UN Convention on the Rights of the Child – ratified by the UK in 1991 – included articles that promote the principle of inclusive education.
- 1990 World Conference on Education sought to universalise primary education.
- **UK** 1992 The Alliance for Inclusive Education produced *The Inclusive Education System – A National Policy for Fully Integrated Education*. They currently publish *Inclusion Now* in partnership with Parents of Inclusion and Disability Equality in Education.
- 1992 Italy abolished special schools. Since 1993 all disabled children have been educated in mainstream schools.
- 1993 UN Standard Rules on the Equalisation of Opportunities for Persons with Disabilities represented a strong moral and political commitment of governments to take action to achieve equality of opportunity for people with disabilities.
- **UK** 1993 Education Act – supported the education of more children in mainstream schools.
- 1994 UNESCO's Salamanca Statement included the following: 'Mainstream schools with this inclusive orientation are the most effective means of combating discriminatory attitudes, creating welcoming communities, building an inclusive society and achieving education for all. Moreover, they provide an effective education for the majority (without special needs) and improve the efficiency and ultimately the cost-effectiveness of the entire education system' and it urged all governments to 'Adopt as a

matter of law or policy the principle of inclusive education, enrolling all children in mainstream schools, unless there are compelling reasons for doing otherwise'. 94 governments have adopted the Statement.

- **UK** 1996 Education Act – as the 1993 Education Act.
- **UK** 1996 The Council for Disabled Children published their *Policy Statement on Inclusive Education for Children with Disabilities and Special Educational Needs*.
- **UK** 1998 White Paper, *Meeting Special Educational Needs: A Programme of Action*.
- 1999 OECD publication, *Inclusive Education at Work: Students with Disabilities in Mainstream Schools* acknowledged the growing acceptance of inclusive education.
- 2000 The World Education Forum held a conference in Dakar, Senegal to review advances in basic education in the 1990s. 1,100 delegates from 164 countries adopted the Dakar Framework for Action, committing themselves to achieve good-quality basic education for all by 2015.
- **UK** 2001 Statutory guidance *Inclusive Schooling – Children with Special Educational Needs*. SEN Toolkit provides information and resources to schools to complement the SEN Code of Practice.
- **UK** 2002 Centre for Studies in Inclusive Education published the second edition of their *Inclusion Charter* (first published 1989). With government backing, they also produced the *Index for Inclusion*; this was distributed to all primary, secondary and special school in England as well as all LEAs. The index contained materials to support schools in their development of inclusive practice by breaking down the barriers to learning and participation.

Crucially, inclusion is a policy supported by both Conservative and Labour governments. In 2000 the Audit Commission reported that providing education for pupils with learning difficulties in a mainstream school did not incur a greater financial cost compared to special school provision (Audit Commission 2000). Six years later, the Labour government published their *Comprehensive Spending Review: Aims and Objectives*, which included the aim for the DfEE: 'To give everyone the chance, through education, training and work, to realise their full potential and build an inclusive and fair society and a competitive economy'.

Now we have to work towards the targets identified in *Every Child Matters* and *Healthy Minds* (DfES 2003b; Ofsted 2005), inclusion is an aim for every teacher, irrespective of subject speciality or type of school.

The moral and economic arguments for inclusion were thereby confirmed and this has acted as the bedrock from which to develop improving services to children and families and the following as educational policies are already changing the educational landscape. The 'five outcomes' of *Every Child Matters* (2003), of being healthy, being safe, enjoying achieving and economic well-being so as to be able to contribute as a full citizen, highlight this evolving new world.

The Centre for Studies in Inclusive Education published their *Inclusion Charter* in 1989. In 2000 and with government backing, they produced the *Index for Inclusion*; this was distributed to all primary, secondary and special schools in England as well as all LEAs (Booth *et al.* 2001). Inclusion was defined as: 'the process of increasing the participation of students in, and reducing their exclusion from, the cultures, curricula and communities of local schools'. The index contained materials to support schools in their development of inclusive practice by breaking down the barriers to learning and participation. The assumption is that inclusion is a continuous process; it is not a target that is achieved. The Index has been used increasingly widely in other countries and has recently been translated into French.

The government offered statutory guidance in November 2001 (*Inclusive Schooling*) and described inclusion as 'a process by which schools, local education authorities and others develop their cultures, policies and practices to include pupils' and 'actively seek to remove barriers to learning and participation'. In this sense, inclusion is an active, evolving process. If it has an ultimate goal, then it is surely to reach fully inclusive mainstream settings. Indeed, those who doubt this as even a theoretical possibility should know that in parts of Canada some school boards have no special schools. All children are educated in the mainstream with appropriate support, wherever possible.

Like any policy, inclusion will be most successful when it is supported by sufficient resources and training. Unfortunately, inclusion is sometimes associated specifically with behavioural problems and the debate as to how students with behavioural problems should be included in mainstream education is a lively one. The issue of behaviour and its association with inclusive practice is ongoing and it was the 1993 Education Act that introduced legislative changes with regard to the education of children with challenging behaviour. 'The 1993 and 1996 Acts said that children should be educated in mainstream schools so long as the child's needs are properly met, other children's education is not adversely affected, resources are used efficiently, and parents are in agreement' (Rustemier 2002).

In fact, the way we deal with students with behavioural problems is subject to incremental change. The use of special schools, for instance, has been part of an evolving process. There are many good reasons for this, for instance:

The policy of inclusion has acted as a pressure upon the use of special school placements. Is it too harsh to substitute the word '*segregated*' for the word 'special' in this context? Try using the phrase 'segregated *schools*' and see how it feels. Other specific factors have supplemented the pressure, for instance:

1   The cost of provision in boarding education has increased markedly. This increase has resulted from improvements in provision. The experience of one particular independent special school is illuminating. From 1982 to 1986 the London Borough of Newham was its biggest customer and this was at a time of recession so they weren't spending money unless they had to. The school provided education and care for 44 pupils with severe and complex learning difficulties. At the end of each school day one, or occasionally two members of staff would take a group of students for a 'walk and talk' through the surrounding country-side in order to discuss and hopefully resolve issues that had arisen during the interactions of the day. The requisite resources amounted to a torch and a pair of wellington boots. In order to undertake a similar activity today, it is necessary to provide two staff (at least one should be trained in first aid), a written risk assessment, two torches, a lifeline (in case anyone fell in the river), a mobile phone etc. The school still accommodates 44 pupils; the total number of staff though, has increased from 31 to 144. The school's fees have increased correspondingly.
2   Parental choice has been given a much higher status. If a parent chooses that their child should be educated in a mainstream school, then this choice is given high regard.
3   There has been an increasing reluctance to separate young people from their families and this has increased the pressure to secure a place in a local school.

A sense of the scale of segregation comes from the Statistics of Education, *Special Educational Needs in England* (DfEE 2001) which shows that 36 per cent of the 258,000 school pupils with Statements of SEN were placed outside mainstream education; this compares with 44 per cent in 1996.

'Research has indicated that the longitudinal outcomes for students placed in special education is questionable, particularly given the increased level of investment in these students' education' (Scott *et al.* 2001). This is particularly so when comparing the most 'socially excluded', former 'excluded-from-school' (EFS) and 'looked-after children' as young adults. Despite expectations, it was the former EFS who had a far worse psycho-social and criminal outcome (Pritchard and Butler 2000a, b). As we know, the 'awaiting' costs as it were of a 'failed ' education are associated with astronomic costs in early adulthood, at approximately £80,000 at 2001 prices for each educationally alienated young adult up to 28 years old (Scott *et al.* 2003).

In action, inclusion is a process. As an idea, inclusion is about seeking to empower the citizen to maximise his or her potential, because it recognises that some citizens are not equal and therefore, by inference, it sees the totality of all forms of social and health services as compensating for their disadvantages, thus enabling them to fulfil their obligations and exercise their human rights as envisaged by the UN Declaration on Human Rights, which was itself a philosophical pointer to economic globalisation (UN 1948).

Relating the idea to mainstream education, inclusion is to have recognised, by whatever means in the school, what it is you bring to the feast; an analysis of what you have. Out of that you define need and define that in terms of what the child needs in terms of his or her development now and as an adult; plus shaping the service to meet the need.

Extended schools

Extended schools are a key component within the government's new agenda for children and they will be central to the delivery of improving services to children and families for many years to come. Crucially, extended schools are at the forefront of the ambition to develop the integrated working practices among the children's services.

There are plans for up to 240 full-service extended schools by 2006. These full-service schools will include, in addition to childcare provision, lifelong learning; health and social care services; community use of the sports, arts and ICT facilities; adult and family learning, as well as parental involvement. Schools can choose to develop as lead schools and thereby become the centre that leads a group of other schools and children's facilities e.g. neighbourhood nurseries and children's centres. A school can also choose to develop as a developing extended school: a school that can become a part of the Big Lottery Fund bid for out-of-hours learning e.g. for sports, arts, ICT-related training.

One of the main features of extended schools is their development of childcare provision. By 2008, it is intended that one thousand primary schools will offer childcare from 8 a.m. till 6 p.m. All parents should have access to good-quality childcare and pre-statutory education and this provision should have the flexibility to adapt to the needs of families.

When all these are being provided, then a school has become a full-service extended school. This policy dovetails with the government's ten-year strategy for childcare, *Choice for Parents, the Best Start for Children*, which was published in December 2004 and sent out for consultation. Its key elements were outlined as:

- availability;
- affordability;
- quality;
- choice and flexibility.

An example of a local authority's experience of developing extended schools is as follows.

In autumn 2004, the DfES consultants visited and explained they wanted a full-service extended school and outlined how much money they would make available to the authority. Local officers went away and did the planning and calculated that for the same money they could develop three schools. Six months later, in 2005, the DfES returned to explain they wanted the local authority to use the same amount of money to fund an extended school strategy to include all the authority's schools. The officers identified areas of deprivation based on the Index of Multiple Deprivation (IMD) from the last Census. The IMD breaks up the data and identifies areas called Special Output Areas, which are smaller than wards. Then, using this information, a formula was created to apportion funding to areas of need. Schools based in these areas were asked to express an interest in developing as an extended school and the local authority provided one-year start-up funding for:

- lead schools for at least one year to fund the management structure and start-up costs of an extended school;
- raising awareness e.g. training for school governors and senior staff as well as for developing multi-agency practice.

Additional funds are for use by the lead schools' steering groups (comprised of people from the local community, the school and interested agencies) who will decide how money should be spent, e.g. by appointing an Extended School Co-ordinator.

All of this is part of the modernisation and reform of public services that the Labour administration has placed at the heart of their political agenda. It's not tinkering; this is serious and fundamental change and there will inevitably be resistance to some of this change, e.g. how to persuade a traditionally successful, popular school (plenty of good SATs scores and/or GCSE A–C levels) to change. What is in it for them? There is now a change management process. Each local authority will have an Extended School Remodelling Adviser whose remit is to work on the schools' leadership and management structure and their roles and responsibilities. Governors are responsible for developing their school's extended school strategy.

Each local authority will stamp their own identity on their area's strategy and each school and surrounding area will develop in their own unique way. There are barriers to these changes:

- Schools are restructuring and this affects people's career, status and income, e.g. responsibility points paid to teachers are evolving into teaching and learning responsibilities (TLRs) alongside the remodelling of staffing structures.
- There are widely differing priorities shaping the development of extended schools, e.g. attainment focuses on league tables and special needs focuses on the individual.
- Who pulls the purse strings? Whose agenda (and therefore whose targets) predominates? Some children's services will be dominated by education, some by social services and some will create an enlightened balance.

The order of priorities being handed down from the government seems to offer a specific emphasis to:

- primary schools that will develop wrap-around childcare, which is why Sure Start is a lead agency;
- secondary schools that will develop out-of-hours learning.

It is very clear that the extended schools initiative is about significantly more than schools adding facilities and services; it is very much about joining up and opening up existing provision. This is demanding a fundamental shift in ethos. Full-service schools can evolve by developing and extending their existing provision to meet the needs of their pupils and their local community. The following example of a feeder primary school in the Healthy Alliance's local authority gives a sense of what can happen.

In 1999 the school's Key Stage 2 SATs results were approximately 54 per cent English, 48 per cent maths, and 48 per cent science at level 4 and above. These results were not good and within a period of months a series of events occurred that galvanised the school, led by the head teacher, into a programme of school improvement.

First, the school failed its Ofsted inspection and was placed in the category of 'Serious Weakness'. This placed a clear responsibility upon the senior management (the head had been in post for just six weeks) to lead the school improvement and to raise standards in the school.

The Registered Inspector of the Ofsted team sat with the staff team and told them they had no understanding of pedagogy and that they needed a theoretical framework from which to understand and develop their practice. The Inspector encouraged the staff to use Maslow's Triangle to provide the theoretical framework and, in doing so, demonstrated the essential first priority to meet the pupils' physiological needs: food, water, shelter and warmth. From this point the school introduced a breakfast club staffed by parent volunteers; drinking water in all the classes; hot meals at lunch time with healthy free school meals as opposed to the rubbish that the pupils had been given beforehand. The Neighbourhood Management scheme had been developed to identify nutritional needs of children as a priority and they supported the school's actions.

Children had to be taught to use a knife and fork and the social skills that are a part of eating together. The school had identified speech and language delay as a significant factor for children entering the school and the daily routine of sitting and eating together must surely impact upon these skills. The teachers had experienced a deterioration of behaviour in the afternoons, including lower concentration levels. Behaviour improved, concentration levels improved and the queues of children lining up to be told off ended.

Maslow's Triangle, as a broad guide to human needs (1998), looks something like this:

Self-actualisation
Being oneself at the ultimate of one's potential

Self-expression
Being able to express ideas, values and beliefs

Status
Being a valued member of a group

Social needs
Being a member of a group; connecting with other people

Safety needs
Income – secure housing – pension

Physiological needs
Food – water – shelter – warmth

Clearly, the physiological needs needed to be met before beginning to progress through the hierarchy of needs and thereby impact on attainment. While children continue to begin their school day on an empty stomach and to be offered rubbish for lunch then we will inevitably continue to fail to meet optimum attainment targets for our most vulnerable children.

The head teacher used research being published by the Community Educational Development Centre that demonstrated the importance of improving the educational opportunities of parents in raising the educational attainment of their children. Realising that the pupils had reached a plateau and that their parents were a crucial factor, the head teacher introduced a variety of initiatives such as parenting classes, additional personal support for parents and a weekly newsletter to communicate values and information. One member of staff took lead responsibility to develop the pastoral link to parents.

This was just the beginning and many aspects of the school have evolved, including the following:

- the pupils chose the school's new uniform and wear it with pride;
- there is an active student council;
- older pupils as members of the school council attend governors' meetings;
- pupils run the Green School Award;
- pupils who also raise the funds and undertake the purchasing and choose the play equipment;
- Key Stage 2 SATs results have risen to 80+ per cent English, 80+ per cent maths, and 90+ per cent science at level 4 and above.

The drive and the vision of the head teacher proved pivotal. The staff are fully supportive of the school policy. After all, they are working in a successful and improving school. The head teacher, when asked her understanding of inclusion, explained that: 'It doesn't mean treating people the same; it does mean taking account of people's varied life experiences'.

Flexible curriculum

The Department for Education and Employment (DfEE) published a circular, *Social Inclusion: Pupil Support* as guidance in the late 1990s (DfEE 1999). This encouraged local education authorities and schools to implement policies and practices to reduce exclusions, to improve inclusion and to engage the disaffected. Schools began to create individualised packages of education for young people who were disaffected, or at risk of disaffection. There was extra money, from the Standards Fund, to help move the work-related learning policy into general practice. The Standards Fund acts as an extra pot of money that schools receive from central government, often via the LEA. It is ring-fenced for spending on a specific provision. The funds in this case came into schools as the 'Pupil Retention Grant'.

The process of developing greater flexibility has continued; for instance, by September 2004 the number of compulsory subjects in KS4 were reduced to english, maths, science, ICT, citizenship, religious education, sex education and careers education. In addition, schools must provide access to humanities, design and technology, modern foreign languages and arts if students wish to take courses in them. This does not necessitate individual schools offering all the provision themselves; indeed, schools can make arrangements with other providers such as a neighbouring school to provide GCSE music.

For a small but significant minority of young people, it is in their interest to create a highly individualised educational programme to meet their learning needs and to assist their transition from school. It is always beneficial to ensure the full support of parents and to consult as widely as possible. Indeed, the process can be a complex one to manage from within school. For instance:

Moses (throughout the text all names used are pseudonyms)
The flexibility to create an individually tailored curriculum permits the school to meet needs in depth. In Moses' case, the strategy produced a successful outcome. He was in the school's ninth year and had become increasingly aggressive as the academic year had progressed. He became increasingly difficult for people to teach, e.g. he would regularly refuse to work, walk out of class, verbally abuse a teacher in front of a full class, threaten other students etc. He spent a lot of time with me but this made it no easier for others to teach him; at best, he became increasingly difficult at a slower rate. As is often the case, when he was removed from the classroom setting, his behaviour was much less problematic. He never swore and was always polite to visitors e.g. parents and was trustworthy in terms of his never stealing.

There were lots of people involved to help him, including his parents. They were always willing to review his progress with us and to take part in any plans that might benefit their son e.g. in working with the Children and Adolescent Mental Health Team. Both parents were very supportive of the school and fully involved. Moses was allocated an excellent social worker and a very able youth offending officer and we worked closely as a team (including Moses' parents). The sorts of strategies we employed in school were:

- **Additional teaching assistant support in the classroom.**
- A report card to monitor his behaviour in class.
- A reward system agreed with Moses and his parents that linked, daily, to his performance in school.
- Twice-weekly one-to-one sessions with his year head, with whom he had a good relationship.
- Referral to, and interview with the educational psychologist who assessed him for learning difficulties.
- Referral to the local education authority for a multidisciplinary assessment
- Referral to and meeting with the careers adviser to gain advice on future career opportunities and the advisability for Moses to access a work-related learning package.
- A personalised timetable that included sessions in the student support base.
- **Fixed-term exclusions.**
- An extended work experience placement.
- 'Taster days' at the local college of further education to sample different courses.

Moses' behaviour became ever more challenging. Some people felt genuinely threatened by his confrontational and unpredictable behaviour. The head teacher was being pressurised to exclude him permanently; even the police suggested that he should be permanently excluded.

Meanwhile, the school had a teacher who was responsible for pre-vocational education. She understood that academic success in school is not a secure predictor of success after school; neither is academic failure a secure predictor of failure after school. Also, she believed that for a significant minority of young people, something other than, or additional to school is sometimes necessary to keep young people included. This is a key point, because this teacher continued to persevere with Moses when others sought his permanent exclusion. This perseverance was not prompted by different skills; instead it was her beliefs and philosophy that were different – her belief that Moses had equal value and that the school should continue to act on his behalf, whatever the probability of failure. Her beliefs and philosophy significantly affected her ability to work with Moses.

This teacher continued to seek opportunities for Moses to succeed. When Moses was sacked from a work experience placement because he was rude to his boss, she continued to work with him and found him another placement. He was then excluded from his placement with a training provider. Eventually, she secured another place for him at another training provider (an FE college) to undertake a second course, yet again of his choosing. Success at last, including arguments drastically reduced at home. Work experience was so successful that Moses' boss paid for him to attend a training course. Moses even joined his local library to help with his course at the college. Surely this would not have happened if one or two key people had not kept plugging away on Moses' behalf.

Moses' mother was actually so impressed that she wrote a letter to the Chief Constable to extol the virtues of work-related learning.

While the outcome was successful for Moses, it also had a financial cost. The college course cost £2,500 per year and the cost of previous failures amounted to over £650. The cost in terms of time and effort of colleagues was also significant. The saving to the public purse, particularly in terms of the criminal justice system, is potentially enormous.

A school can radically develop its curriculum to take account of the needs of groups of pupils; this requires vision and innovation.

Work-related learning

Crucially, from September 2004, schools have been required to include work-related learning in their curriculum for all pupils in Key Stage 4. It is not intended to be taught as a specific subject; rather it is encompassed within other subjects and training opportunities that contribute to all pupils developing their knowledge, understanding and skills. The motivation behind the policy is to encourage young people to develop a better understanding of the world of work and their own ability and confidence to take an active role within it. For some young people it is a lifeline into their future and offers them hope at a time when being at school seems a constant trial.

9 Special vulnerable groups: education and social inclusion

If we understand inclusion as a process, it will be helpful to consider where to focus our attention in practice. Which groups are currently experiencing exclusion and could therefore become the beneficiaries of the training and resources to improve their situation? This chapter will look at some of the issues relevant to groups of people who fit into this category.

Gypsies

If you want one phrase to encapsulate Gypsies' cultural ethos, it is 'Family First', and we explore two such examples. The following will focus upon two groups of people: Travellers of Irish Heritage and Romany Gypsies. Both of these groups have an ethnic status that will be used to record ethnicity in a school's data system. Travellers of Irish Heritage are recorded as WIRT; they prefer to be known as Travellers (please use a capital 'T'). Romanies are recorded as WROM; they prefer to be known as Gypsies (please use a capital 'G').

We start with Gypsies, not least because they are known to be one of the longest and most discriminated against groups in British society (Thompson and Pritchard 1987).

Within their culture, children of Gypsy and Traveller families become adults at the age of 11 or 12 and therefore expect to be accorded the respect of an adult. Tradition in the Gypsy culture is that the eldest daughter becomes the owner of the vardo (caravan) and becomes responsible for it. The vardo is emptied and cleaned every day; different cleaning vessels must be used for different purposes e.g. food in one vessel, clothes in another, washing the body in another and so on. Animals are not permitted in the vardo; in fact the Gypsies view the Gyordio (non-Gypsies) as having filthy living conditions in that they let their animals inside.

When you meet a Gypsy over the age of 11, greet him or her as an adult equal. Frame the child in terms of adult education. Don't get excited about jewellery; a Gypsy's jewellery can be culturally significant and taking it off can be like asking a Gypsy to walk naked – do not dishonour them. If it is a Health and Safety issue, then make the request as such; if it is a concern about security, suggest to parents that rather than leaving such (a) valuable item(s) in a kitbag during PE or games, they might be safer left at home. Respect is the key.

Gypsies will not raise their hand and ask for help; they will not want to admit to a weakness in a foreign (school) setting. Sit the child next to somebody who gets on with things and from whom a Gypsy can work out cues. Gypsies are very able with people; the notion of 'looking for a fight' is a myth. Gypsies have good communication skills, which have been partly developed by dealing with the oft-repeated experience of being received with abuse.

Gypsy men tend to do the talking. Do not be fooled; the balance of authority is fairly shared between men and women. There is no misogyny. Families are cherished. When the women speak, listen: it must be important, or they would not be telling you.

Gypsies will often be terrified of schools. The adults' own childhood experience of schools has often been a bad one. Face-to-face contact is so important. Meet parents at the gate or, better still, make a home visit. There are so many reasons why the parents are reluctant to come into school and the biggest reason of all is fear. Remember, Gypsies place a huge importance upon their family. Indeed, this will explain why the parents often ask for their children to go in the same class, irrespective of age. It's worth reminding others that Gypsies have been persecuted for a very long time, not just by the wholesale slaughter of hundreds of thousands by the Nazis; and modern-day British politicians and press seem to use the issue of Gypsies as fair game for negative exploitation. Indeed, they were fellow victims of the holocaust, along with physically and mentally disabled people, gays, German political opponents of Hitler, as well as Jewish people (Gilbert 1998).

If you want to get advice, then Friends, Families and Travellers are an independent group who can be contacted on 0845 1202980. Have a look at their website first; it's really quite informative (www.gypsy-traveller.org).

African–Caribbean boys

In order to write with relevance about the successful inclusion of African–Caribbean boys I have read more, talked to more people and worried a lot more than for any other part of this book. There is a plethora of material describing continual failure to facilitate successful outcomes of black boys relative to other ethnic groups. For instance, the 2002 annual pupil census reported 30 per cent black Caribbean children gaining five A–C GCSEs; this compared to 51 per cent of white children and 64 per cent of Indian children. In 2003, just 9 per cent of black boys in Hackney gained five A–C passes.

Diane Abbott, the Jamaican-born Labour Member of Parliament, took her son out of the state system to place him at the City of London boys' school; she took a lot of criticism. However, as we have seen, her actions were evidence-based. There is clearly scope for improvement and this was evidenced by The Learning Trust (the not-for-profit private company that has the contract to manage the Education Department in Hackney) when the schools within its field of responsibility looked at the prior attainment of their pupils. Significant numbers of black boys were found to be failing to maintain their rate of attainment through their secondary education.

Who, then, are the role models that these boys relate to? It is striking to realise that in 2003 the proportion of black pupils in London's schools was 19.5 per cent, yet by comparison the proportion of teachers in London's schools who were black was just 2.9 per cent. It will of course be some time before this ratio is improved. There are, however, alternative methods of role modelling. It was instructive to listen to a colleague (currently a Head of Children's Services for a local authority) tell me about what was initially a well-funded programme introduced in Birmingham during Tim Brighouse's tenure as Director of Education during the 1980s. Mentoring of Caribbean boys by members of the Caribbean community was a central feature of a programme that produced a 50 per cent reduction in exclusions among African–Caribbean boys in its first year.

More recently, policy decisions in Hackney have taken account of the fact that the lack of role models may be linked to poor educational outcomes. One of the strategies employed by The Learning Trust has been to introduce a programme of mentoring for black Caribbean pupils and this may be linked to progress that the boys are making in Hackney. Indeed, 'Black Caribbean boys' improvement at GCSE rose this year by more than twice the national average' (*TES*, 11 March 2005). In addition, there are favourable trends being reported from Birmingham City Council via their School Effectiveness in Cities Unit's *Excellence in Cities Evaluation 2003* (BCC 2004); where African–Caribbean boys' GCSE results have risen to 28 per cent in 2003, from 20 per cent in 1999.

In addition to the above, acknowledgement must be given to the effectiveness of everyday good practice. For example:

- the use of relevant materials to support progress in reading has always made a positive difference to any group of students;
- applying the knowledge that mothers of black Caribbean pupils

want the best for their children, just like any other mother, and will be able and willing to respond supportively;
- knowing that when a young person looks down when being admonished it can often be the body language of respect;
- arguing and questioning by a young person can be reframed to encourage a sense of justice, and so on.

It seems that the truth is that there has been no significant, sustained and widespread improvement. There is clearly a political will to see progress; after all, improving the educational outcomes of black Caribbean boys, especially in London, will impact significantly upon the overall improvement in GCSE results and that will be a feather in any Education Minister's cap, as well as adding to social inclusion by providing the boys with greater life chances, which would also be likely to lead to a reduction in overall crime figures, so strongly associated with educationally alienated youngsters (DfEE 1999, 2000; Smith and Farrington 2004).

The DfES paper *Aiming High: Raising the Achievement of Minority Ethnic Pupils* (2003a) is worth exploring.

Pupils with a disability

The Disability Discrimination Act 1995 focused upon people's access to services and legislated for reasonable physical alterations to property. It considered service provision; for instance, if a venue hosts a concert, then an elderly person with diminished mobility should be able to get into the concert and be comfortable, have access to appropriate toilets and so on. This Act did not encompass education but the Disability Discrimination Act 2001, in two parts, did include one for pre-16s and one for post-16s. In the context of pre-16s there is an obligation to consider a child's disability and for a child with impaired mobility, the school should have a responsibility to bring education to the child of the same standard as that provided to his or her able-bodied peers.

A local authority (LA) has the responsibility to produce an Accessibility Strategy and this is a published document. Each LA must have a programme of works to undertake the recommendations of an access audit and schools have an Access Plan that has three strands to it.

1 Communication – sending out information to parents using clear print.
2 Curriculum – how to promote it in an accessible way (room layout, for instance).
3 Physical – how to make the building more accessible.

The local social services department will hold a register of disabled young people; hopefully this will be reviewed for changes of address and changes of school placement etc. A child with a disability is automatically a 'Child in Need' in the terms of The Children Act 1989 and if a child is 'in need' then the social services department is obliged to help that family. One example of help was helping a blind pupil attend a youth club by providing a volunteer to transport him and to be with him for each session.

The strategic purpose of the register is to support health, education and social services departments engage in strategic planning that ensures young people have access to services when they become adults. Part of this process is that, for Year 9 pupils with a Statement of SEN, schools seek clarification from their local SSD as to whether the pupil should be registered disabled. An example of this was when the school was informed that we would be very likely to admit a student who was educationally blind as part of the normal primary transfer, i.e. into Y7. The prospect of this admission and my own sense of accountability for this student's welfare, as well as for his educational progress, left me feeling so daunted that it is hard to describe.

Our colleagues' thoughts were polarised in two directions. On the one hand we wanted him to be fully included into the social and educational fabric of the school, to experience no discrimination on the grounds of his disability and to access the full breadth of the national curriculum. On the other hand we wanted him to wear bright red clothing, preferably with a flashing light strapped to his head and that he should go nowhere near the playground during free association times – school playgrounds can be pretty hectic, if not potentially, physically dangerous to people of impaired mobility. This probably expresses the conflict between my head and my heart. Our school's beliefs and philosophies were firmly entrenched within the policy of inclusion. I was concerned that my ignorance and fear were encouraging a path towards exclusion and prejudice. It is this conflict that many teachers must deal with regularly and their mature response is, appropriately, to seek the necessary education and training to support their work with the students and the resources that are necessary to provide for students with special educational needs.

Sajed (educationally blind boy)

The planning that was involved in Sajed's admission was lengthy and detailed. The first meeting took place in the December before his transfer the following September, at his primary school. I was invited to meet with a specialist teacher who worked with Sajed. She showed me Sajed working in class and then took me to another part of the school to put on a pair of goggles that had the effect of replicating Sajed's visual experience. I needed to be guided and I could determine nothing specific, just an awareness of a small amount of light but that was about all. I left the school with mixed feelings. He was doing really well, so I could see that progress was attainable, but this meant that anything less than such a rate of progress could not be acceptable.

During the Spring term, many people with a stake in Sajed's ongoing progress contributed to an example of good practice; **Sajed**, who was really positive about moving to a secondary school, was actively included in the planning, as were his parents.

At his primary school two **teaching assistants** (TAs) shared the support for Sajed, this having been organised to ensure continual, experienced support, and the **specialist teacher** for students with visual impairment had been working with Sajed for eighteen months. She had a comprehensive grasp of all the issues involved, which thankfully included the practical preparations that needed to take place prior to Sajed joining our school.

The range of staff, outlined below, is a good indication of possible resources the teacher can call upon in such situations.

The **head of service** to students with visual impairment was keenly aware of the strategic issues, including the responsibilities that lay with other agencies, such as the social services department who provide mobility training for Sajed in his home area (inside his home and in his local area e.g. local shops and crossings).

A **special needs casework officer** worked in the special educational needs team of the local education authority (LEA). The responsibilities of this post include the monitoring of whether a school meets the needs of a young person with special educational needs and, specifically, the responsibilities that are written down in a statement of special educational needs.

The **disability officer** was another officer in the LEA, whose responsibility extended to the negotiations with the school as to the financing of resources to support students with a disability. There was the **access officer** who was employed by the local authority and gave the school practical advice to help it become accessible to Sajed.

A **social worker** who, as a member of the social services department's disability team, had to negotiate within her own agency to secure additional resources for, e.g.:

- local holiday activities and the one-to-one support that Sajed needed to take part;
- mobility training from home. This may have been a statutory entitlement, but with no mobility officer in post for eighteen months, it was a source of continual frustration;
- a volunteer helper to support Sajed in his desire to be included in normal social activities e.g. scouts and visiting friends.

Other professionals had specific responsibility for ophthalmology, information technology and even designing and adapting the internal school building to accommodate Sajed's equipment.

The first hurdle to Sajed's full inclusion was focused upon the question 'Who pays for what?' This was overcome by some fairly robust negotiating between the finance officer of the school and colleagues in the LEA and it did not take long. The hardest part for me was to provide a projected figure for the number of hours of additional TA support that Sajed would need, over and above that provided by the LEA, i.e. to be funded by the school. The difficulty was that no one knew the answer, partly because, at the time, there was no other student with a comparable level of need in a mainstream secondary school within the three local LEAs. We decided upon 15 hours in addition to the 25 provided by Sajed's statement of SEN. This would take into account the need for additional help required for the following times and activities:

- meeting him on arrival in school and guiding him to his tutor room;
- differentiating all his class work;
- supporting Sajed in class;
- providing support for him during his free association times.

The next difficulty was to find a space within the building that could be adpated for use by Sajed and those colleagues using the resources dedicated for his support. This was not easy and I will explain one of the strategic issues affecting the search for a solution.

During the last few years, many responsibilities and considerable amounts of money to meet these responsibilities have been delegated from many local education authorities to schools e.g. education welfare; budgeting; special needs provision; behaviour support and so on. Indeed, local authorities have targets to achieve in terms of the proportion of money they delegate to schools, compared to the amount that they hold centrally. Some services are not yet available for delegation e.g. educational psychology. The exact proportion of delegation and the amounts of each service that has become the responsibility of schools is probably as diverse as the number of local education authorities. Nevertheless, the trend has been to delegate funding to schools.

While this has been occurring, there has been an increasing pressure upon schools to accommodate these activities, that is, to provide office space. For example, in my authority, the education welfare service was held centrally until about two years ago. The LEA then arranged to delegate the funding for secondary schools, with certain provisos, e.g. that the funding should be used to employ only qualified social workers (later revised to qualified or qualifying social workers). The LEA kept sufficient funds to undertake specific educational welfare activities, such as the monitoring of schools' performance and the monitoring of child protection arrangements. The school duly appointed a committed and dedicated EWO. The question of office space then arose. Schools are bound by a formula as to how much office space they can provide and this formula has created additional pressures as the additional responsibilities have been delegated. This school's solution was to use an interview room that had previously been used for teachers to meet with parents during the school day.

To return to the matter of finding a room for Sajed's equipment, I decided that expediency dictated that we take a piece off the learning support room and that this 'piece' should be Sajed's and his helpers' support base. The room also had to be soundproofed to take account of the electronic Brailling machine, which, I was advised, sounded like a machine gun (when used in an enclosed space).

By the end of the Spring term, the head of service to students with visual impairment was visiting the school once a week, on Thursday afternoons, to help Sajed become familiar with the site. At this time the Senior Management Team took part in a training session, undertaking a similar exercise to the one that I had taken part in at the primary school. It was a grand sight, all the senior managers groping their way down the admin corridor, each wearing a pair of the specially adapted goggles. However, no one baulked at the prospect and they all gained a realistic insight into Sajed's level of disability and therefore why we needed to prepare so thoroughly.

Each subject area has a member of its team who takes a particular responsibility for SEN issues. At one of the regular meetings we discussed Sajed's admission. Heads of department were similarly informed and colleagues were generally interested. No one had previous experience of working with a student who was assessed as 'educationally blind'. The overwhelming reaction from colleagues was favourable and fully supportive of inclusion. Many expressed concern and in the same sentence asked what training they could access and what level of support Sajed would receive. Only two people expressed any depth of antagonism (both have since left the school). They based their argument around the issue of finance, based upon the belief that it was inappropriate to spend the money on Sajed's education and that as Sajed was not a British national he should return to his country of birth and cease being a burden upon the British taxpayer. These were the lone voices of exclusion and prejudice from within an otherwise positively inclusive staff team.

One of the teaching assistants who worked with Sajed at the primary school applied to work with him at our school. This was a fortunate event as there would be pressure from the very first day, as Sajed would need all his work to be fully differentiated from the first lesson on the first day. Consequently, textbooks were sent by subject heads to the TA at the primary school in May, so that she could begin the task of differentiating his work for the following September.

The new term started and a teaching assistant colleague was waiting to act as Sajed's sighted guide and to walk with him from the reception area to his tutor base. When he arrived, he walked down the corridor looking animated, smiling and chatting away to the TA. Seeing this made all the previous effort worthwhile.

Sajed's head of year played a crucial role, within the school, to enhance his inclusion. With Sajed's superb helpers, TA and teacher, the head of year organised awareness-raising sessions with Sajed's tutor group and they learnt about the experience of being visually impaired and how Sajed could be supported in school, for example how to act as a sighted guide. Throughout all these sessions, it was made clear that no student would ever be expected to take responsibility for Sajed, such as in enabling his movement around school, but that acting as a friend would always be appropriate. Later in the term the whole year group were involved in further training.

All the teachers who were due to teach Sajed were provided with training sessions during the Summer term, and teachers new to the school were provided for during the first two days of the Autumn term, which of course extended their professional experience, especially in learning what being visually impaired means.

Sajed has gone on to access the whole national curriculum. His Brailling speed has improved, as has his Braille and typing speed. Within eighteen months of joining the school, he has met one particular target that I negotiated with him. A prospective student visited the school with her parents. Sajed met them in the reception area and took them, independently, on a tour of the school.

To summarise: accessibility is about how a child uses a school on a day-to-day basis. Some solutions are common sense, for example a school can provide access to English lessons for a young person in a wheelchair if one of its English classrooms is on the ground floor. There is a very good short video called 'Talk' that can be ordered free from the Disability Rights Commission (DRC).

One golden rule is to involve the young person in the planning. The following was quoted to me; I'm unsure of the originator, but it is worth repeating:

'It's not the person who has the disability; it's the environment that disables them'.

Students with English as an additional language (EAL)

There are probably over a quarter of a million pupils with EAL in England so the chances are that children may come to you fairly regularly with no English language. The good news is that the best place to learn a new language is in a language-rich environment such as a school.

It makes a positive difference when you take the time to learn how to spell and how to pronounce the young person's name and check with the child that you have got it right. If you are the pupil's tutor or pastoral head, then the 'buddy system' is a great way to start. Each new child should be given access to a set of words and phrases to help him or her to cope with the first few days. 'Hello' and 'goodbye' could come first, followed by 'please may I have' and 'thank you'. 'I need to go to the toilet' is a priority and 'I do not understand' is very useful.

Crucially, a child with EAL needs to be given a place in a group that is suitable to his or her cognitive ability and not in a lower ability group to compensate for the language gap. When a young person joins our system they can appear to fall below their peers with English as a first language (EFL) in measured ability. This can easily be a reflection of their difficulty in accessing testing materials in a foreign language. This is especially true where the young person's home alphabet is not the western alphabet.

In the classroom, explain how you praise, criticise and mark as well as any rules that you operate within your sphere of influence. Children with EAL may need longer than others to respond to a question, so allow for this and be aware that patience may be required as the young person will most likely take time to gain the confidence to communicate. When you are asking questions, make sure you do not sound threatening.

A science teacher told me that to learn science to GCSE level and to gain an A–C grade necessitates learning the equivalent of a new language – imagine doing that in another language. It is easy to see, therefore, how helpful it would be to have a set of materials that link a picture to an English word and to the word in the child's original language. It helps to use visual materials and ideally, if possible, it is very good to develop sets of materials for different subject areas and put them in rooms which are frequently in use.

Here are some affirmative actions that will help to enhance inclusion:

- Involve pupils and their families in the learning process.
- Use prior knowledge, e.g. use assessment for learning techniques.
- Match the curriculum to the pupil's cognitive ability.
- Find out rather than make assumptions.

The young person's progress is likely to be a quiet six to eight weeks followed by their demonstrating acquisition of language at an increasingly rapid rate. After two years, on average, pupils with EAL are on a par with their peers with EFL and after four years they may be outperforming their peers.

Among the many websites that you may find useful are:

- http://babel.altavista.com/ offers translation of 150 words to and from French, German, Greek, Italian, Japanese, Korean, Portuguese, Russian, Spanish, Dutch and Chinese. It also allows you to translate whole websites.
- www.languages-on-the-web.com supports an extraordinarily wide variety of languages; it has MP3 sound files that allow languages to be heard as well as read. The bilingual texts are worth considering as accessible materials.

Asylum seekers and refugees

Asylum seekers will have escaped from their home country and will have sought refugee status in another country. Asylum is 'protection granted by a state on its territory against the exercise of jurisdiction by the state of origin, based on the principle of non-refoulment and characterised by the enjoyment of internationally recognised refugee rights, and generally accorded without limit of time'. Refugees will have fled their own country and will be judged to have, 'a well-founded fear of being persecuted for reasons of race, religion, nationality, membership of a particular group or political opinion' (UNHCR 1968).

In the UK, the Immigration and Asylum Act 1999 introduced a national dispersal policy for asylum seekers, to ease pressure on specific areas in the South East of England. The numbers of people subject to this process is difficult to ascertain; however, the Independent Race and Refugee News Network reported that in 2003, the European countries that received the largest per capita number of asylum seekers (between 3 and 4 per 1000 of their population) were Luxembourg, Sweden, Austria and Norway. By comparison, the UK's figure for the same year was 1 per 1000.

The proportion of asylum seekers can vary significantly from school to school and the support offered by local authorities can also vary significantly. One example of an excellent website, created to support an education service that successfully includes asylum seekers, is that of Portsmouth LEA's EMAS (Ethnic Minority Achievement Serial). This site is very well put together and is a fine example; it is well worth looking at on www.blss.portsmouth.sch.uk/asylum/leaguide.shtml. An admissions policy should recognise that many pupils join a school mid-term. It makes a positive difference to undertake an effective initial assessment and to seek information about a whole range of factors, for instance:

- the family's requirement for an interpreter to facilitate the admissions process;
- the family's first language;
- the young person's knowledge of the English language;
- length of time out of education;
- the support network in place for the family and their contact numbers.

Families seek asylum for many different reasons and the circumstances of each will need to be treated individually. As an example, when Armand was admitted as an asylum seeker from Kosovo, the admissions process failed to bring to light the information that was eventually uncovered on a joint home visit with the EMAS teacher. Armand had spent over a year hiding in a cellar during which time many of the male members of his family had been murdered. The most immediate problem that Armand faced was dealing with Post Traumatic Stress Disorder (PTSD) in a school that had to learn very quickly how to help him.

PTSD is characterised by flashbacks; and intense fear of stimuli associated with the trauma; for example, if a child has seen the rape of a woman in a red dress, the child may continue to be frightened for the safety of women in red dresses. A classic way of behaving is to avoid the stimulus; for instance, if the teacher is wearing a red dress, the child could leave the room, hide under a desk, cause a disturbance in order to be sent out, stare at his feet. The stimulus may be more complex than the red dress: it could be a tone of voice or the child feeling uncertain. Imagine being woken up in the middle of the night and being told to get up straight away and to leave your home without making any noise, leaving behind all your precious possessions, being aware of the tension in the adult's voice, not knowing what the danger is, but having a gut-level knowledge that danger is present. Now imagine yourself as that person a year later, in a new school, in a new town, in bed and breakfast accommodation. How secure do you feel on a day-to-day basis? How easy is it to give your trust and attention to a teacher delivering a lesson? It's all right to say to a child 'Are you having difficulty concentrating today? What would make it easier?'

PTSD has a major influence upon people's ability to concentrate; it actually has an impact on brain cells and the connections between them (the physical underpinning of thinking, learning and memory). The people from whom to seek advice are your local Child and Adolescent Mental Health Service.

Ofsted produced a very positive report, *The Education of Asylum-seeker Pupils*, in 2003 and it is most encouraging to read.

Drugs and alcohol

The changing pattern of drug experimentation was discussed earlier and drug use, along with binge drinking, continues to be a problem for a substantial minority of pupils. As we outlined earlier, there is no such thing as a 'safe drug' and too many of our young people are taking risks (Pritchard and Cox 2005) which are often minimised by people who perhaps had experience of drugs that did not overtly damage them.

The government published *Drugs Abuse: Guidance for Schools* (DfEE 2002) as comprehensive guidance to schools. It makes clear that a measurable reduction of drug misuse by young people can result from a good drugs education policy. It also confirms that there are specific groups of young people who are vulnerable to misusing drugs and alcohol – young people who have been excluded, those who truant and young people who have been abused. Another high-risk group for substance misuse is children whose parents are, or have been abusers of drugs and/or alcohol. This acknowledges that drug misuse is, for some young people, a coping strategy or a means of escaping from their pain and misery.

Each school should have a drugs incidence policy and this is going to become a statutory requirement. It will describe, for instance:

- What a school's level of tolerance will be concerning drugs. Will pupils be excluded for possessing drugs, or only if they are dealing?
- What are the rules for a teacher who hears a conversation alluding to drug misuse?
- What are the medical guidelines should a teacher find a youngster under the influence of something that could potentially be dangerous?

The policy should be very clear to the young people, who should have some ownership of it. That is, it should be written with the meaningful involvement of the young people and their parents. They will therefore understand exactly what the consequences will be. This becomes quite a challenge for the inclusive practice of a school. One of the difficulties is that problematic young people are often seen as the enemy and we cannot get rid of them quickly enough, because that will mean that all the others will settle down. This is rarely the outcome, however.

When a pupil has been excluded, the questions that need asking are 'What is it that this youngster needs?' and 'Can they cope in this school context?' In other words, use the process that you would implement for any other problem. We need to believe that this young person is our responsibility; that we are not going to pass him or her onto someone else. They will only go somewhere else if they are really unable to cope, and therefore our reintegration should prescribe that.

The National Centre for Social Research and NFER (NCSR 2003) published the results of a survey that found that 24 per cent of 11- to 15-year-olds had consumed alcohol in the previous week and that this included 5 per cent of 11-year-olds and 47 per cent of 15-year-olds. This becomes of increasing concern when put alongside the *Young People's Drinking Factsheet* (Alcohol Concern 2002), which reported that young people aged 15–16 are consuming greater amounts of alcohol and doing so more frequently. Crucially, the practice of binge drinking is increasing. There is increasing evidence to suggest that the long-term negative effects of alcohol are greater on the brains of adolescents than on those of more mature people (Gabriel 2000). And, as was shown earlier, we have a mini-epidemic of liver disease in young adults, revealing the extreme consequences of starting to drink earlier and consuming stronger drinks (WHO 2005).

The school had one student who was already addicted to alcohol when she entered Y7, and I learnt more about the pain of alcohol addiction and withdrawal while my colleague was supporting her than at any other time. Sadie had been the victim of physical abuse by her father and she was clearly a young person within the 'vulnerable' category. By the time she was 15, admission to the local Accident and Emergency Department had become a regular weekend occurrence.

Sadie, however, realised that her life, including her education, was being ruined by her habit; so she attempted a self-imposed and self-regulated withdrawal. It was at this point that she learnt that withdrawal from alcohol can involve convulsions and fitting and can be a very dangerous process. Sadie was admitted to a dedicated residential provision that was able to supervise the appropriate medication and offer the necessary professional monitoring. She came through the process and is living independently while attending a local FE College. Clearly, most children do not reach this stage. The range of preventative measures that are available to a teacher will include:

- knowing who is the person with responsibility for coordinating drug issues;
- accessing the training provided by the school;
- knowing who are the young people assessed by the school as being vulnerable;
- having access to, and knowledge of the school's Drugs Policy and therefore knowing the referral routes for student(s) causing concern and the range of partners and services embodied within the Policy.

Four rules that are worth mentioning are:

1 A member of staff should not carry out a personal search. Personal property should not be searched without prior consent.
2 If a young person asks a question or converses in such a way that indicates that he or she may be at risk, then the school's Child Protection Policy should be followed. A teacher cannot and should not offer a young person total confidentiality.

3 An unconscious child should be gently moved into the recovery position so that the tongue cannot fall back and prevent breathing; basic first aid training is essential.
4 If you are going to talk to young people about this topic, then know your facts and be aware of your own self-medicating tendencies such as use of caffeine, aspirin, exercise and nicotine.

In 2001 the Office for National Statistics and the National Programme for Substance Abuse Deaths reported on Volatile Substance Abuse (VSA) – the inhaling of volatile substances such as glue, aerosols and lighter fuel. Crucially, they reported that VSA is responsible for more deaths among those young people aged 10–16 in England and Wales than illegal drugs.

Clearly, good-quality training is a prerequisite to good practice. In addition, there are a variety of sources of high-quality, easily accessible information, such as the National Drugs Helpline (telephone number 0800 77 66 00). There are, after all, currently a bewildering plethora of harmful substances available, all of which have different effects.

In conclusion, a good Drugs Policy is essential and it will become a statutory requirement. Good in-school drugs education can have a small but significant positive effect. This positive effect will be greatly enhanced by a school being successfully inclusive, for example by reducing exclusions and by embracing the *Every Child Matters* agenda, with effective coordination of services to those young people who are deemed to be vulnerable.

Sexual development

While physiologically young people are maturing earlier, they are, as a consequence, relatively less well equipped in terms of 'emotional' maturity to deal with the impact of burgeoning sexuality. Indeed, as one colleague said, 'We're dealing with youngsters who are hormonally challenged'. Conversely, some pupils are relatively late developers. Imagine what it's like being the shortest and most physically immature boy in the class? What concerns go through your mind? What is the last thing you need your teacher to say to you? I well recall from my schooldays an inconsiderate master yelling at the 'runt' of the 15-year-old class ' "Smith", go back and bring your body with you'. Few of us laughed. Research has indicated that late maturers, particularly boys, have lower self-esteem and lower attainment than their peers who enter puberty at an average age (Holle 2004; Lundgren *et al.* 2004; Storch *et al.* 2004). Those later to mature will be keenly aware of:

- their vocal range when reading out loud;
- their strength e.g. in a physics experiment on forces;
- being picked last by their peers for a team event in PE.

Remember that those who mature late and those who mature early will feel different.

At the opposite end of this spectrum is the early developer, who might well be embarrassed by misunderstood early hair growth or their genital and breast development, which has surpassed their emotional competence. Indeed, 'body image' is of vital concern to children, especially adolescents exposed to all the ideal 'body beautifuls ' of media advertisement, which affects children of every ethnicity (Furman and Thompson 2002; Iyers and Haslam 2003; Holle 2004; Lundgren *et al.* 2004; Storch *et al.* 2004).

Sexual orientation

Do you believe that a person is born gay or straight? The majority of young people who suspect or know themselves to be homosexual experience 'internalised homophobia', i.e. they share the culture's derogatory attitudes. We need to be aware of our own attitudes and beliefs about what is normal. What is clear is that within different cultures and in different times our sexual norms have varied considerably; for example, in Victorian times no 'respectable' women would admit to having a sexual appetite and D.H. Lawrence's *Women in Love* can remind us just how fluid and different is our thinking about sexuality.

This is still a sensitive issue in many local authorities, and to argue that a homosexual orientation (gay and lesbian) has been present throughout history is irrelevant to some of a particular moral position. They cite, for example, verses from the Bible that 'condemn' homosexuality – Leviticus 20:13 for example – but relatively ignore even more strongly condemned behaviour such as adultery (Leviticus 18:20, 18:10) and the ever-popular fornication (Leviticus 18:20, Deuteronomy 22:23); it is noteworthy that homosexuals are sixth in the list of death sentences passed for 'abominations'. Yet there is not the same venom against heterosexual falling away and one cannot fail to recall Gertrude's remark 'Methinks they doth protest too much' (*Hamlet*). Moreover, few would wish to give equal authority to the biblical sanction against children born out of wedlock 'A bastard shall not enter into the congregation of the Lord, even to his tenth generation' (Deuteronomy 23:2), which is diametrically opposed to Jesus of Nazareth's injunction 'Suffer the little children to come unto me'. This is, however, a serious issue, for despite the changing liberal tolerant attitude of today, adolescents and youths with an uncertain or homosexual orientation still have a significantly higher suicide and suicidal behaviour rate than their heterosexual peers, and often the fatal event is triggered by teasing and bullying homophobia in schools (e.g. Cata and Canetto 2003; Crawford *et al.* 2003; Savin-Williams and Ream 2003; Fitzpatrick *et al.* 2005).

Sexual behaviour

There is still more talk than action, but young people are becoming sexually active well before the age of consent as our figures showed: 19% per cent of the boys and 29 per cent of Y10 and Y11 girls – clearly the girls are having their experience with older boys, which itself can be problematic (Pritchard and Cox 2005). The child protection rules haven't changed for a teacher whose knowledge of a child's sexual activity prior to the age of consent will have to be referred to the appropriate designated teacher. The responsibility of judging whether a child is safe does not rest with the classroom teacher or the form tutor; use the designated teacher. There is a case to be put for acknowledging that our young people might sound more streetwise than they once were, but are they? Not if we remember that Britain has the highest teenage pregnancy rate in Europe and that chlamydia rates for the under-25s are scandalous: 8 per cent in young people under 20 in the UK and rising (Adams *et al.* 2004; La Montagne *et al.* 2005; MacCleod *et al.* 2005). Furthermore, the level of HIV infections continues to rise, especially among heterosexual people and in 2001 0.11 per cent, i.e. 11 young mothers in a thousand, who gave birth were HIV-positive (Dougan *et al.* 2004). This leads us to question the impact of sex education when the nation awaits the first live copulation on Big Brother with baited breath – or have we already missed it? No wonder young people are sceptical at our ambivalent and often hypocritical attitudes when it comes to their sexual behaviour, yet sadly they often do not appreciate the power and the consequences of being so intensively 'hormonally challenged'.

Pregnant teenagers

In the 1970s, the UK had a similar teenage birth rate to other European states. By the late 1990s the UK rate was twice as high as Germany, three times that of France and six times that of the Netherlands.

More recently, Britain has continued to record the highest rate of teenage pregnancy in Western Europe. In 2002 Unicef's Innocenti Research Centre researched the birth rates among 15- to 19-year-old teenagers in 28 of the world's wealthiest nations. They found that the United States had the highest number, 52 per 1000 and that the second highest number was evident in the United Kingdom where the figure was 30 per 1000. By comparison, Switzerland, Sweden, Japan and the Netherlands recorded less than 7 per 1000. The Office for National Statistics reported that in 2003 the number of 15- to 17-year-old girls who became pregnant was 42,173 (from 39,286 in 2002) and that this equated to a ratio of 42.3 per 1000 (ONS 2005). Just think of the restricted life-chances for these girls and consider the life-chances of their children, which are often the sad consequence of unplanned and unprotected sexual activity after drinking alcohol (Bonnell *et al.* 2003, 2005).

The government has set itself a target to halve the rate of conceptions among young women below the age of 18 by 2010. There is also a commitment to increase the proportion of teenage parents in education, training and employment. The legal position in terms of statutory education is that a young person who is pregnant and at school should continue her education until she reaches school-leaving age. There is an entitlement to 18 weeks' maternity leave and this leave can be taken from 31 weeks into the pregnancy. It can be considered bad practice if a young person is 'forced out' of education before she feels ready.

If a teacher discovers that a child is pregnant and she is under 16 the first responsibility is to talk to the designated child protection worker, because the pupil has had sexual intercourse below the age of consent, so a teacher would have a duty at least to pass on the information.

To improve the overall quality of provision, one of the first things to overcome is the prejudice about health and safety. If a teacher becomes pregnant she is normally able to continue working without any difficulties, but if a pupil becomes pregnant and wishes to remain in school, there are often concerns about her physical well-being. First we have to remember that this is not an illness; this is a young person who requires our support. What we should do is make arrangements so that there are facilities available in school if she becomes unwell. Secondly, we should not ostracise the pupil. One thing a young mum-to-be needs is continuity amongst her peer group. Thirdly, we need to address the issue of childcare. A young mother is not going to leave her youngster happily unless the baby can be cared for by someone she trusts, so if possible we need to give her some independence by actually putting childcare in place; that's what one new project, 'Care to Learn' is all about. Schools can opt into the scheme and there are allowances made to the mother for childcare so that she can continue with her education; the childcare can even be arranged on the school site.

Next, there needs to be an assessment of how many hours the pupil could spend in school, and an attempt made to meet at least the young mother's basic needs. All pupils need to have literacy and numeracy skills and then you look at the ability of the youngster and encourage her to take courses according to her ability. If she was heading for university, she can still do so. In this way you actually personalise the learning and you build the timetable around the youngster. A school can make sure that the sexual relationships education that is put in is now appropriate to the experience of that youngster.

A pregnant teenager will often benefit from mentoring support from an adult in her school. Find the person to fit with the young mother; keep it simple for her – she's got enough problems. It can happen that many people want to be supportive at the outset, but this support drops off and the teenager can feel let down. There are all sorts of issues to consider, for example a timetable should take into account that working before 10 a.m. can be difficult. The young person may have many issues to deal with in addition to her education; for instance:

- being scared of telling her peers;
- fear of teachers' attitude;
- parents putting boundaries up against the father while telling the father that he has to take responsibility;
- wondering where she is going to live;
- not knowing how she is going to provide for her baby.

Planning for parenthood is a lot to be dealing with at any age. In the case of a pregnant teenager, we need to be especially wise in how we act to support a new life within our community.

10 Attendance and truancy

> The whining school-boy, with his satchel and shining morning
> face creeping snail-like
> Unwillingly to school.
>
> (Shakespeare, *As You Like It*)

We are all familiar with Shakespeare's (Shakespeare, *As You Like It*)
evocation of the reluctant schoolboy, but unless children attend school
they cannot be educated. And the one constant we find in cohorts of
'socially excluded' people is educational failure and underachievement
(Pritchard and Butler 2000a, b; Smith and Farrington 2004). Hence
attendance is a major issue for all concerned with the well-being of
children.

Behaviour and attendance are brought together at ministerial level;
for example, the DfES has implemented the Behaviour and Attendance
strand of the Key Stage 3 Strategy. The implication of this and related
policies is that improvements in behaviour and attendance will lead to
the raising of educational outcomes and more effective inclusion.
Crucially, where schools deal successfully with the issues of ethos and
organisation as well as strengths and weaknesses in teaching and
learning, then improved standards of behaviour and attendance will
ensue.

Truancy: key indicator of educational alienation

Improving school attendance is integral to the 'every child matters'
agenda. The five outcomes include, 'enjoying and achieving', and
achieving in school can only be undermined by poor attendance.
Another of the outcomes, 'achieving economic well-being' is a core
priority for Connexions, for whom a core function is to reduce the
number of young people not in education, employment or training
(known as NEETs).

The need to improve pupil attainment and to reduce youth crime
has brought together the Home Office and the DfES to develop policies
to reduce truancy and improve attendance; it is very clearly a
government priority.

Not so long ago, in the 1960s and 1970s, the School Attendance Officer was nicknamed 'The Bunk Man', 'School Bobby' or 'The Wag Man' and it was the remit of the SAO to enforce attendance at school. Nowadays, the terms Education Welfare Officer (EWO) or Education Social Worker (ESW) are almost universal in their application and most local authorities employ EWOs or ESWs to help them fulfil their responsibilities on attendance. The main job of the Education Welfare Service (EWS) is to 'work closely with school and families to resolve attendance issues, arranging home visits when necessary' (DfEE 1999).

Attendance at school is compulsory. The ages for which attendance is a legal obligation are from 5 years of age until the date announced by the DfES that slots in somewhere between the end of GCSEs and the end of the students' Summer term of their eleventh year of statutory education. Some years ago, when Michael Forth was an Education Minister, there were rumours that serious thought was being given to putting the eleventh year leaving date at the end of the Summer term i.e. about six weeks after the end of the GCSEs. As a way of increasing truancy statistics, this would be a certain success.

Much of the rhetoric written and broadcast about attendance in school is dominated by the anti-child propaganda that is a common feature in the media; local papers are a classic example. The inside pages can be full of stories about primary and secondary school pupils engaged in good works, but any chance to sensationalise a negative story about children on the front page will be grabbed with open arms. This was evident when a local secondary school cooperated with the local Community Health Team in a 'drugs awareness' initiative; they had handed out leaflets and done some group work with the pupils to promote healthy lifestyles among the pupils. The headline that reported this on the front page of the local paper read 'School Encourages Drug-taking' and the headline named the school.

On the political front, it was former Home Secretary Michael Howard who made the overt link between truancy and youth crime. Since Michael Howard, other ministers have spoken upon the matter of attendance at school. The link between truancy and crime was restated in the 2004 MORI Youth Justice Survey. When Michael Forth was Secretary of State for Education under John Major in 1996 there were rumours of Education Welfare Officers having the power of arrest and a uniform to reflect this newly authoritative status within the criminal justice system. It sounded like the ravings of extreme politics at the time. Who knows? It may yet happen. We've now had the imprisonment of a parent in 2002 as a result of her daughter's unauthorised non-attendance at school. This reached the national press and it surely had repercussions around the country. Indeed, there have certainly been a number of instances when an EWO has written to threaten court action, and this threat was taken more seriously than would normally have been expected.

Successive governments have taken the matter of truancy very seriously, as I do because it is the fastest route to early 'social exclusion' a youngster could take. According to the National Audit Office (NAO), the DfES spent £885 million on schemes to tackle truancy during the first two terms of the Labour administration to 2005; a further £560 million is available for the following period to 2006 (NAO 2005). On 25 August 2004, David Miliband and Ivan Lewis wrote to all Chief Education Officers and Directors of Children's Services in England. Their intention was to highlight the need to improve attendance and to tackle truancy; 450,000 children were cited as being absent from school every day. They clarified that the DfES held data that demonstrated a strong correlation between absence and attainment for individual pupils. This is a considerable investment. Ruth Kelly told BBC Radio 4's *Today* programme that a 'hard core of persistent truants' represent around 2 per cent of the country's 6.7 million pupils. The NAO suggested that the Behaviour Improvement Programme (BIP) had impacted in such a way that absence rates in schools taking part in the programme fell twice as fast as the national rates.

The BIP began in 2002 as part of the 'Street Crime' initiative and is part of the government's Behaviour and Attendance Strategy; this programme will have invested £342 million by March 2006. The programme supports local initiatives as well as encouraging key developments. One of its key strategies is to allocate key workers to young people deemed to be 'vulnerable' i.e. at risk of exclusion, truancy or criminal behaviour.

Truancy sweeps are a feature of provision in the vast majority of local authorities. They started in 2002 and are carried out nationally twice a year, undertaken by a range of professionals acting together, e.g. EWOs, Connexions staff and school staff. When the police undertake a sweep with the EWS they are empowered under the Crime and Disorder Act to pick up children who are truanting and to return them to their school.

The legal sanctions as they apply to children and families and the legal measures to help improve attendance can be summarised as follows.

Fast Track to Prosecution: This strategy was designed to prevent 'drift' in casework and in court action. For instance, if parents are not working with the professionals involved, e.g. school staff and EWO, then the EWS can move for prosecution. The case will be reviewed six weeks later, before the court date, and the level of progress will dictate whether the case goes to court or is withdrawn.

Prosecution: It is an offence if a child fails to attend school regularly and these absences are unauthorised. These cases are brought under Section 444 of the Education Act 1996.

Penalty Notice: Section 23 of the Anti-Social Behaviour Act 2003 gives a local authority powers to issue Penalty Notices where a parent or carer is considered capable but unwilling to secure an improvement in his or her child's attendance at school; this is an alternative to prosecution. It is designed to act as an early warning. Each local authority should have a code of conduct agreed by police and schools, to ensure that implementation is consistent and fair. A Penalty Notice has to be requested by a head teacher or by the police. Parents get a warning letter from an EWO seeking improvement in their child's attendance within three weeks. Failure to improve leads to a Penalty Notice which results in:

- £50 fine per parent per child if paid within 28 days;
- £100 fine per parent per child if paid within 14 days and before 42 days.

When there is non-payment of the fine then this results in a court appearance under the attendance legislation. The spur for this policy was the publicity that surrounded unauthorised holidays and led to penalty notices against parents.

Education Supervision Order (ESO): The Children Act 1989 empowered a local authority to apply for an ESO with respect to a young person of compulsory school age who is deemed not to be properly educated. Before it makes such an order, the court has to be satisfied that to do so is in the best interest of the young person. The Order will last for twelve months (with a possible extension for up to three years as a result of a lack of success in the first year) and a Supervisor will have a duty to assist, advise and befriend the child and offer support to parents. The working relationship between the Supervisor, the young person and the parent(s) is as a partnership and the objective is that the young person should access an appropriate education.

When an Order is made, then the young person to whom it applies has to attend school on a regular basis, meet regularly with the Supervisor, follow any reasonable instructions imposed by the Supervisor and discuss any matters that are preventing his or her attending school.

Parenting Orders: Parenting Orders were included in the Anti-Social Behaviour Act 2003. They can be issued by the court and are often more useful than a fine. These orders formalise a Parenting Agreement/Contract and give it some teeth. Parenting Orders can be issued for pupils who have been given a fixed-term exclusion more than twice or a single permanent exclusion in an academic year.

DfES targets

For the academic year 2002/03, the DfES set attendance targets for both the primary sector and the secondary sector.

Primary schools	
Unauthorised absences	0.3% maximum
Overall attendance	95% minimum

Secondary schools	
Unauthorised absences	0.6% maximum
Overall attendance	90% minimum

When a school has reached the overall attendance target, then the figure for the following year is raised by 0.2 per cent.

In 2003 attendance targets had to be agreed between LEAs and schools. The next year individual schools were set targets. For the following year, 2004/05, individual schools were set targets that placed an emphasis upon their Free School Meals (FSM) levels. In other words, higher FSM levels equate to lower standards.

The practice of target setting is clearly a sensitive process; after all, LEAs and schools are judged by Ofsted on their performance in meeting attendance targets. Interestingly, the DfES reminded many Principal EWOs on the last day of the Spring term 2005 that they needed to send in targets for the next year by 5 May 2005, i.e. during the Easter holidays, without time for consultation with schools. Apparently, the DfES claimed they had sent out their requirement to Chief Executives during the previous December; nobody had responded. Even more surprising, the Behaviour and Attendance Strategy Leaders in the local authorities were told to set attendance targets for schools using one formula, while the Principal EWOs were told to set targets using a different formula. The truth is, it gets a bit frantic when there's a strong emphasis coming from a government who all the while receive criticism in a hostile, national press for spending money without achieving results, for example, on 4 February 2005 BBC television news reported that truancy in England had not fallen 'even though £885m has been spent on boosting attendance'.

A working definition of attendance at school is that when a student arrives for registration (one registration in the morning and one in the afternoon) the register is open for a specific period of time, usually thirty minutes; after this thirty minutes, then the registration period is deemed to have finished. Arrival after this time should be marked in the register as 'late' and this will count as an absence from school. Note that the attendance register is a legal document, so correction fluid should not be used.

There are, as you would expect, instances when the issues are not as clear-cut as the attendance register might lead us to believe. For instance:

Mary

Mary came to the school in her eighth year, having moved from another English city. There were a number of family issues e.g. recent family violence, current homelessness and previous attendance problems. The Social Services Department had been alerted to their arrival in our city and had duly notified the school of their residence in our catchment area; in other words, there was good interagency liaison. Mary was admitted to the school and ten hours of in-class support were put in place to help her settle in. This was quite a large amount of support and was, in part, an acknowledgement of her lack of numeracy and literacy skills, which had been exacerbated by her frequent absences from school.

Mary arrived in school on Monday and there was no honeymoon period. The immediate problem was her very strong reaction to females, both in her peer group and to staff. There was nothing aggressive in her reaction to males. Her peer group was quite frightened of her and, unusually, there seemed to be no efforts made by her peers to test her out. Then, after ten weeks, she simply disappeared. There were various rumours as to where she, her mother and her younger brother had gone. Under normal circumstances the word on the street can be quite informative, but all our best efforts to trace her whereabouts proved unsuccessful. After a few weeks the assumption was made that she had left the area. Her name was circulated on the list of missing children.

Then, after a few months, there was a call from another social worker to inform me that Mary was being 'looked after' by the local authority. She was in residential care in a local children's home and it was hoped that we would be able to agree a reintegration programme. We held a meeting in school and Mary was fully included. She had a Key Worker from the children's home with whom she had developed a good relationship. In fact, Mary had obviously thrived since being accommodated by the local authority. She took part in all the decision making; it was Mary who set the date for her initial return to school on a part-time basis and who set the timetable for a return to attending full-time.

Mary's mother had little direct influence over her daughter and gave the impression of having no immediate interest in Mary's education. She attended three review meetings in school. Crucially, as Mary's parent it was more than a legal obligation to include her at every stage; it was a moral imperative – they would be mother and daughter long after she left school.

Mary returned home on 23 of February, at which point her attendance at school reduced from 96 per cent to 35 per cent. The threat of legal action did, initially, have a positive effect. This wore off when it became obvious that the magistrate would not convict because Mary's mother was acting to the best of her ability and that she had no money to pay a fine. Home visits were undertaken to her home at least twice per week, just to bring her to school; it is really hard for her just to enter the building, and much more so to fit in with lessons. When she requested a change of option to do GCSE PE, the Head of Department and the teacher agreed straight away. Life is so much easier when colleagues are flexible. In part, this conforms to the guidelines that recommend teachers should listen to the preferences of students with SEN. Efforts were made to organise a training course for her; she wants to be a decorator. It proved increasingly difficult to engage her because her attendance was so poor and it was difficult for any agency to make reliable contact with her.

Currently, the school is working with the Connexions Service, EWO and social worker to arrange a work experience placement for her and enable her to work towards a GCSE in maths. Mary has been placed on the Child Protection Register under the category of neglect. Her attendance at school currently stands at 31 per cent.

Tutoring and attendance

A tutor is able to have an impact upon individual students' attendance. When looking at the attendance statistics for different tutor groups, there are marked differences that are not explained simply by the nature of the group or the chronological age of the students. Tutors who are prepared to make an effort make a difference. The efforts that can be made will vary from school to school depending upon differing policies. However, students will benefit when a tutor does some of the following:

- develop a special teacher/student relationship that is slightly more relaxed than the normal teacher/student relationship;
- set clear boundaries when it comes to their punctuality and their attendance; enforce the making up of lost time;
- make it clear to the students that they matter to you and that the discipline that you provide for them is for their own good and for their future development;
- keep in regular contact with the parent(s) and guardian(s) of the students who cause you concern;
- show an interest in their 'whole school experience'; make the time to find out about and to acknowledge their successes and their failures. Apply the same principle to their experiences outside school;
- reward good punctuality and attendance e.g. with praise, certificates, sweets;
- remember that the students appreciate being liked and respected and this can be expressed openly;
- when writing references, do this in consultation with the student. Show an interest in their future placement i.e. school, college, work.

It has been interesting to listen to colleagues at the forefront of work in this field. The message that comes across loud and clear is that there is a common factor among the overwhelming majority of cases where attendance is causing significant concern. This common factor is that the needs of the young person have not been appropriately met and/or there is a lack of available provision.

Tracking students can be problematic. Clearly, it is the intention of government that the Common Assessment Framework will act as a supportive, preventative measure for children and to encourage agencies to intervene before things go wrong in children's lives. Also, it is the intention that information will follow the child and will be passed on promptly to their next school. There will need to be a considerable improvement in data transfer for children at the margins of social inclusion. For instance, children who are poor school attenders and whose families are difficult to engage can 'disappear' and move to a new location. There is then a pressure on school because these children's absences impact on attendance statistics and may continue to do so until confirmation is received from their next school that they have enrolled. Files can take time to transfer; collating a file and sending it off for a child who has left can become a reduced priority in a busy school and, when the file does arrive, the child may have moved on again.

It may help us to resist temptation to remove a child from a school roll if we heed the advice of one ex-Principal EWO who warned that any such child 'may have gone to live with today's Fred West' (David Bowen, Personal Interview 1996). We need to ensure the child's whereabouts to ensure his or her continued safety and education.

Behaviour

Behaviour and learning are inextricably linked. Self-evidently, anti-social, disrupting behaviours undermine the learning of the individual and can also affect the learning of others in the classroom and beyond. The underlying causes of behaviours exist at different levels within a school, as well as outside the school, and therefore require different solutions. At one level, for instance, pupils' behaviour may be partly physiological in origin due to their poor nutrition and/or dehydration. Improvement actions will most likely relate to school-wide policies such as breakfast clubs, improved access to drinking water and healthier lunches.

It is, however, very unusual to read anything about improving the management of behaviour, or to attend a related training event, without the word 'consistency' being a key word in the discussion. This is because young people feel most comfortable when they feel they are being treated fairly; when discipline is applied in such a way that the young people know where they stand, when adults implement rewards and sanctions consistently and fairly and where pupils have been included in the development of a school's behaviour policy.

To attain a reasonable level of consistency, then the whole staff team needs to apply a school's behaviour policy. To achieve this effectively, the staff team and the pupils will need to have taken part in developing the policy and be familiar with the policy; in other words, everyone will have a sense of owning the policy. They will also need to take part in reviewing the policy and the opportunity to access appropriate training focus upon its application. In this way, then the whole staff group can be accountable for, and take responsibility for the behaviour of the students in the school.

Each new member of staff should receive at least a basic programme of induction that includes advice and guidance on the application of the behaviour policy, before being expected to manage a classroom full of students; this should include supply teachers. With a commitment to the above, the whole team will benefit and, most importantly, so will the young people. These are functions of the organisational constraints that fall beyond the remit of the classroom management of an individual teacher; this refers to the school's Management Team getting the fundamentals right, i.e. managing an effective whole-school behaviour policy while simultaneously monitoring and improving the quality of teaching and learning.

Meeting the learning needs of pupils in a classroom is one significant contribution that good teaching makes to improving behaviour. A child whose needs are not being met and whose opportunity to experience success is being limited is more likely to avoid the experience of failure by behaving inappropriately e.g. disrupting or truanting.

Differentiation

All teachers have a responsibility to teach pupils with special educational needs and this has implications for the time needed to spend on preparation. The government acknowledged this during negotiations with the professional associations, which produced the Workload Agreement. This has removed the number of administrative tasks that teachers are required to perform e.g. collecting dinner money and doing bulk photocopying, as well as removing the requirement for teachers to invigilate the government exams, such as SATs, GCSEs. Teachers are now required to have 10 per cent of their teaching hours as non-contact time to facilitate their marking and preparation. All of this is within the 1265 hours per year of directed time that a teacher may be contracted to work.

A teacher is expected to help students with a range of learning difficulties to make progress. In a class group this can include students with:

- moderate learning difficulties;
- specific learning difficulties;
- speech and language difficulties;
- visual impairment;
- hearing impairment;
- autism;
- emotional, behavioural and social difficulties.

There are many other categories of special educational needs and those mentioned above are broad categories. They are, probably, the learning needs that are more frequently experienced by a teacher in a mainstream classroom.

All teachers have their own ideas and their own skills. What follows are a very few of the ideas that are available to be employed.

Assessing the reading level of text

Knowing the reading age of students is of limited use without a measure of the reading level of text. One way of calculating this is as follows.

From ten consecutive sentences of the chosen text:

- Count *every* word over two syllables.
- Multiply this number by three.
- Find the nearest square root of this number.
- Add this number to eight.

Now you have the reading age of the text. It is extraordinary to note that very few educational texts provide information relating to the reading level of their text.

There is another way to work this out, and this is especially useful when you are using Microsoft Word to produce materials. You can request a readability score if you take the following steps:

1 Click on 'Tools'.
2 Click on 'Options' (at the bottom of the box).
3 Click on 'Spelling and grammar' (on the top right of the box).
4 Click on 'Show readability statistics' (the small box at the bottom) to put a tick in the box.
5 Click 'ok' (at the bottom).

Having done this, you will need to do the following to get the readability statistics for a piece of text:

1 Click on 'Tools'.
2 Click on 'Spelling and grammar'.

The software will then do a check on your spelling and grammar and when it has completed this process it will display a box of statistics. At the bottom of this box is the Flesch-Kincaid Level; add 5 to this level and you have a reading age for your text.

Teaching materials

Pupils with learning and particularly reading difficulties need written materials such as books and worksheets that take account of their difficulties. Many students are at a level where they may need differentiated curriculum materials to take into account their reading skills. The following are suggestions to consider:

- Use a larger font; it's easier to read. A minimum font of size 16 is ideal.
- Different coloured paper makes a difference. Don't use anything too bold; pastel colours are effective. Some coloured paper costs little more than standard white.
- Put in easily seen, clearly comprehensible pictures in appropriate places. This breaks up the volume of text and appears less daunting.
- Be aware of the spacing of your processed text; there's no point in using a good font and then squashing the words together.
- Make an effort to provide a glossary of words and pictures.
- Try to use a mixture of activities to meet the needs of students with different concentration spans.
- When you set targets, it helps to negotiate the targets with the student(s), and you can guide them with setting attainable ones.
- It helps to revisit topics in order to reinforce skills and concepts.

Key words and flash cards: Each subject has its own key words. To learn science to GCSE standard, for instance, necessitates learning the equivalent of an entire new language. Most classes will include children who are visual learners and flash cards can assist the learning of key words.

When A4-sized flash cards are displayed around a classroom, then a teacher can read out the definition of one of the words and students can move towards the word that they believe the definition refers to. This can be done as a class of individuals, or perhaps in pairs/groups who nominate one student to go towards the chosen word. This type of activity engages the visual and the kinaesthetic learners.

When you design the cards, avoid the use of capital letters. If possible, only use capital letters when the word demands it e.g. London, Macbeth.

Pairs: Cards with key words written on each one and a similar set of cards containing the definition of each word. These can be used individually, or in pairs or groups to match the word to its definition. Placed upside down on a table the cards become a memory game.

Bingo: Each student has a card with a answers to the test/quiz written on it. The teacher reads out the questions and the students write the number of each question next to the answer that they believe to be the correct one.

Wonder Wall: If you can adapt something from TV then all the better. For instance, Wonder Wall has its antecedence in the National Lottery. Using an overhead projector, words are put along the top row and their definitions are put along the bottom row. The students write down the matched pairs.

In all of the above, using additional visual clues for the students will often be appreciated, so if the materials are useful, laminate them.

Worksheets: When preparing worksheets for groups of students with mixed ability, there are some fairly simple guidelines that are useful to follow. The list that follows complements the previous advice. It is not exhaustive but it does contain a degree of common sense.

- Use simple, not compound sentences.
- Write positive statements; negatives confuse and double negatives confuse absolutely.
- Keep sentences short; seven to ten words long as a maximum.
- Use monosyllabic words whenever possible and disyllabic words when necessary. Words of greater length should be introduced sparingly.
- When using technical or subject-specific words, try to introduce them as key words e.g. on flash cards.
- Provide clear, unambiguous instructions. For instance, avoid 'You may prefer to organise yourselves into groups or pairs and go into a separate space'; it is preferable to say 'Work in groups of four students, the person next to you and the two in front, working from the back of the class'.
- There should be a minimum of 40 per cent of 'white space' on the worksheet.
- Avoid using capital letters; students find text with capitals much more difficult to read.
- Use bullet points or a numbered sequence where possible.
- Avoid questions that may be answered 'yes' or 'no' if you require a longer answer.
- Boys in particular respond better to precise instructions, such as 'Find five examples of . . .', rather than 'See how many examples you can find.'

'Tracking back'

'Tracking back' benefits students in KS3 and KS4 with general learning difficulties e.g. whose national curriculum levels are two levels below the norm for their age. This requires secondary schools to have access to the primary curriculum materials. It is a fairly straightforward way of going back from Year 6 to Reception for literacy and numeracy and then into the 'P' scales, in order to ensure curriculum entitlement and access for all students.

Emotional intelligence

The importance of emotional intelligence is that schools need adults with high levels of emotional intelligence to deal successfully with pupils who are challenging, whose ability to manage their own emotions is a daily struggle and who lose control because they experience feelings of anger, fear and hostility that overwhelm them. These distressed and distressing children need to be managed by adults who are able to manage their own emotions.

Academic ability alone is not a reliable predictor of success and happiness in the adult world. Indeed, IQ alone may contribute just 20 per cent to the factors that determine success in life and Daniel Goleman in his book *Emotional Intelligence* (1997) explores the possibility that emotional intelligence is a key contributor to the other 80 per cent.

Yale psychologist Peter Salovey (Salovey *et al* 2000) suggests five key areas of emotional intelligence:

- knowing one's emotions: being aware of one's own emotions e.g. anxiety and being able to influence them;
- managing emotions: controlling emotions such as anger can significantly enhance the ability to manage anger in others;
- motivating oneself: positive thinking, channelling anxiety and so on;
- recognising emotions in others: developing the skill of empathy greatly assists in the ability to read verbal and non-verbal cues;
- handling relationships: using empathy, the emotionally intelligent teacher acts as the leader and can negotiate solutions and help put pupils at ease.

Mark Whitby works as a head teacher in Sussex. He has a fine grasp of what is necessary to work successfully with the most vulnerable pupils, whose behaviours can be challenging in the extreme. His ability to manage and support staff and to work directly with pupils combine with a clear understanding of the crucial role of emotional intelligence in the most effective practitioners. What follows is an attempt to impart a sense of his understanding (while acknowledging that it cannot compare with) his own training.

What is set out below sits alongside the concept that **behaviour and learning are not only linked; they are the same thing.** We know that a child has learnt something because he or she behaves differently; which is different from knowing something but not changing your behaviour. For example, I know that exercise is good for me but I remain passive and take no part in exercise. It can therefore be argued that my knowledge has changed but my learning hasn't (maybe I doubt the knowledge that I have). Semantics maybe, but it works well in the field of child development.

We judge children's progress by what they do, not what they say, and we also believe children judge us (the practitioners) by what we do and not what we say. Therefore, our actions and our ability to manage our emotions and apply them strategically are paramount (emotional intelligence). It makes a mockery of the old saying, 'Do what I say, not what I do'. One of the aims of practitioners is to transfer appropriate 'skills' from adults to children. To achieve this, the adults need to guide pupils in how they react, think, interact and feel. How the adults manage stress acts as a model for the stressed child. The extent to which we can control emotional pressure will determine how well we manage stress; how well we manage stress will determine how effectively we can apply the strategies available to us. Some things, like challenging children, or people who drive dangerously, are beyond our immediate control. We must learn, therefore, that if we cannot directly control events then we need, instead, to govern ourselves and control our thinking; this will include the way we characteristically perceive, think about and speak to ourselves about stressful events, such as our reactions and responses and the way we organise time and plan for situations.

On an individual level, there are different types of practitioner. For instance:

- Passive: the appealer, the best friend, justifying instructions with 'Because I'd like you to'.
- Aggressive: the imposer, being demanding, justifying instructions with 'Because I'm telling you to'.
- Assertive: the enabler, being decisive, justifying instructions with 'Because that's what we've agreed to'.

The assertive approach is developed through a team philosophy, a culture that sustains the integrity to forego moaning and blaming and whose focus is on solutions, not problems. The behaviour is the problem, not the child; that this becomes obscured is indicative of the need to appreciate and to value emotional intelligence.

Exclusions

The opposite of inclusion is exclusion and it's exclusion that is the ultimate sanction available to a head teacher. Exclusions are used in response to inappropriate behaviours e.g. aggression, verbal abuse, theft and so on, and they come in two types, when they are legally applied. They are:

- fixed-term exclusions;
- permanent exclusions.

Fixed-term exclusions: Fixed-term exclusions are for a specific period of time. No student may be excluded on this basis for more than 45 days in one academic year. After 15 days the school is responsible for the provision of full-time education for the child and this does not mean sending home some books. It might, however, mean purchasing a place at the local Pupil Referral Unit and this brings the issue of money into the equation. If the student is particularly difficult then the charge could be over £35 an hour. Extrapolate this into 25 hours per week and the notional figure comes to £875 per week. Admittedly, this would be an extreme case, but one can appreciate the financial concerns of a bursar and the tensions this can produce in a school if the school has to pay for the placement.

The fixed-term exclusion can offer time for colleagues to come together, to meet with the child's parents, to plan and to put in additional educational provision. The example of 'Sarah' illustrates this.

Sarah
Sarah came to the school from Manchester, where she had been living for two years. She was admitted into Year 8. When she was screened on entry the following results were gained:

Reading age	12.04
Reading comprehension	12.02
Numeracy percentile ranking	42
Non-verbal reasoning percentile ranking	39

There were no school records indicating that anyone had expressed any concern that Sarah had special educational needs. Her Key Stage 2 SATs results were commensurate with the national average i.e. maths, English and science all at Level 4. The conclusion was that on the basis of her previous records, her literacy, numeracy and non-verbal reasoning and her most recent SATs results, Sarah would be able to access the National Curriculum from within a mainstream classroom.

A planning meeting was held to plan her admission. This was because there had been a six-month gap, prior to her joining our roll, during which time Sarah had received no formal education. Sarah's family circumstances had previously become increasingly difficult and she had been sent to live with a relative in another city. This had not been a successful placement and by the time she came to the school, she was being looked after by the local authority and was in her second foster placement in two months.

The discussion during the planning meeting acknowledged that Sarah would be likely to demonstrate emotional behavioural and social difficulties. The evidence for this was gleaned from her behaviour in her foster placements, where she had physically threatened two of the adults and physically attacked one of her peers (the son of the foster parents). It became apparent that Sarah was a young person with very low self-esteem, who had experienced rejection by her parents and still felt very hurt. She felt very angry because of this rejection and because she felt very strongly that she had been unfairly treated.

It seemed reasonable to predict that Sarah would 'test' those adults she came into contact with, in order to find out whether these new adults would also reject her. This pattern of behaviour will be seen by adults who work in schools, because of the number of children who feel rejected by their parents during the upheaval caused by family breakdown; it can be demonstrated by people of all ages following rejection. Sarah's rejection was made worse for her by the fact that she had been physically abused by family members and had disclosed this to no one, fearing the disruption that a disclosure can precipitate. Despite her silence, she had been forced to leave her family by those same family members. The sense of injustice that Sarah was living with can only be imagined. While her rage was challenging to deal with, there was no doubting its sincerity.

During her first three months in the school, Sarah was placed in three different foster homes. Given the local and national shortage of foster parents, just finding this number of new placements was an achievement and was a testimony to the commitment of her social worker. The placements had broken down because Sarah was becoming increasingly adept at 'testing' the adults and, with no intended criticism, the adults were failing her tests. Indeed, she was becoming increasingly demanding and the question implicit within her escalating behaviour, 'Will you still be there for me if I do this?', was becoming an increasingly rapid 'No'.

The most difficult task facing the school with Sarah is to be able to build a relationship with her that is based on trust. One person needs to be able to make a start with this and Sarah needs to be part of this. Sarah has been placed in more secure residential care and continues to attend mainstream school. The potential drawback inherent in institutional care is evident where young people may be placed in a situation where their peers are able to confirm each other's inappropriate behaviour. Sarah learnt that destruction of property is an effective strategy to employ as an avoidance tactic. For instance, when she asked to go home, during the second lesson of the day, it was explained that she was committed to a full-time timetable. Sarah's response to this was swift and effective; she picked up a chair and threw it across the room. At this point, a fixed-term exclusion became advisable, to achieve three outcomes:

1 to let Sarah know that her behaviour was not acceptable;
2 to let other students know that such behaviour was not acceptable;
3 to provide time for a planning meeting to be convened.

The planning meeting was a good one and Sarah took part in it. It was acknowledged that those working with Sarah had not been able to provide her with a vision for her future and that this lack of direction was unsettling for her. It was clear that her placement at the school was viewed as an important part of her future. The difficulty was this: when a pupil is most vulnerable and disruptive, this is a time when those around him or her will be confronted by the most challenging behaviours. In school, colleagues have to respond to the needs of the individual as well as to the needs of the group and such behaviours put pressure upon the head teacher to 'act decisively'. In practice, the teachers and support staff, acting as corporate parents, need the flexible support of external colleagues such as social workers and Youth Justice Officers.

The teachers in the classroom had the most difficult task. Sarah tested each and every one of them. Every effort was made to keep each teacher informed of what was occurring in Sarah's life. This way she was more than just a disruptive element; she was a person in her own right. Also, the teachers knew that there was some back-up available and that any concerns would be listened to and taken account of. It takes greater effort to implement the behaviour policy evenly when students are 'at the margins'. The efforts are, however, worth making because sanctions for inappropriate behaviour are most effective when there is certainty in the student's mind that they will be applied. Therefore, when Sarah's maths teacher placed her in an after-school detention, it was necessary to do the following:

- make time to locate and listen to the maths teacher;
- support the maths teacher's decision by discussing with Sarah the reason for her detention;
- telephone her foster parents and agree that Sarah would do her detention;
- telephone the taxi company and rearrange Sarah's transport to arrange a later taxi;
- telephone the social worker to inform him that Sarah might be very resistant to the implementation of normal school discipline;
- agree the social worker's visit to the school to support the school's decision and to support Sarah;
- use the time during the detention to confirm the normal consequences of cause and effect that correspond to inappropriate behaviour and detention.

It would have been so much easier not to bother. Nevertheless, education in its wider context dictates that the effort should be made.

It was to Sarah's benefit that the social workers working with her were highly committed and their practical contribution e.g. organising and implementing rewards for appropriate behaviours, meeting regularly with Sarah and teaching staff, mean that Sarah remains on roll and with the realistic hope of remaining in mainstream school.

Permanent exclusions: Permanent exclusions are much less common. There are two main reasons for this. First, they represent extremes of behaviour and these, by definition, occur less frequently. Secondly, and here we return to the issue of money, there is often a financial penalty to bear. For instance, a local education authority may rule that a school that permanently excludes a student will provide £6000 to go with the student to his or her new establishment as well as the Age-Weighted Pupil Unit (AWPU) money.

There are schools that have progressed so far towards inclusion that they do not exclude at all. It is interesting to note one example of an LEA which has been highly rated by Ofsted and has, until recently, had a very low rate of exclusions. However, there has been a significant reduction in its allocation from central government, schools' budgets are under enormous strain and staff are being made redundant. While this is happening, the rate of permanent exclusions is rising; inclusion has to be resourced reducing – resources increases exclusion.

There are many aspects of a school's provision that impact upon the behaviour of children.

Parents

The majority of people who work as education professionals experienced success at school when they were children. By contrast, it can easily be forgotten that some of the parents that schools work with previously experienced educational failure as children, at a time before league tables, before Ofsted, before SATs tests, before 'inclusion', even before targets. These 'children' may have been members of a significant minority who were simply discounted because they were not academic achievers and were not predicted ever to be successful. There were no attendance targets, so when they voted with their feet and truanted it may have been frowned upon, but it happened. Times are very different now.

On leaving school people rarely renegotiate their relationship with school in general and with teachers in particular. Imagine, then, what it can be like for those adults who previously experienced failure at school and who had felt written off. For those adults, teachers remain in the same authoritarian category as members of the police force. This helps our understanding of the regular non-attendance of some parents at parents' evenings.

All parents want the best for their children. In addition, a major area of concern shared by most parents is bullying and while everyone has their own definition of what the term means, one working definition is that bullying is evident when a person's experience is of being bullied. Bullying affects the whole family; it generates anger, frustration and a sense of powerlessness and dealing with individual cases of bullying can be immensely time-consuming, as the following example shows.

Myung
Mr and Mrs Choi complained on behalf of their son Myung. They wrote to the Chair of Governors expressing their concern

that Myung was being bullied, that he felt unsafe and that staff in the school had been negligent and ineffective in their response to previous expressions of concern during recent months. This complaint precipitated a lengthy investigation by the head of lower school that included interviews with students, parents and colleagues, including the head teacher, and an action plan was created with, and agreed by, the student's parents. This included:

- Myung's immediate, full-time inclusion in the Student Support Base until both parents and student were satisfied that appropriate arrangements were in place;
- assurances that Myung would be able to undertake all ongoing work in his core subjects while in the Student Support Base;
- referral by the school to the educational psychologist for impartial advice and contribution to the action plan;
- 'no blame' interviews with all eight students identified by Myung as being those who had given him a, 'hard time', each interview concluding with verbal assurances that those incidents of bullying would cease;
- daily contact with parents at the end of each school day for two working weeks;
- daily contact with parents prior to the start of the school day for two working weeks;
- individual supervisory arrangements for Myung during free association times;
- planning meeting that included school-based staff, Mr and Mrs Choi, Myung and the school's link educational psychologist. This meeting agreed that:
  - Myung would register in the Student Support Base every morning and afternoon, where he reported himself to feel safe consistently;
  - Myung would be offered additional support in his lessons for maths and French;
  - the educational psychologist would meet with Myung to assess whether Myung had any special educational needs that had not been previously identified and would report back to the special needs coordinator and Myung's parents;
  - Myung would be introduced to a Circle of Friends (a system of support originating from work in Canada). The head of lower school would manage this Circle;

- Myung would be allocated a place on one of the school's confidence-building groups, which were led by a team of independent counsellors;
- The pastoral leader would coordinate the programme, liaise with Myung's teachers, monitor his progress and contact Mrs Choi weekly throughout the term, to provide regular progress reports.

Within two months of the original complaint, Myung and his parents were satisfied that Myung's situation had been resolved successfully and the Chair of Governors sent a formal, written response to Mr and Mrs Choi, to confirm the satisfactory completion of the process.

11 All our children

What is child abuse?

Child Abuse is when a child suffers harm or even death because of physical cruelty, emotional cruelty, sexual abuse or neglect by an adult. Often the adult is a parent or someone the child knows and trusts. In many cases the child may be subjected to a combination of different kinds of abuse, for example, neglect and sexual abuse. Bullying and racism are also forms of child abuse, as are uncaring professionals who fail to meet young client/patient needs, organisations that put corporate needs before those of children, and governments who ignore the reality of established levels of need because they lack the political will to overcome them, i.e. a passive abuse of 'sins of omission', as much as 'sins of commission' (Pritchard 2004).

Section 175 of the Education Act 2002 raised the responsibilities of school staff in both public and private sectors to report child protection matters appropriately. It is not yet widely appreciated that if it can be proven that a teacher or a social worker has not passed on information about abuse of a child, or the risk of such abuse, then the teacher or social worker can be taken to court. It may never happen, but it does demonstrate that the lessons learnt from the Victoria Climbie Inquiry have been instrumental in shaping recent reforms. Remember, each human being under the age of 18 years is a child.

Before anyone starts works in a school it is essential that they know who is the teacher with designated responsibility for child protection in the school. It is normal for the teacher with specific responsibility for child protection to attend the child protection conferences. There should be training and/or information made available to every member of staff, as this area of practice is of the highest priority.

The impact of child abuse upon the life of a young person should not be underestimated. A very experienced colleague provided one of the most memorable techniques used during a child protection training course; she had provided training on behalf of a national organisation, at the highest level, for over two decades. On this occasion she had a group of about twenty social workers and police officers from a variety of child protection teams. They were about to embark upon a five-day course and most of them were strangers to each other.

After they had registered and had their coffee, the trainer instructed them to split into pairs, choosing a partner they had not met prior to that day and to find a place in the room where they could talk quietly to each other. The next instruction was to take it in turns, taking no more than ten minutes each, about the most humiliating and embarrassing sexual experience they had ever had. Apparently you could virtually hear people's jaws drop and most trainees were unable to engage with this task. The trainer let the implications of such an instruction be appreciated for a few moments, and then drew a parallel with the expectations we make of children and young people during their disclosure. Obviously, highly trained practitioners sensitively handle joint investigations (police and social services working together); nevertheless, it's a tough time for the young person.

Victoria Climbie's death in 2001 has led to strategic changes in the delivery of child protection services in England and Wales. Lord Lamming's report advised the *Every Child Matters* Green Paper (DfES 2003b) for consultation, resulting in *Every Child Matters* and the Children Act 2004. Although much of the thinking behind *Every Child Matters* is not new for many schools, their influence and collaboration will be essential in the development of new local authority Directors of Children's Services and Children's Trusts.

The 2004 Act clearly sets out the importance of local agencies working collaboratively to ensure children do not fall through the net; for example, new rules state that the disappearance of children from registers *must* be followed up and reported to either the Police Child Protection Units or Social Services Department. The setting up of the Common Assessment Framework (CAF) enables all practitioners involved with children to tackle and identify problems for children before they become serious; the CAF is particularly useful to the education and health services in their role as universal services. All school staff will need to be familiar with the CAF, which will support their school's ability to identify and deal with problems at an earlier stage and enable key staff in schools such as teachers, EWOs and nurses to liaise more effectively with other professionals.

Talking in confidence

Children must be made aware, in schools, that there is someone they can turn to at times of crisis. Ideally, all schools would have an independent counsellor, but in reality any teacher could be asked for advice by a child and it is important that:

- the child is heard and action is taken if appropriate;
- the teacher/member of staff feels confident enough to listen.

A good practice guide can include the school providing a leaflet for all children setting out the ground rules for confidentiality. All children should be aware that if they share with any member of staff information which means they could be at risk of serious harm then that *has* to be passed on. Any other information or confidences can be shared, but only if it is thought this will be necessary to protect the child. The child will then be made aware there is someone to turn to. Normally staff will look out for indicators of concern such as absences, neglected appearance, withdrawn behaviour, acting out, distressed behaviour. Staff will be able to assess, at some point in the discussion, where they need to inform the child that the information must be passed on.

Looked-after children

Looked-after children (LAC) is the phrase used to describe young people who are looked after by the local authority and in 2003 there were approximately 58,900 such children (ONS 2003).

Schools have a duty to provide data that measure the progress of looked-after children. Local authorities provide returns to government that show various measures for LAC, including:

- those having over 25 days off school per year;
- the number of exclusions applied to LAC;
- the number of LAC who have been moved more than three times in a year;
- proportion of KS2 results attained at levels 4/5;
- number of LAC with 1+ GCSEs on leaving school.

There is also a target that 75 per cent of LAC should achieve one or more GCSEs. It would be sensible if local authorities did not have to include pupils with severe learning difficulties in the cohort to be measured. As a teacher, it is worth knowing that there will be people in the local authority with responsibility for LAC. These people will have resources and a budget; so if you think a revision guide or a software package would help the pupil, ask the designated teacher for LAC to ring them up and recommend they buy it, or just do it yourself. Look up the 'Education Protects' section on the DFES website and you will find the contact details for the colleagues to contact in your area.

LAC are, by definition, looked after by the local authority and in most schools teachers and support staff are employees of the local authority. So, if you work in a local authority-maintained school, as most teachers do, then remember that 'looked after by the local authority' means looked after by you. This duty of the whole local authority to 'safeguard and promote his [or her] welfare' (1989 Children Act S22(3)(a)) is called 'corporate parenting'. Schools have received guidance from the DfES that they should maintain a Register of LAC; there has been concern that not all schools disseminate this effectively to staff.

Successful educational inclusion can make the key difference, leading to meaningful life choices. For all of us as citizens and taxpayers, it is in our self-interest to help our looked-after children become self-determining responsible adults who can become net contributors, rather than be excluded and become long-term drains upon the public purse.

Len Davies was a Senior Lecturer in Social Work at Brunel University in the early 1980s and he spoke movingly of the experience of children in care. He spoke of children whose damaging experiences were legion and that in responding as a carer there is a moment to forget the jargon and, instead, to redress the balance with good experiences. It's rarely simple in practice, but sometimes a simple framework can aid understanding when caring becomes burdensome.

Young people in school who are looked after by the local authority frequently carry a great deal of emotional baggage. Imagine being in a school where the local authority has accommodated a young person because her mother has been murdered; an extreme example, but so many of the real cases of young people being separated from their parents and families are traumatic. Imagine how hard it is to take seriously a dress code when what is dominating your thoughts is when you will be able to see your mum again, and you are 11 years of age, or 8 or 14. Are these pupils really expected to cope like all the others?

There may be a perception within schools that there are two different categories of LAC. First there are those young people who are victims of child abuse and then there are the very naughty children, and this can encourage the notion that LAC are associated with problematic behaviour. Yet the truth is frequently so different. For instance:

> The head teacher had waited after school with colleagues to hear from a social worker as to whether a foster placement had been found for a family of four siblings attending his school. The eldest boy, Paddy, aged 10, had used the number he always carried with him to contact the social services department to explain that their mother was descending into depression again and that the family was not coping. By early evening mum had been found and was staying at a local psychiatric facility. Paddy

had done this before; he had been the victim of abuse at a very early age and he had done all that he could to keep the family together and to understand that his mother sometimes needed extra help to make her well and able to look after her children. So Paddy was at home, with a neighbour, waiting to find out where he and his brother and sisters were going to sleep that night. Two emergency foster placements were found; two children were to be placed in each home. Staff drove them from the school and they were able to help settle them in to their emergency placements.

The children were in school next day and they all completed their schooling at the local mainstream schools. Many people worked very hard to support the family: housing officers, social workers, psychiatrist (for both the children and their mother), family support workers, community psychiatric nurse, Education Welfare Officer, police officers, foster parents, LAC officers, probation officers, general practitioners, teachers from primary and secondary schools (who were a constant and stabilising factor in their lives) and others. The schools were key partners in flagging up concerns and assisting in the delivery of services.

The number of agencies and their representatives working to support LAC can bring its own complications. It has been estimated that a single young person can have over forty adults to deal with and the two things that LAC consistently complain about are

- being moved from their foster placement;
- their social workers moving on and having to get used to a new one, when their case is allocated.

The number of moves is reducing but social workers keep moving. It's a very stressful job, the hours can be very unsocial, and the pay is significantly less than, for instance, that of teachers.

Who should know that a child has become a looked-after child and when should they know it? Both these issues should be discussed and negotiated with the young person.

When a child is accommodated under Section 20 of the Children Act 1989, the only people who have parental rights (PR) are the natural parents. This means that social workers and foster parents do not have PR and the parents should be involved in all decision making. Foster parents, for instance, would not sign a school admission form in this case. Also, from December 2003, if the father's name is on the birth certificate, then he has parental responsibility.

When a child is subject to a Care Order, then PR is held by the local authority and the natural parents; the natural parents only lose PR when the child is freed for adoption. PR is legally held by the Adoption Panel during this period.

Schools must maintain contact with all the parents, ensuring that reports are sent to them unless specifically advised otherwise, e.g. by a court order. Some of the parents of LAC will feel undermined when they see other people succeeding with their children, such as foster parents or teachers. It can become easy to judge parents of LAC, but that needs to be guarded against. We can help families retain their relationships by giving their responsibilities the respect they have a right to in law.

Government guidance bolsters the oversight of LAC in school by giving responsibility to a designated teacher to take responsibility for these pupils, without there being any additional ring-fenced funds to provide free time to carry out these duties or to offer responsibility points. This is why, in primary schools, the head teacher often carries the responsibility.

So what training do teachers receive? In general, the priorities for in-service training do not often place LAC at the top, so little training is offered. Yet the government has now placed a duty upon local authorities, via the Children Act, to improve the educational outcomes for LAC.

In terms of the advice and guidance available to schools in general, and teachers in particular, there is one excellent document, *Education of Young People in Public Care*, available free from the Department for Education and Skills.

It's not easy to imagine what many of these children have seen, what they've been through and what they've experienced. What we can do is make the time to learn from them and make the effort to understand.

Clearly, there is a need to act responsibly when a child has made a disclosure. The work that is undertaken to support a young person and his or her family is not time-limited; the duration of any intervention is based entirely upon the needs of the child. This period of the child's life may be the most traumatic he or she will ever experience and how successful people are in working together to meet the child's needs may be likely to shape significantly the rest of his or her life. Each case will have unique and stressful circumstances and will test the ability of different agencies to work together effectively.

The complexity and the severity of circumstances that are experienced by some young people mean that the issues of child protection and looked-after children are featured together, as shown in the following example.

Winston

When Winston came to us, it was at the end of the Autumn term of his first year at secondary school, three months later than we had planned for. He had a fairly new Statement of SEN and a planning meeting had taken place during the previous Summer term to plan his transfer from his primary school. Winston was on the child protection register, in the category of emotional abuse. During his last year at his primary school things had obviously become very difficult. His timetable was reduced to one hour per day and then, three weeks before the end of the term, he was excluded for the rest of his time there. This exclusion took him up to the maximum permitted in any one academic year, 45 days.

The meeting to agree the plan for his admission to secondary school was somewhat strained. It was clear that the primary school's representative did not believe that Winston should, or could, make progress in a mainstream secondary school. Winston had been involved in incidents of physical aggression against both his peers and staff at the school. This school had been affected by a change of intake over a period of five years; indeed the increasing social deprivation experienced by the local catchment area has attracted several millions of pounds in government aid. So this was a school under pressure and coming to terms with the need to become a more effective, inclusive school. Winston's placement was associated with:

- complaints from parents of the students that he had assaulted;
- staff time taken up by attendance at child protection conferences and the attendant report writing;
- additional cost to the school of increased individual, one-to-one support;
- reduced staff morale attributed to Winston's aggression towards adults;
- the sense of frustration that other children were being adversely affected both educationally and emotionally by his behaviours towards them.

As far as the school's targets were concerned, Winston had a negative effect upon their numbers of exclusions, their attendance figures and their Key Stage 2 SATs results.

Let me state quite clearly that this was not, and is not a bad school (they have recently received a very positive Ofsted report). What this describes is the sort of discussion that exists in many schools and staff rooms and is definitely a feature of the debate that is stimulated, in schools, by the policy and practice of inclusion and the need to meet targets and balance budgets.

Winston didn't transfer in September; his mother moved away to try for a fresh start. This new beginning did not work out as hoped. The housing department in her new city assessed the family as having made themselves intentionally homeless and therefore ineligible for access to social housing provision. After three months of bed-and-breakfast accommodation and an unsuccessful trawl of the private housing stock they returned to the city they knew and to the people who knew them.

A phone call from the SEN Case Officer informed the secondary school that Winston had returned to the area with his mother and that his admission to the school was back on track. Another planning meeting was held; Winston took part in the meeting and an early admission date was set. The plan was that he should attend school full-time. This was his entitlement, albeit that his last experience of school was for just one hour per day for twelve weeks, prior to his final exclusion at the end of the Summer term. Also, and quite understandably, there was considerable pressure to have him safely occupied in school, rather than unoccupied and free to wander the city's streets. Consequently, it had been difficult to arrange the dedicated support that he was entitled to. This meant that he would have a combination of four teaching assistants supporting him in lessons.

Then look at it from Winston's point of view. Whatever else was going on in his world, his only experience of school was at one primary school where he was taught by two, maybe three teachers each year for six years and one of these would have done the lion's share of the teaching. Now he was about to move to a school where he would be coping with:

- twelve teachers (approximately) over his two-week time-table;
- one tutor for morning and afternoon registration and his personal development and citizenship sessions;
- one year head with overall pastoral responsibility for his year;
- one head of school responsible for Years 7, 8 and 9;
- four teaching assistants;
- this author as special educational needs coordinator.

On the positive side, he would experience greater variety in his daily routine and would meet people who had few or no preconceived opinions about him and who were informed as to his needs. These needs may be summarised as emotional behavioural and social difficulties; numeracy and literacy skills that both scored at approximately the tenth percentile but with a non-verbal reasoning score that scored within the average range and expressive language skills that scored in the first percentile. This latter was significant in that Winston had great difficulty expressing his feelings verbally e.g. his anger and confusion.

Then Winston arrived for his first day. The head of lower school had arranged for two 'buddies' to help him settle in. All of his teaching assistants had their timetables prepared to support him in his lessons and the school was as ready as reasonably possible. For the first week all went well, but in the second week an ashen-faced teaching assistant explained that Winston had been running around the classroom during his humanities lesson stabbing everyone he passed with his newly sharpened pencil and refusing point blank to cooperate with the teacher. This had provoked a less than favourable reaction from his classmates. He spent the rest of the afternoon in the Student Support Base; a facility supervised by very able support staff. They spent time with Winston with the aim of:

- confirming that assaulting his fellow pupils was wrong;
- finding out what precipitated his actions;
- preparing Winston to begin the task of making amends for the pain he had inflicted upon other students i.e. to express appropriate remorse;
- mediating between the humanities teacher and Winston;
- informing Winston's parent of the day's events and of the school's responses;
- encouraging Winston to explain his version of what had happened and to record this, if necessary writing it for him using only his words;
- interviewing students who were closest to the incident and ensure a record of their observations is included in the final report;
- collating a report of the incident in its fullest possible context;
- advising the head of year as to whether any additional parents, other than Winston's, should be contacted and informed of the incident and the school's response;
- informing the Case Responsible Worker at the Social Services Department.

This, then, was the short-term aim, but how much time was available to achieve this? An hour and a quarter was the maximum amount of time that could be allocated, so which of these tasks could be compromised and what would be the risks?

Confirming that assaulting his fellow pupils was wrong. Basic rule number one: give a clear, consistent and measured response to the child confirming the core values inherent in the school's Behaviour Policy. It's not reasonable to compromise on this one.

Finding out what precipitated his actions. A common error is to fail to make the time to explore the context of an action. Children will most often be truthful, albeit with their version of the truth, and we understand an action only when it is placed in its rightful context.

Preparing Winston to begin the task of making amends for the pain he had inflicted upon other students i.e. to express appropriate remorse. If we don't do this then we are not including Winston in the process of education. This one's a must.

Mediating between the humanities teacher and Winston. A common complaint heard from the most reasonable and experienced of teachers is the lack of mediation and appropriate reparation that follows a significant incident and which should precede the student's return to the classroom. Another must.

Informing Winston's parent of the day's events and of the school's responses. Absolutely no way that this can be omitted. Failure to do so would be unprofessional, discourteous and risk undermining the relationship between home and school.

Encouraging Winston to explain his version of what had happened and to record this, if necessary writing it for him using only his words. It is the school's responsibility to act as his advocate. Remember that his expressive language skills are in the first centile and although his literacy skills are better, they are still only in the tenth centile. Winston's future successful inclusion may well depend upon the ability to actively earn his trust.

Interviewing students who were closest to the incident and ensure a record of their observations is included in the final report. It's not just Winston who expects to be treated fairly and to be listened to; so do all his classmates.

Collating a report of the incident in its fullest possible context. Someone in authority – the year head, the head of lower school, the deputy head teacher, maybe even the head teacher, will have to act and be seen to act; these colleagues must have the information needed to make a professional judgement.

Advising the head of year as to whether any additional parents, other than Winston's, should be contacted and informed of the incident and the school's response. Good communication with parents is plain good manners. When the effort is made to let parents know the truth about what has happened, even when the news is painful, schools usually earn their trust and respect.

Informing the Case Responsible Worker at the Social Services Department. The Education and Social Services Departments have a statutory duty to work together and their good working practices will always be beneficial to the child. Poor communication quickly fosters mistrust and professional disrespect.

In reality, all of the above were attempted. Winston was able to say he was sorry, that he had done wrong and to talk about what would be a fair punishment for his behaviour. The social worker had a message left for her via the Duty Team. Winston's parent's mobile phone was switched off. Of the other students, there was time for only two pupils in the class to be interviewed and their parents contacted. Winston's teacher made the effort to find Winston and was able to speak with him at the end of the day. He talked through the incident and explained that Winston would be welcome in his lesson next time and confirmed that he wanted to help Winston deal with things differently and more successfully. Winston's views were written up and this and all the other papers were duly passed on to the deputy head teacher. It's a lot of work, with many opportunities for getting it wrong and it's the sort of pressure that comes with including our most vulnerable young people. It's at such a time when the beliefs and philosophies of colleagues are most keenly tested.

To attain the professional standards required, most teachers already have the skills. It's whether we have the values that support inclusion that determines the degree of success. Take this humanities teacher for instance. He came looking for Winston at the end of his last lesson. He came in quietly and spoke gently with Winston, beginning by reflecting upon the good lessons that he had previously had with him. He talked about how such an incident could be avoided in the future and how much he wanted Winston back in his classroom. He told Winston that the behaviour was wrong and made it clear that it was the behaviour and not Winston that was unacceptable. Good work, good practice, high professional standards and a pleasure to recall here.

Winston would arrive at school at 7.45 each morning (he wanted to avoid meeting other children on the way to school) and he would leave at 5 p.m. (to avoid them on the way home). There were daily incidents of physical aggression towards his peers and defiance towards staff. With the enhanced clarity of twenty-twenty hindsight it is obvious that Winston was behaving like the frightened little boy that he was. With the dominant influence of his past experiences, he became highly distressed when there was anything that upset him, such as children being noisy in class or a perceived slight. Winston had a way of creating this reality around him and stabbing people with a sharp pencil was one of a range of strategies he employed to create a reality that only went to prove how accurate his fears were. Colleagues in the school had the task of continuing to provide Winston with an education, to act meaningfully and purposefully and to work in partnership with Winston's parent and the Social Services Department.

School staff had a number of advantages.

- The SEN team in the local authority is a very effective group of officers who remember what it's like to be doing the work 'at the chalk face'. This team was quick to increase the level of support for Winston, with immediate effect. In practical terms this equated to an additional five hours of TA time, per week, to complement the school's provision and the LEA's own, existing contribution of ten hours' TA time.
- The head of lower school was fully aware of Winston's needs and very willing to do anything to help.
- Every single one of Winston's teachers was willing to help and to include him in their lessons and the Learning Support Department would provide an additional adult in each of Winston's lessons.
- The school had invested in resources that offered a range of provision, such as Student Guidance, where a small number of students could be accommodated for a short time, access curriculum materials and have the time to discuss any problems in a calming environment.
- The social worker was receptive to Winston's needs and willing and able to come to the school at short notice to spend time with him and to support the work of the

school. He was also trying to arrange an assessment of the risk that Winston represented to others and to find a foster placement for him.

- The teaching assistants were actively seeking to help Winston and to work with him in his lessons.
- The head teacher was sympathetic to the notion that a formal exclusion was unlikely to help Winston and that, with the extra free time that would accrue as a consequence, he would be a very vulnerable child.

It was very difficult to predict his behaviour, but there were likely to be a number of incidents in any one day. We tried a number of strategies in addition to the above, for instance:

- his use of an exit card from lessons, which he could show at any time and be allowed to leave a lesson to go somewhere he considered to be safe;
- a reward system (his choice was sweets) for defined, appropriate behaviour in class; his punishment would be the lack of a reward;
- a personalised timetable that concentrated upon his areas of success e.g. French lessons where he was consistently successful in his work and in his interactions with others in the class.

While each of these and other strategies had some minimal success, they were insufficiently effective to offer much hope that Winston would be able to make good progress in the school.

While all the disruption was going on he could be quietly charming at particular times. Most days Winston chose to eat his lunch with a member of staff, in the school canteen. He would go without food rather than go to the canteen without 'adult protection'. He understood good manners and explained, 'I know to say please and thank you and I always say thank you to those people' (he gestured towards the people serving) 'because they're always polite to me.'

He had no positive control over his life and never really had had, so he was told by those supporting him that he should always have a choice. For instance, if he had an English lesson, then he could go to the lesson, or to Student Guidance or to the Student Support Base. This way, whenever he had a lesson and said that he wouldn't go to it, then staff could simply explain that he had choices and that no one was telling him what to do. This made a significant difference because the number of confrontations was reduced and it also gave the breathing space needed to start building a meaningful relationship with him.

Nine months later he is still in school. He's had a couple of exclusions. He is now a looked-after child, being accommodated by the local authority, so the school staff are acting as his corporate parents. He spends a lot of his time in school word processing a project of his choosing. This has entailed his supervised use of the internet and he is becoming increasingly proficient in the use of Microsoft Word. He has to maintain a good relationship with the librarian so that he can get onto the internet and he needs to ask a TA to take him there. We still 'do lunch' when time permits. Winston always has an adult with him in school and as he requests this, it does not become an imposition.

Future plans include Winston's referral to a specialist NSPCC resource for a full assessment of the risk he represents to others and staff from the school will need to travel to London to take part in this process. Foster placements, especially the specialist ones, are incredibly hard to find and very expensive to purchase. A lot of good interagency practice and a lot of resources will have to be in place for the months and years ahead to give hope for Winston.

12 Practical development for mainstream schools

Finding out what strategies work in teaching and learning is like embarking upon a journey that lasts as long as a career does; developing the practice of teaching and learning is an ongoing process. To this end, a new strategy is unveiled every few years, sometimes more frequently. If they're any good, then they get to stick around and they become part of accepted practice.

Assessment for learning

Often known as A4L, this teaching strategy was brought to prominence by Black and William in their publication 'Inside the Black Box' (1998) and its follow-up, *Children's Behaviour: Beyond the Black Box* (ARG 2000) Crucially, it helps to clarify the positive difference between assessment of learning and assessment for learning.

Assessment of learning is an assessment of the level of a pupil's performance i.e. summative assessment. The results of this type of assessment are, for instance, used in school reports.

Assessment for learning (A4L) is an assessment that is integral to the process of teaching and learning and is used as a tool to actively shape the teaching and learning process; it is used as an ongoing feature within the classroom. The theory is that pupils will make optimum progress if they understand the aims of the learning, their own position in relation to the aims and how they can best work towards achieving the aims i.e. formative assessment.

There are five basic principles associated with A4L:

- feedback to pupils, which offers the pupils advice on how to improve their work. It avoids the comparing of students' attainment with that of their peers;
- self-assessment by pupils, which will necessitate their being taught to understand why they are learning and what they have to do to make progress;
- opportunities for pupils to talk about what they understand;

their interaction with others forms a key component of the learning process;

- dialogue between all parties is essential and as such should be reflective, should explore their understanding and should involve everyone in the classroom;
- tests and homework should contain feedback that advises students on how to improve their work and there should be the opportunity to act on the advice and thereby improve their work.

The question is, can assessment really raise standards or is it all about league tables and memorising facts that will soon be forgotten? 'Assessment is one of the most powerful educational tools for promoting effective learning, but it must be used in the right way. The focus needs to be put on helping teachers use assessment as part of teaching and learning, in ways that will raise pupils' achievement' (Assessment Reform Group 2000).

In practice, A4L is a way for a teacher and pupils to find out how much the pupils already know, because there is no point in teaching what they already know or already understand. A lot of A4L is done in pairs or small groups, so that pupils feel less intimidated in front of a peers or their teacher and they can learn from each other. For example, something that their friend says can trigger the thought, 'I do know something about this', as opposed to being fearful of responding to a teacher's question in front of a whole class. Examples of materials and how to use them would be, in order:

1   Have different facts on different cards.
2   In pairs or small groups, students put them in three piles, 'Don't know', 'Definitely do know' and 'Not sure'. Alternatively, the pupils can 'traffic light' them, i.e. hold up a red card for 'Definitely don't know', amber card for 'Not sure' and a green card for 'Definitely do know'.
3   Teacher picks up on the ones in the 'Not sure' piles and opens them up for explanation.
4   The rest of the class try and explain these because there will be other groups who can and the class teaches itself.
5   When that is completed the teacher can focus the teaching on the, 'Don't know' pile.

Another example is Dominoes. The skeleton of a story can be created on domino-type card, for instance:

rising from the dead	Christians believe that Jesus was

the son of God	They celebrate Jesus' birthday

on 25 December	The most famous Christian book

is called the Bible	Easter celebrates Jesus

They continue as a normal set of dominoes. Individuals, pairs and small groups can use them. These need to be matched with the intended learning outcomes and can be very useful for kinaesthetic learners.

At the beginning of a topic, the teacher can give all the pairs of students a post-it and they write down something they don't know about the topic that they would like answered; the teacher sticks the post-its on the door. Hopefully, by the end of the lesson quite a few of the post-its can come off and the whole class can answer the questions because they relate to something that has been learnt in that lesson i.e. evidence of their learning.

At the end of a lesson, one favourite activity goes something like this:

'OK everybody, we've got about two minutes left. I want you to write down four things you have learnt today.' Then share them and it will be a lot more than four things that have been learnt. This counters students' feelings that they have learnt nothing in a lesson and helps them see their learning differently.

'Two stars and a wish' is what a lot of teachers use for marking. A teacher writes down two things he or she has done well on a piece of work and one 'wish' to indicate what would be good to change next time, i.e. what could improve the work. Using this strategy, students can mark their own work or they can also mark each other's work; whoever does the marking, students seem to like this approach as it removes the negativity.

In summary, A4L helps to avoid wasting time in a lesson and it helps to ensure that students make progress in a lesson and that a teacher can help students measure their progress against themselves, their partner(s) and against the class. It helps the students to appreciate how much they do know. It is a good approach for all students and works for students with SEN because it concentrates on what they do know, as opposed to what they don't know.

Ofsted are very concerned about whether progress is being made in a lesson, so if you begin with an A4L starter, then it gets rid of that problem at the beginning because you can assess where the pupils are in their learning and go on from there. Also, for a newly qualified teacher (or an experienced teacher), it can be a cracking starter for a lesson being given on interview when you don't know specifically the children you are teaching other than their general ability range.

Preferred learning styles

Education in general and schools in particular have become increasingly interested in the concept of accelerated learning. Clearly, there is an onus upon education professionals to encourage students to reach their highest potential. There used to be a commonly held notion that the ability of a young person was limited by a fixed ceiling. We have been encouraged to disabuse ourselves of this notion and, instead, to explore methods by which we can improve the performance and therefore the educational outcomes of our young people. Consequently, schools have been using staff training resources to develop colleagues' understanding of accelerated learning and to apply theory to practice. This has led to a number of developments. We have learnt that dehydration affects learning and that students need access to water. Hence, there has been a plethora of water dispensing machines in schools and most schools now allow students to have access to water during statutory examinations.

There has been considerable research into finding out how people learn best. It can be frustrating for some people, for example, to be expected to learn from an instruction manual, but if someone sits down and shows them how to do it, then it can be much easier for them to learn. There are many learning styles and it can be very helpful to know what they are and how to apply this knowledge to the process of improving teaching and learning. A brief introduction to seven of the different intelligences might help.

Intelligence	Strengths	Qualities	Encourage with
Interpersonal	Able to see someone else's point of view. Willing to adjust one's own behaviour to take account of another person. Able to sense changes in mood.	Builds good relationships with others. Listens to and understands other people's views. Influences others.	Pair work. Group work. Use of empathy. Problem solving in teams. Interviewing others. Listening. Sharing and cooperating.
Intrapersonal	Good self-knowledge. Well motivated. A clear understanding of their own selves with ability to express and use their own feelings and emotions.	Self-motivated. Likely to hold a strong set of beliefs and a willingness to live by them. Aware of own feelings and emotions.	This person should be encouraged to set their own targets and to monitor them themselves. Enjoys discussing issues of a moral nature. Working alone.
Kinaesthetic	Enjoys physical movement. Likes working with tools. Physical activity encourages learning.	Enjoys learning using physical movement e.g. by touching. Building and making things. Good sense of balance and timing.	Break up lessons with reviews. Touching and moving. Field trips. Role-play. Making things. Allow moving about appropriately.
Linguistic	Well-developed understanding of the use of words.	Will learn through discussion and listening as well as reading and writing. Likely to be more auditory than visual.	Use word games and any exercises involving language e.g. flash cards. Hearing and seeing words.
Mathematical	These are people who can solve problems. They enjoy order and logic.	These people will understand the concept of cause and effect. They will be able to see patterns in relationships. They will be able to think mathematically.	Encourage working with numbers. Problem solving activities. Brainstorming is a good opening activity, leading to an ordering of data/ideas. Sequences, hypotheses, analogies etc.
Musical	These people often have musical patterns with them at all times.	These people will be affected by sounds and changes in rhythm. Hear and enjoy playing with sound patterns. Have a sense of rhythm.	Use music to positively affect the atmosphere in your room. Use opportunities to create raps and any types of song. Link music to revision.

Visual/spatial	These people will be able to remember things they have seen and to be able to draw upon these memories.	Will understand visual materials e.g. maps and graphs. Will learn through looking and observing.	Use visual tools like memory maps to support learning. Working with pictures. As a prelude to activities e.g. discussions, provide an opportunity to visualise solutions. Using their mind's eye.

Multiple Intelligence Questionnaire

5 = This is exactly like me
4 = This is quite like me
3 = This is a bit like me
2 = I am not very much like this
1 = I am hardly ever like this
0 = This is not like me at all

	5	*4*	*3*	*2*	*1*	*0*
1 When I am doing a project I usually do things one step at a time.						
2 I am good with words and can explain what I mean.						
3 I can remember TV programmes and see the scenes in my mind.						
4 I know why I behave the way I do. I understand what makes me do things.						
5 I like working in groups and cooperate well when working with others.						
6 I like my music lessons. It is fun to be able to make my own music.						
7 I see things other people miss. I am good at noticing things.						
8 I understand how maths can help with science and how English can help with other subjects.						
9 When my mates are arguing I am able to help them sort things out.						
10 My music can make me feel all sorts of things, from sad to happy.						
11 I wish I could move around more in class. I do not like sitting in the same place for a long time.						
12 If I don't see the point in a lesson I can often lose interest and do things like look out of the window.						
13 If my friends don't understand something in class, I can often help them understand.						

Table (contd)

	5	4	3	2	1	0
14 In technology, I am good at working with tools.						
15 It is easier for me to learn when I am given diagrams and things to look at.						
16 When I listen to music I can tell which instruments are being used.						
17 Maths is one of my favourite lessons. I enjoy working with numbers.						
18 When I am running or playing I have a good sense of balance.						
19 I really look forward to going to parties.						
20 When I first came to the school, I found my way around quite quickly.						
21 It's great when a teacher gives us word searches or crossword puzzles.						
22 When I play my music I can remember most of the words.						
23 When I revise I use the notes I have taken in class.						
24 When it's quiet and I am alone I can think much better.						
25 When my mates are in a good mood it makes me feel good; if they are unhappy, it brings me down.						
26 When the teacher is talking and explaining things I can learn easily.						
27 When the teacher lets me work on my own e.g. in the library, I learn really well.						
28 Working on my own is how I learn best. I am happy working alone.						

Intelligence	Statement number	Scores	Total score
Interpersonal	5; 9; 19; 25.		
Intrapersonal	4; 12; 24; 28.		
Kinaesthetic	11; 14; 18; 27.		
Linguistic	2; 13; 23; 26.		
Mathematical and logical	1; 8; 17; 21.		
Musical	6; 10; 16; 22.		
Visual and spatial	3; 7; 15; 20.		

The higher scores indicate a student's preferred learning style.

Home visiting to engage parents

There are parents whose active interest in their child's education significantly reduces on their child's entry to secondary education, sometimes before. Teachers are keen to engage with these parents and guardians in order to deal with problems at the earliest stage and to gain the active collaboration of the responsible adults at home. Indeed, teachers are very good at predicting which parents and guardians will not arrive for parents' evenings. As an experiment, during one week leading up to a parents' evening, home visits were made from our school to all the families that had been identified as likely non-attenders. The responses were enlightening. After all, why would anyone do a home visit, in the evening, from a secondary school? On each occasion, the adult who answered the door, on realising this was a visit from the school, moved backwards, if only a little way. When it was explained that the purpose of the call was to make sure that everyone knew about the parents' evening and to offer transport if it would help, they moved out and engaged in a conversation, asking for more information about the evening. That year, the school had 100 per cent contacts from parents; it was a remarkable result.

Sometimes it pays dividends to go out and bring parents into the school, as well as getting them more involved in school life.

Special educational needs

Mary Warnock, in the late 1970s, chaired the committee that established the framework for special educational needs, as we understand them today. Interestingly, the committee never considered the issue of money; this was, after all, pre-1979.

We talk of entitlement today as if it is a new idea, yet the Warnock Report recommended providing all children, whatever their needs, with a meaningful education. Before this time there were children languishing in special hospitals and residential provision who had received minimal if any formal, regulated education. This cannot happen now and we owe a debt of gratitude to the Warnock Committee for this change.

In January 2002 a new, revised Special Educational Needs Code of Practice established three levels of action that schools should use to describe their levels of support to students with SEN.

School action

School action describes the level of action that uses resources available in the school, for instance, a student who has a numeracy score at the tenth percentile could have daily access to an individually tailored software programme to support progress in numeracy. This level of special educational need is a high-incidence need, i.e. it is a relatively common SEN. At this level teachers adapt their teaching with differentiated materials such as adapting work sheets to ensure they have a reading age that matches the reading levels of the students.

School action plus

This describes a level of action that utilises resources from additional sources that are applied in addition to those at school action. For instance, a student with emotional, behavioural and social difficulties could be accessing a social skills group in school (from the school's resources) and be accessing additional support from the Child and Adolescent Mental Health Services.

Statements

For students with low incidence needs, i.e. the most severe and complex cases, a Statement of Special Educational Needs may be appropriate. The statement is written following several months of expert assessment. The LEA takes advice from a number of professionals such as educational psychologists, School Medical Officer and so on, and the statement includes the following:

- a description of the student's special educational needs;
- the provision prescribed to meet the special educational needs;
- the objectives that the provision is designed to meet;
- the arrangements for the monitoring of the statement.

The statements are very expensive pieces of paper, in that the cost of the students' assessments, the writing of the reports and the collating of all these reports, including those from the parents, is in the region of £2000–£2500. Each statement is reviewed at least annually and progress is measured against the objectives that are laid down in the statement.

General descriptions of SEN

Special educational needs cover a very wide variety of categories. What follows is a brief introduction to some of the more common categories of need that may be more likely to be evidenced in mainstream classes and the simple advice that may help to develop the strategies to include and thereby engage such students.

Specific learning difficulties (SpLD)

This is a generic category that includes dyslexia and dyscalculia. Those students who have been assessed with specific learning difficulties will have significant difficulties with one or more of the following:

- reading accuracy;
- reading comprehension;
- spelling;
- writing;
- numeracy.

The progress attained in one or more specific area will not be typical of the student's general level of performance. Many students with specific learning difficulties will score above the lowest quartile for their non-verbal reasoning; however, their progress is undermined by their specific learning difficulties.

Speech and language difficulties

These difficulties include the following:

- language delay: when a student's language develops more slowly than in most children;
- language disorder: this occurs when language does not develop normally;
- communication difficulties: these affect a student's social use of language.

One of the simple ways you can help these students is by being aware of how you speak to a class group. Many people move around the room when they are speaking. Try to avoid this remain in a place where you can be seen.

Autistic spectrum disorders (ASD)

These disorders describe a variety of social interaction and communication difficulties. There are more students in mainstream school with features of autism than there are specifically diagnosed with autism. There tends to be a reluctance to place a specific diagnosis of autism i.e. attach a label; however, the fact that these disorders are on a spectrum implies that we all fit on it somewhere (Rutter 2005). For instance, a colleague of mine used to manage a Behaviour Support Service. Whenever he was under stress it was easy to tell: his desk would be immaculate, every piece of paper perfectly filed, not a speck of dust anywhere near him and his clothes cleaned and pressed, with knife-edge creases in his trousers.

Some of the more commonly observed features of autism include:

- an inability to empathise, with little or no awareness of the needs of others;
- poor understanding of the rules of language;
- obsessive and/or repetitive behaviours.

Asperger syndrome (or Asperger's Disorder)

Asperger syndrome is sometimes described as high-functioning autism. Students with Asperger's will most likely demonstrate difficulties with non-verbal communication and pragmatic language. There are characteristics that are similar to those in autism. For instance:

- a lack of imagination;
- significant difficulty in relating comfortably with peers and adults;
- the need for a familiar routine;
- specific interests;
- poor social and communication skills.

There are helpful strategies that can be usefully employed to benefit these students. First, though, it is helpful to have an understanding of the student's needs.

We now know that autism and Asperger's have a complex aetiology and we are long past the time of assuming it is the 'parents' fault'. Modern research evidence points to some form of neurological deficit or delay, with psycho social concomitants quickly following (Gilchrist *et al.* 2005; Rutter 2005) . In a sense it is like 'emotional deafness' but, like physical deafness, is neither the 'fault' of the parents nor of the child.

Imagination

Abstract thinking can prove difficult. Concentrate on more factually based learning. Questions like 'How would you feel if ...?' Or exercises that begin with 'Imagine you are on a desert island' can be very unsettling. For instance, when Mick's class group was told to imagine themselves on a desert island, he spent the rest of the lesson pursuing the teacher with questions like 'Is the island in the Pacific Ocean?' and 'Does anyone live on the island?'

In imaginative play, it will be easier to join in with others if the activity is seen by the student to be play on his or her own terms, in other words, he or she has the idea, and/or leads the activity.

Communication difficulties

Students may have a sophisticated vocabulary. However, it may be difficult to take into account the reaction of the person to whom they are speaking. The social behaviours that communicate a lack of interest, or even anger, can be difficult for someone with Asperger syndrome to identify. Students may receive language and interpret it literally, for instance:

> When Ray came to the school in Y7 he came with a reputation from his primary school as a pupil with behavioural difficulties and the willingness to act aggressively towards his peers. He was being looked after by pastoral care staff following a couple of incidents when a meeting was held with the educational psychologist (EP), with the agreement of Ray's parents. The EP and Special Educational Needs Co-ordinator (SENCO) naturally discussed Ray, and he introduced himself to Ray and asked him two questions:
>
> *EP*:   Which school were you at before?
> *Ray*: St Andrew's Junior School.
> *EP*:   Was it very different there?
> *Ray*: Yes, it was all on one level.
>
> Eventually, following a referral to the Consultant Paediatrician and further assessments, Ray received a diagnosis of Asperger's.

When you speak to/with a student with Asperger's, or even a group with one or more such students, it may help to:

- be clear;

- be brief;
- keep sentences short.

In class, it may well help to provide:

- written instructions;
- flash cards for key words;
- appropriately differentiated work sheets.

A picture is worth a hundred words.

Relationships with peers and adults

This is an area where students with Asperger's may be different to those with autism. These students may well wish to be socially accepted and enjoy the experience of being with others. The difficulties in such situations come from their inability to interpret the facial expressions of those around them or other social rules of communication such as body language. Students may find social situations confusing and unsettling. Unable to read body language or to interpret facial expressions, students may find themselves unable to act or reply without appearing gauche or awkward.

The structure of a formal lesson is relatively comfortable. The social rules are more straightforward. Free-association times are significantly more problematic. It can be *very* helpful to negotiate appropriate, safe space(s) for a student to spend his or her break times and to eat lunch. For instance:

Peter
This is a special plea to acknowledge the difficulty experienced by students during school break times. When Peter came to us at the beginning of Y8, he was moving with his family from another city. He had a diagnosis of Asperger's and he first came to the school with his parents for a planning meeting to arrange his admission. Peter's parents were as nervous as he was and clearly Peter was loved and cared for. He was a well-behaved boy who was never going to break a school rule. Listening to his parents, it was obvious that Peter would need somewhere to go during break times. Like many students with Asperger's, he felt comfortable in well-ordered classrooms where he could feel secure within a familiar structured routine. When the bell went, this could signify disorder and chaos and be a frightening experience.

The solution was, and remains, simple. A supervised room was kept open at break times and lunchtimes. The difference that this made for him is evidenced by the fact that he came to this room every morning break and lunchtime for the four years he was on roll and his attendance at school never fell below 98 per cent in one academic year.

Students with Asperger's are sometimes happier to interact with younger children and also with older, kind children. There are fewer girls than boys diagnosed with Asperger's and this has been explained as the result of the more supportive nature of many groups of girls acting in a nurturing capacity. Supporting each other, they are able to create an environment that truly 'includes' their peer whose Asperger's is not as accentuated as it could be within a more competitive group.

The need for a familiar routine

Students may find routines very comforting. They may be unsettled by unexpected change such as supply cover, or a change in what is planned for a lesson. If you are aware that a change is going to occur, such as doing an experiment rather than the test you announced previously, it is important to give the student as much notice as possible. If we have to close the room to students where Peter spends his break times, then the teaching assistants take it upon themselves to ensure that Peter is allowed in and thereby catered for.

Specific interests

These are sometimes labelled as obsessions. The interests can take any form, such as collecting specific items or some kind of a hobby. There is often a common feature of accumulating facts and figures e.g. collecting bus timetables. It is very helpful to accept this interest and to incorporate it positively within the student's programme. In time, such interests can form the basis of a means of employment e.g. in working with computers.

In the long term, students with Asperger syndrome can experience success and this will be enhanced by a combination of the following factors:

- a mentor for guidance and inspiration;
- a life partner to provide support, affection and commitment;
- achievement at work or in a special interest;
- coming to terms with one's own strengths and weaknesses.

Semantic Pragmatic Disorder

Semantic Pragmatic Disorder (SPD) is a communication disorder. If you have a student with SPD in your classroom, please be aware that he or she will find it difficult to take in all the information and to process it. Their responses may also be inappropriate: for instance:

> On one occasion a PE teacher, who was normally accustomed to considerable respect from the students, was speaking to a group of about forty boys, when one student with SPD in the group shouted out loud the fact that the teacher 'smelt horrible'. This caused nervous giggles and embarrassment amongst the group and, fortunately, the teacher had the confidence and experience to tactically ignore the incident. He dealt with it later, away from the group, having sought advice from the SENCO. It was clear to the teacher that the boy was not intending to be rude and this assessment guided his approach to the boy when dealing with his behaviour, which simply noted the teacher's perspiration.

To help students develop the skills to use socially acceptable responses, teachers with appropriate training can deliver a course called 'The Social Use of Language Programme'. The course progresses through different levels and provides students with the skills to deal successfully with social situations that others would deal with automatically.

Students with SPD have difficulty when they are required to receive and to process information, particularly when this information is delivered verbally. The disorder relates to autism in that it involves difficulties in the same three areas: socialising, language and imagination.

Most children absorb information easily, processing and analysing it, discarding what is unimportant or uninteresting and storing the rest. They are able to build up a memory bank of words and their meanings, including those that relate to concepts such as time and personal feelings, which may not have a visual reference. They use this data, together with their past experience of the world, to predict how other people will react to certain things, to understand their intentions and forecast what might happen next.

A child with Semantic Pragmatic Disorder has an imperfect 'information processing' system and will have problems in knowing what to say, sometimes appearing rude or outspoken and not realising that the listener has 'had enough'. He may talk at great length about something that interests him, but not realise that the listener has 'switched off'.

A child with Semantic Pragmatic Disorder may demonstrate a combination of these characteristics:

- speaking fluently, sometimes in a mature manner, frequently on the student's own terms;
- difficulty in giving specific information;
- the appearance of arrogance or rudeness; 'appearance' because the intention is often not to cause this effect but is caused by the student's lack of understanding of social conventions;
- the tendency to be easily distracted;
- difficulties with motor skills;
- a particular sensitivity to certain noises etc.
- difficulties when confronted with abstract concepts. It helps to limit the numbers of instructions that begin with such verbal commands as 'imagine', or 'guess'.

In school, these children need:

- straightforward, specific and unambiguous instructions such as 'Put the pencils in the blue box', not 'Tidy up';
- practical, hands-on tasks;
- a quiet, orderly working environment;
- predictability in the classroom routine – give clear signals for any changes;
- time to reply when asked a question;
- specific activities to help with socialising;
- clear rules on how to behave;
- regular reminders supported by visual/written information;
- an adult to interpret what the child 'means' rather than what he or she actually says, when this doesn't make sense;
- explanations about sarcasm, metaphors, and jokes – don't take for granted that they understand;
- a teacher to double-check their understanding;
- to be taught the meanings of idiomatic expressions and appropriate language for different situations;
- constant encouragement and praise.

The best teachers make mistakes, as when Paul was new to the school and had a teaching assistant with him in a technology lesson. The teacher was showing Paul the equipment, electric drills, power saws etc. and Paul was clearly in awe of some of this. This was compounded when he was told, 'There's almost nothing to worry about, and we've only lost a couple of arms during my lessons'. Paul's face went as white as a sheet. He had taken it literally and had to be reassured. When he knew he was safe he went into a celebratory salute and a cry of 'yeeeaaah' as he danced around the room – which speaks for itself.

Emotional difficulties

The school has around a thousand students on roll at any one time. This is like a thousand years of life every year. No wonder, then, that every year, members of our school's community experience a wide range of challenging experiences such as death; family breakdown; emotional, physical and sexual abuse; neglect; homelessness; poverty; illness, or rejection. Indeed, it needs to be remembered that the most severe form of 'abuse' is not physical or even sexual, but emotional, where relationships are involved and are exploited or manipulated (Pritchard 2004).

Thinking about this list reminds me that the emotional impact upon the students of any one of these experiences may be significant. It is not reasonable to expect feelings, and the effects of these feelings, to be left outside the school gates; they need to be acknowledged and given due respect.

A student's tutor or favourite teacher will sometimes be the first person in school to be told of an event by a student, or to notice something is wrong, or even to be told by the friend of the student that there is something wrong. It can escalate the teacher into the role of significant carer. Remember that a tutor could see a tutee twice a day, every day, for thirty-six weeks of the year. There are going to be times when the tutor will have concern for a student and will want to help. Using counselling skills can be effective. This is distinct from actual counselling, which is undertaken by colleagues who have undertaken a programme of training that can include education to graduate level and beyond and hundreds of hours of supervised and documented counselling sessions before attaining accredited counsellor status.

Counselling skills are directly applicable to working in schools, for tutors and teachers, and include:

- open questions;
- paraphrasing;
- summarising;
- reflecting.

It is worth remembering that, for many children, their foremost experience of adults is of being told what to do. The culture that exists in many schools, whereby students have to do what they are told with minimal choice, is much the same as it has been for a long time. Yet this is wholly at variance with the culture these same young people experience outside school, which includes a vast array of choices, from the range of television channels to the choice of fashionable clothing and on to the best mobile phone contract.

Crucially, in the context of a counselling overview, young people need to be in an environment where they have a right to own their feelings and for their feelings to be acknowledged. Incorporating counselling skills into dialogue with young people can enhance this.

The key thing about using counselling skills is that, when in conversation, it is important to avoid a predetermined agenda about where the conversation is going. Hear what the other person has to say and be able to do this without going through the process of prejudging. By doing this, it will be more likely that the child will have the experience of being heard.

It can be very easy to make assumptions about what a student's experience of an event will be, e.g. divorce. A tutor can hear that a tutee's parents are divorcing and assume that the pupil will be upset because of the family split. The tutor is therefore sympathetic: 'It must be awful'. Whereas, if he used counselling skills, the adult would look to be empathetic, which means getting inside the student's experience. This could be done with an open question: 'What's it like for you at the moment?', followed by reflecting back the summary of what the student has said, or paraphrasing it, to give confirmation to the child that he or she has been properly heard, because on rare occasions the divorce can be a relief for the child.

Paraphrasing is useful because it gives listeners the opportunity to check out whether they have understood what they have been told. Summary passes on the message that 'This is what I've got so far', and this leads naturally on to 'What next?' Reflection sounds easy, but is hard, because it requires giving back in the child's own words, the content of what he or she has said. It can also be a way of sensitively focusing on the feelings underlying what they said. Either way, this process should not be added to by anything of yourself.

The tone of voice and body language matters, i.e. a critical tone of voice negates the benefit of using any of the counselling skills.

When a student says 'I'll never be able to understand this' and receives the response 'Of course you can' this will be perfectly ok, sometimes. If the student in question suffers with low self-esteem, it might be better to say something like 'You really think you can't do this,' which gives the student the opportunity to express how he or she feels about the activity and to move on from this point.

Just think about the last time you were fed up and how it felt to be given one of the following responses:

- 'I know how you feel';
- 'poor you';
- 'what you need to do about it is . . .'.

For students with low self-esteem, their experience is often that when they express what they feel, they have people trying to fix it, or telling them that they are 'wrong' or, 'Don't be daft; you can do this easily'. These responses can come with good intent, but students will walk away from this interaction with the affirmation that they are wrong.

For a tutor, the greatest difficulty in using counselling skills is to be able to find the time to spend with tutee, especially time without constant interruptions and tutor tasks such as literacy programmes. It's at this time that the tutor needs to make an informed judgement to refer on, to a pastoral leader for example.

Attention Deficit Hyperactivity Disorder (ADHD)

The characteristics of a student with ADHD are often expressed in terms of inappropriate behaviours with the implication that the student is 'naughty' or 'badly behaved'. This attitude is unhelpful, but if we ignore it or talk over it then we will undermine the opportunities for the child with ADHD to succeed and to make progress.

There is often a Health Service dimension to students with ADHD and this is because of the medication that is sometimes prescribed in these cases. The most common forms are Ritalin or Dexedrine. The more common of the two is Ritalin. The dosage is tailored to the student's need and to his or her physiology. The active ingredient is amphetamine, which can have implications for side effects, for instance:

- blood pressure: the consultant paediatrician must closely and regularly monitor this;
- weight: this must be monitored because the effect of the amphetamine can have a negative effect upon the student's appetite.

Also, there must be regular monitoring of the student's behaviour to review the efficacy or otherwise of the medication. There is a tendency to employ the use of slow-release medication. This can overcome specific difficulties, for instance:

Sally was diagnosed with ADHD when she was at her primary school. She is perfectly aware of the diagnosis of ADHD and understands the effect it can have upon her behaviour. Her medication is taken twice per day, once before she comes to school and again at midday. Anyone who teaches Sally for her third lesson knows that her educational needs may have to be carefully considered between 11:30 and 12:00; her behaviour will most likely indicate a high level of need. Slow-release medication does have the beneficial effect of avoiding these pressure times.

There are many strategies that may be helpful to consider when you are including a student with ADHD in your classroom. The following may act as a simple, common-sense checklist, which you can refer to at any time.

- Maintain classroom rules that are clear and simple.
- Minimise the opportunities for external distractions e.g. use focal points away from the window view.
- Work sheets should be in large type e.g. size 16 font.
- When pictures are used in work sheets, ensure there is an obvious link with the text.
- Vary the activities in the lesson by providing activities that involve movement, interspersed with 'at-desk' type activities. Movement activities can occur at the beginning of the class with the recall of the previous lesson's learning and the student can have responsibility for recording on the white board.
- Whenever possible, ask the student to repeat instructions to you.
- Monitor carefully the effect of group work activities.
- Be aware that the student may have difficulty with self-organisation and you may derive benefit from maintaining spare kit for the student.
- Be aware that change is particularly upsetting. If you know that there will be a change of routine e.g. doing a practical lesson, not the planned test, then give as much warning as possible to the student.
- Maintain eye contact when you give the student verbal instructions.
- Make every effort to ring the student with 'better-behaved' peers at least of equal status in the pecking order.

As with any student, the better the quality of your relationship with him or her, the better your ability will be to help the student to manage in your classroom. Also, as with any young person, the first rule is to praise good behaviour and to achieve this with your attention.

Dyslexia and dyscalculia

Dyslexia and dyscalculia are sometimes included under the heading of specific learning difficulties (SpLD), because children experience specific difficulties in learning to read and/or in understanding numbers. These are lasting difficulties but do not affect all learning skills. In many cases, children who have dyslexia can achieve at or above the average level in other areas.

The term dyslexia means having difficulties in learning to read. These difficulties usually affect reading, writing and spelling. When the ability to recognise and manage numbers is affected it is sometimes called dyscalculia.

Definitions of and support arrangements for dyslexia may vary from one local authority to another. The differences can be based on testing arrangements, different policies, financial pressures, different beliefs and philosophies and on different SEN arrangements. As a consequence, the definition of dyslexia can change over time as these factors come into play. There are probably at least 10 per cent of the student population whose learning profile includes elements of specific learning difficulties.

In parenthesis, in the early 1960s we used to have a condition described as 'minimal cerebral dysfunction', which described in effect hyperactive and/or clumsy or attention-deficit children. We knew it was organic in origin although the psychological impact on child, family and school could be profound. It was, however, less than 0.1 per cent of the caseload. In today's child psychiatric service caseload, the figure is more than 10 per cent and in the USA it is estimated that there are 2 million children under treatment (Daley 2004). The cause of this mini-'epidemic' seems to centre around some biological underpinning, sometimes with or without psychological causes, but always with psychological ramifications, as well as the possible effects of diet (Richardson and Puri 2000; Rutter *et al.* 2004). In view of other changing patterns of neurological morbidity (Pritchard and Sunak 2005), it is feared that this may be an increasing problem for children, parents and teachers for many years unless the underlying causes are tackled.

Developing reading skills

The development of the ability to read is influenced by a number of factors and the skills involved in learning to read are thought to involve the following:

- the ability to remember what is seen or heard in order;
- the ability to identify sounds in words e.g. rhyme, similar sounds and syllables;
- recognising letters/number shapes and being able to write them;
- speed of reading and understanding;
- concentration;
- coordination;
- the ability to put things in order, e.g. letters, groups of letters, days, months, stories or information.

These weaknesses can be shown through common mistakes in reading and accuracy, for instance some letters and numbers are swapped or back-to-front. The connection between letter shape and sound is difficult to learn and remember. When these pupils are learning to read some ways of working out an unknown word are harder for them than others. More able readers will recognise a word through its shape, or by looking at parts of the word, letter groups, syllables or the meaning of the sentence. Dyslexic children often have difficulty with one or more of these methods. When they start to write, the letters are often drawn wrongly and writing may not flow. In addition, people with dyslexia can also find problems with directions, map reading, recognising left and right and reading music.

What does it mean for the child? Dyslexia affects some children very little. Others find that they face real difficulties in learning and their confidence and self-esteem take a battering. Pat, for instance, is a classic example. He is very bright and he can answer questions orally, demonstrating a depth of understanding, but he cannot read beyond c–v–c words (consonant–vowel–consonant words) and his writing is totally unintelligible. Each day in school is a major effort for him. One of us has a special sympathy as being left-handed and slightly uncoordinated and a very poor speller as a child was all due to being slightly dyslexic, and not just being deliberately difficult and stupid.

Visual dyslexia

Visual dyslexics include students who have vision problems, can wear glasses and are sometimes referred to an optometrist. You may see the use of a coloured overlay being used to help these students and the use of different coloured paper can help. Students will have difficulty following words along a line and, when they reach the end of the line, will have real problems working out where the next line starts. These students will tend to read one line as an entity in itself, then go to another line and read that as a separate entity i.e. the normal punctuation aids are irrelevant and of no purpose.

Perceptual difficulties

Some students will score very low on their non-verbal reasoning, yet you will know that their underlying ability is higher than their score indicates. This may be due to perceptual difficulties. The reason is that many non-verbal reasoning tests concentrate on pattern-based activities, like the old IQ tests. Some students may see things differently, e.g. in reverse, so that the usual tests cannot reflect their underlying ability. This is overcome by using a wider battery of tests, such as those available to educational psychologists.

Organising difficulties

Students may have difficulty with time sequences e.g. before, after and next. This difficulty with sequencing will affect comprehension of the timetable and the months of the year. Additionally, instructions that are of the type 'before lunch we will do this, then during lunch we will do something else and afterwards we are going on to there' are very hard to follow. The two-week timetable is unhelpful, as is the habit of having two teachers to teach one subject, sometimes in different rooms. These difficulties are more readily observed following the transfer to secondary education where the teaching environment is more complex – there is more moving about and more teachers. Knowing which day to bring the correct kit can be very difficult. Some students revert to carrying everything with them; some revert to carrying nothing at all.

How bad can it be for the students?

Sometimes it is pure hell – ritual humiliation, hour after hour. Some develop work-avoidance strategies e.g. not going to school, talking in class, forgetting homework diaries so they can't write in them, forgetting their kit.

What do schools do to exacerbate their difficulty? Ask them to:

- copy from the board
- copy from a book;
- write an essay;
- record their homework, especially at the end of the lesson;
- expect their written work to be legible;

- do tests without support;
- read undifferentiated work sheets.

Strategies that help include:

- flash cards;
- games, e.g. pairs;
- sequencing activities. For example, when you've done the science experiment, give the groups a set of flash cards (about eight to ten) depicting the experiment. The first might be 'get equipment ready' and there would be visual clues when possible. The students then put them in the right order to tell the story. Some could copy them out for themselves. Others could have a pre-prepared sheet with a few words missing and have the task of completing the sheet;
- using audio equipment to put text etc. on tape;
- reasonable homework expectations. Write it in their diaries for them or have it on a pre-prepared slip to stick in;
- homework clubs to help complete work in school so that they have a stress-free time at home;
- accept homework on tape or word-processed by a parent.

If these strategies are in common use, then the student with SpLD will feel less 'different'; it will reduce the sense of stigma.

Flexibility will always play a role because pupils and their circumstances are unique. The following example illustrates this.

Jack

Jack came to the school from another English-speaking country, joining the school roll at the end of Year 9. His parents had requested that he should be the subject of a statement of SEN. This was turned down by the LEA because his SpLD were a high-incidence need i.e. a need that was relatively common and was a need that should be met from within the school's delegated budget for SEN.

His parents were very supportive and were committed to his education, probably more so than Jack was. He never did any work at home; it was, he explained, more than he could cope with. He wanted to go home and relax.

With the specialist SpLD teacher, he spent the first year (Year 10) concentrating upon his literacy skills, using a combination of ICT and direct teaching. During this one year his reading accuracy rose from eight years seven months to ten years three months. During his second year, the teacher looked at his predicted GCSE grades and compared this with what he needed to progress onto his preferred college course. He had been predicted a grade 'E' for maths and he needed a 'C' so they worked together on his maths.

Then there was science. The day before he was due to hand in his course work, his teacher pressed him yet again for evidence of his 'it's at home, I'll bring it in tomorrow' work. He had to reveal the truth; there was no work to hand in because he hadn't done any. During the ensuing twenty-four hours, with many hours of one-to-one support, he had it completed. He attained a double C for science and a C for maths.

It takes time, effort and flexibility as well as willingness to get to know the student and to accept the student's frustrations. Yet again, teachers need good training and good resources and these resources include the time to prepare and to differentiate.

Thankfully, it is unusual to find a pupil whose learning difficulties have been missed; however, it does happen, as Stephen's example demonstrates.

Stephen

Stephen arrived in May 2002. He had been in mainstream schools until Y7, then had spent a few years in a special school and then he had returned to mainstream education. He arrived at the end of Y10, aged 15 years old. A new town, a new school – perhaps he hoped for a new beginning in a new mainstream school.

The school did the usual tests for reading accuracy and comprehension, numeracy and non-verbal reasoning and then did a few more. He came into school and was really quite nervous about going into classes. He went in when a teaching assistant offered to go in with him. Further tests were requested of colleagues in the local authority. They confirmed the initial assessment that Stephen had specific learning difficulties; he was a classic dyslexic.

What does this mean for Stephen? All his life he had been told that he was 'badly behaved' or, probably worse, 'thick'. He was advised at his previous school that he could not manage to do GCSEs. Now, he might have been an awkward so-and-so in times gone past (a quick scan of his file certainly indicated so), but his non-verbal scores were within the range of 85th to 95th percentile and they probably had been so for the last ten years.

What such a student needs is some or all of the following:

- special arrangements for his GCSE exams;
- someone to read texts for him;
- tapes rather than books;
- someone to write his course work for him;
- access to voice-recognition software;
- a reader for class tests;
- a scribe for his class tests;
- teachers to prove to him that he is an intelligent young man;
- to experience success for himself;
- help in organising himself; remember, he can't read his timetable.

Dyspraxia

Dyspraxia is a specific difficulty that affects the brain's ability to plan sequences of movement. It is thought to be connected to the way that the brain develops. The affect of dyspraxia on a child's ability at home and at school can vary, depending on the degree of difficulty. Difficulties may be found in some, or all of the following areas:

- In movement: a child with dyspraxia is not usually good at sport, is often generally clumsy, has poor balance and has difficulties in learning those skills that involve coordination of limbs, such as riding a bike or swimming.
- Smaller movements: poor handwriting, often resulting from too much pressure being applied to the pencil in an attempt to control it. Sometimes a child's writing may be neat, but written extremely slowly, reducing the amount of work that they can do.

Self-help and organisation skills

Dyspraxic children often take a long time to get dressed and organised in the morning. They may find it difficult to remember what equipment is needed and when it is needed, and will typically lose their belongings at school.

Speech and language skills

Dyspraxia can be linked with a delay or disorder in expressing themselves, such as getting words in the right order, or in controlling the movements necessary to make certain speech sounds.

Dyspraxia can affect a child's progress in school on a number of different levels:

- Difficulty with handwriting and this affects both the speed and quality of the student's written work. Difficulties in self-organisation can extend to difficulties in organisation of thoughts, as well as in planning and this can lead to work being disorganised or disjointed. Often students with dyspraxia can appear to have a lot of information in their heads, but cannot record that information in a logical and sensible order. Their written work does not match their apparent verbal ability. These difficulties can lead to frustration and problems with self-esteem, which can further lead to either withdrawn or acting-out behaviour.
- Concentration difficulties are often associated with dyspraxia, but it is sometimes difficult to say whether these are a genuine separate difficulty, or whether they are linked to a child's avoidance of difficult tasks.
- Children with dyspraxia can appear emotionally immature, and are often awkward or clumsy in their social relationships. Students may not make friends easily.

Supporting pupils with SEN

The vast majority of pupils in SEN groups have a long history of slow progress in most areas of schoolwork. The general teaching needs of these pupils will therefore include the need to:

- follow a general teaching approach, which enables skills and concepts to be broken down into small manageable steps;
- provide plenty of opportunity to practise and master each new step before progressing to the next one;
- limit copying from the board;
- provide regular repetition and reinforcement of instructions and guidance, to make allowances for poor short-term memory;
- provide appropriate differentiated resources;
- allow time and assistance for the recording of homework tasks;
- allow more time for some pupils to complete class work and/or homework tasks. Some pupils will be very slow at completing some tasks;
- provide and/or accept differentiated methods of demonstrating subject knowledge, such as audio-taped homework;

- break down lessons into shorter/manageable/effective learning periods, by providing a range of teaching approaches/activities;
- raise the self-esteem of pupils by means of regular positive reinforcement such as credits, commendations and giving verbal praise in front of peers;
- check that the pupils are still on task and still understand what is expected of them;
- avoid asking students to read out loud before checking that they are prepared and confident enough to do this;
- remember that the task of giving out books may be difficult for some students;
- remember that copying from the blackboard/overheads may be difficult. If possible, keep to a minimum, or provide notes;
- avoid dictation;
- provide subject-specific key words in advance of a topic being covered, as an aid to both spelling and writing;
- avoid written tasks when giving homework;
- use cloze exercises/accept oral response;
- encourage self-checking/proof reading.

When children's learning needs are being catered for, this has a direct impact upon their behaviour. All people like to succeed and make progress and most people will try to avoid doing what they can't do; this is simple. Putting this into practice is a career-long challenge and, crucially, successful teaching is the product of hard work, including a lot of planning and preparation, for which training and resources are key factors which will be best utilised by those who believe in and practise inclusion.

13 Interagency liaison

Office for Standards in Education (Ofsted)

Ofsted inspections are a huge deal for a school. The inspection report and the judgements contained within have a dramatic effect upon teachers working in a school.

During one particular inspection in the mid-1990s, when a highly authoritarian leader dominated the team, by day two you could smell the fear in the staff room. The spell was broken for one golden moment when one of the younger students walked up to the head of the team in the corridor, dropped to his knees, looked up at the by now curious inspector and asked, 'Shine your shoes boss?'

The most recent framework of inspections, which was introduced in September 2005, includes a variety of features, including:

- two days' notice of an inspection for schools by small teams who are in the school for about two days for secondary, less for primary;
- regular inspections; at least once every three years, when specific aspects of a school can be targeted;
- a highly significant role for the school's self-evaluation and the 'online' self-evaluation form known as the 'SEF', which has to be regularly updated by the school's management team. (A blank SEF can be viewed at www.ofsted.gov.uk/schools/sef.cfm.) The SEF is frozen as soon as an inspection is announced;
- four grades; outstanding, good, satisfactory and inadequate.

The report will, to a great extent, be driven by the five outcomes laid out in the *Every Child Matters* Green Paper:

1 Be healthy – e.g. school meals.
2 Stay safe – e.g. bullying, child protection procedures.
3 Enjoy and achieve – e.g. pupil progress data, value-added data.
4 Making a positive contribution – e.g. working with local charities and societies.
5 Economic well-being – e.g. improving numeracy, preparing young people for work.

During the inspection feedback occurs all the time. Lesson observations are not necessary; they can be used to check the school's SEF data and to clarify whether the Senior Management Team have appropriately identified the school's strongest and weakest teachers e.g. by undertaking joint observations. There is a strong focus upon how well the head teacher in particular and the SMT in general know the school. Crucially, an inspection looks at the impact of the leadership and the outcomes that result.

The head teacher has one day to challenge the factual content of the inspection report. The report, grades and all, has to be at Ofsted within five days. A letter is sent to students to inform them of their findings.

Ofsted strives to amalgamate issues of inclusion and attainment successfully. It's pretty safe to say that a comprehensive school that has just achieved 60 per cent A–C GCSEs will rarely be hauled across the coals because it has failed to be sufficiently inclusive. It's a very difficult issue to resolve in practice. It will be interesting to see what difference the new framework achieves over time. The changes in children's services are central to the new Ofsted inspection framework and successful inclusion, effective joined-up working and better outcomes for children are clear priorities.

Local authorities are subject to their own framework of inspection. Pre-September 2005, the inspections took place within the local education authority; each department of the LEA was inspected; schools were interviewed for their views and after a few days the team went away and after the appropriate process the report was subsequently delivered. Since September 2005 the procedure has been as follows. The Ofsted team are given the names of 100 children by the local authority and the team choose ten children to track through the authority's children's services e.g. from housing to educational psychology, from school to social services, on to the police, Connexions and health services etc. Just imagine an Ofsted Inspector going into the Town Planning Department to question why a particular student's mother cannot access fresh vegetables without travelling over a mile and on two buses each way. The inspection will look at how different services work together and how effective they are in supporting optimum outcomes for children. This represents a huge emphasis upon all agencies to improve their service delivery to children and families and will certainly impact upon their working practices.

The local authority

When discussing education in general and schools in particular, due regard should be paid to the pivotal role played by the local authority. To achieve this is a simple task – reporting upon the experience of this city in general and, specifically, the vision that is held by a colleague who has a key role in managing services relating to children's support services in developing the authority's inclusive agenda. Following the recent round of Ofsted inspections, this local authority has been placed within the top five in the country for its SEN and for its inclusion.

The role of the local authority is to offer leadership in giving a sense of direction and clear objectives. Wherever possible these are linked to targets which, while not being the be-all and end-all, can be crucial in the areas that impact on issues of social exclusion, such as:

- attainment;
- exclusions;
- attendance.

There can be no doubt that there are people striving towards tangible improvement in these areas. The danger is in compartmentalising the different factors. To avoid this it is crucial that we do not separate special educational needs from social inclusion.

The 'Index for Inclusion' tries to examine the ethos within schools. This is difficult to evidence and we therefore keep returning to the targets referred to above.

Resources

The main role of the local authority is to increase the capacity of its schools to be more inclusive. In doing so, it must look at the irreducible minimum of the government grant retained by the local authority; it must maximise the money pushed out to schools. This process necessitates time being spent with schools trying to find the right formula, e.g. to ensure that the formula takes account of turbulence factors among the student population. The LA should be encouraging schools to become purchasers of services; it can help children by helping schools.

Schools are consequently being provided with the money to provide the services that the local authority used to provide. Our local authority devolved the money to provide the specialist teaching for students with specific learning difficulties (SpLD). When the local authority provided the service, we were provided with two half days per week. After we had the money in our funds we were able to fund 0.75 of a specialist teacher. The fact that the teacher was outstanding was a real bonus. The whole package was vastly improved by giving the money to the school.

The irreducible minimum

The local authority needs to provide skilled advice and guidance e.g. educational psychology (EP). The EP service is moving away from the individual child towards looking at the systemic support to a school. The service is acting more as a consultant to developments. It is using its external view as a critical friend. The local authority is a key provider of training.

During recent years, local authorities have had to meet targets for delegating money. We should, however, be more concerned about the best ways of getting money into schools. The devolution of funding for pupils with specific learning difficulties, mentioned above, is an example of this. The devolving of the education welfare service (EWS) funding is a further example. By devolving this funding, the LA ensured it would be used to maintain standards rather than be absorbed into the general delegated budget. Indeed, the EWS funds were devolved on the condition that they would be used to employ a professionally trained social worker or one who was undertaking the appropriate training.

Monitoring

The LA has a monitoring role and this must be viewed as distinct from a punitive role. In our LA a series of monitoring procedures have been developed, each entitled an 'Opportunity to Excel' (O2E). Ofsted described this as one of the best examples of a local authority supporting self-review. There is, for instance, an O2E for special educational needs. This process can identify when a school is rocking and the LA can act to support the school in a number of ways. The Link Inspector will work collaboratively with LA services to support schools. The Autumn Package plays an increasingly important role in this process (now replaced by the Pupil Achievement Tracker).

The LA encourages multi disciplinary support. It makes sure that all its services work collaboratively. Governors, also, should play an essential role in the monitoring process and the LA must provide training to this voluntary body.

Multidisciplinary working

The school is increasingly being viewed as the focal point for the delivery of services. These services are rooted in the normative base i.e. in schools or with clear links to schools. The LA has a role in bringing clarity and cohesion to the interconnectedness of the disparate services. In this context, the LA should make efforts to use the voluntary services whenever possible. Indeed, the Children's Fund is rooted in the voluntary sector.

Connexions

Connexions transmuted from the old Careers Service. This service does not work within one single model as different areas across the UK have developed their own individual model. Each one does provide:

- Universal Personal Advisers;
- Personal Advisers for individual support.

The Personal Advisers are targeted towards disaffected students. Connexions has developed on the basis of local audits. There is a commitment to work with the local providers to identify and to bridge the gaps in provision to young people. For example, in this authority it was recognised that those students who were excluded for up to fifteen days were entitled to work set by the school. This was identified as relatively inadequate for vulnerable young people who could be denied a supervised structure in their day for three working weeks.

Connexions do work to government targets and these targets are themselves aligned to those set for the LA.

The LA sits on the management boards of different agencies. This practice is used to set up partnerships at a strategic level and has the added benefit of encouraging collaborative working at a practitioner level.

The LA hosts a 'Children Causing Concern' group that meets every week during term time. The remit of this group includes the systematic monitoring of students excluded from school for more than fifteen days as well as those who have been permanently excluded. There is also a systematic monitoring of the progress of looked-after children and of the LA's provision of Education Other Than at School (EOTAS). The group works in such a way as to make people accountable. Group members are clear as to the expectations placed upon them and the timescale in which they have to deliver and when they must report progress to the meeting. Group members are comprised of key LA staff.

In developing EOTAS provision, local authorities have pursued the development of Pupil Referral Units (PRUs) and it is true that the PRU has a key role to play. This LA has maintained the line it has devolved and delegated resources to schools and that the schools have the money and therefore are in a position to make the choice to purchase the provision if they wish to do so. This encourages value for money from the PRU and encourages the school to reflect upon the question 'Why are we paying them to do it when we can do it ourselves e.g. through the development of school-based behaviour support strategies?'

The Youth Inclusion Project exemplifies the process of school-based developments. This was a project based in the Youth Service and was accessed by students who had been permanently excluded. The practice that was developed by the project workers was of a very high standard and the question was posed as to how a broader range of students could access the provision; the answer was simply to make it a provision that could be purchased by schools.

To summarise, it is appropriate to reflect upon the period after the Healthy Alliance concluded, when the research was available for dissemination. The colleague whose shared vision is contained within this section gained a coherent grasp of the lessons provided by the in-depth evaluation. My colleague has been endeavouring to give due regard to these lessons, on the basis of his own conclusion that 'For a whole range of children, on a whole range of indices, it was the right thing to do'.

14 A vision for children

Ten years ago in various studies identifying disturbed and disturbing young adults in the caseloads of health, probation and social services departments, we saw that the majority were educational 'failures', whose problems were part of a cycle of intergenerational mishandling of children, and that many of the 'teacher's pests' were children of damaged and sometimes damaging adults. The response was to create the 'Healthy Alliance' project, which initially provided a school-based social work service to children and their families and, as the project became an integral part of the school, as we have shown, developed into a practical framework, able to meet the immediate future challenges that will emerge from Ofsted *Healthy Minds* as teachers take up the school's task of 'promoting emotional health and well-being in schools' (Ofsted 2005).

We recognise that people do have different abilities, but we can all aspire to 'our personal best performance' and we believe all children should have the opportunity to strive for their own personal excellence so as not only to exercise their 'rights', but to take up their 'responsibilities' as citizens. The late Barbara Castle, a fiery Yorkshire woman and a wonderful Secretary of State for Health, was impassioned by a world vision in which equality, liberty and fraternity could be daily experiences. In response to a political critic who was arguing for a narrow vision of restricted education to the 'able' and for 'excellence', she replied, 'It is not that I am against excellence but rather some people do not recognise that we can find excellence in unexpected places'. It is salutary to recall that in our so-called 'classless society', the grandparents of the majority of today's professional people such as teachers, doctors, nurses, social workers, solicitors) would have left school at 14 and before the Second World War would have been described by *The Times* as 'the lower orders'. It is perhaps the saddest aspect of many adults' lives today that they are functioning sub-optimally and failing to use the talents that they do possess, which then begin to wither.

The new teachers' responsibilities will centre upon Ofsted's drive for 'healthy minds' and will be based upon the 'five outcomes' enshrined in *Every Child Matters*.

Being healthy – this includes enjoying good physical and mental health and living a healthy lifestyle, and here personal, social and health education will be vital.

Staying safe – being protected from harm and neglect; this is a positive 'do' rather than 'do not', and the teacher may well be the first person in line to recognise the need for intervention, as well as enabling the child to be equipped to make better judgements.

To enjoy and achieve – getting the most out of life and developing the skills for adulthood, as well as developing and enhancing the aesthetic and spiritual dimensions of our humanness.

Economic well-being – not being prevented by economic (and educational) disadvantage from achieving their full potential in life, which in former times would not have been possible for many of today's professional people. Here the teacher is vital and central to equip future citizens with an educational base that will enable them to meet the challenge of a rapidly changing world.

Making a positive contribution – being involved in community and society and not engaging in anti-social and offending behaviour; reflecting a core human value of mutual respect for others.

All of these are evidence that the school was able to promote a 'healthy mind'.

We have seen how the realisation that 'every child matters' has implications not only for teachers and parents but for the whole of society, and that citizenship is about being equipped to ultimately contribute to the community as mature adults able to take up their full responsibilities. If we can engage children today so that they enjoy school, then we are fast on the way to reducing educational alienation.

It will not be easy, for example we will have the problem of trying to engage the previously alienated or disaffected parent. Indeed, it is quite clear, while the school can do much to liberate and develop the child's mind and potential, that unless the child's parents are active allies in the process, the child will not maximise his or her potential, which is why the school needs to reach out and include these parents. Another problem for the teacher is the potential pressure from the educationally enthusiastic parent, whose child is being bullied by the child with problems. Few parents would be willing to see the wider picture – that if 'Freddie' is excluded, while it may give short-term relief to their child, Freddie might well be vandalising or breaking into their home this afternoon, or next year. While Freddie will be virtually unemployable, with a local, bad reputation, his easiest 'alternative market' response to his situation is crime, adding to the community's fiscal burden and, still alienated, his children will quickly perpetuate the cycle.

Yet making a reality of *Every Child Matters* is not visionary, though it is a great vision, but it is achievable for the vast majority of children and families. There is a considerable research base of the antecedents of psychosocial pathology, which are identifiable even in the early years of school (Smith and Farrington 2004), and as school is the universal provision, where every child meets the state, it is where we can begin the process of reducing these problems. Moreover, there is a philosophical base, a moral imperative fuelled by the vision inscribed in the UN Declaration of Human Rights, recognising that children have special needs, which can only be met by multi-service provision, which includes the inter-relationship between health, employment, education and the ability of child and citizen to meet their social responsibilities. This was the forerunner of 'joined-up government', and we have found that practitioners are willing to work outside their restrictive organisational 'boxes', and with the encouragement of the new initiatives, appropriately placed within education (Department for Education and Skills), we can see a merging of social work and educational perspectives in the united service to children. It is perhaps not an accident that England's new Commissioner for Children, Alan Aynsley-Green, has a background in health as director of the DoH's 'Children's Taskforce' and is sited in the DfES (Brooks 2005).

He will not be primarily concerned with the rare minority of active abusers, but rather the neglect and therefore the passive abuse of children by sins of omission. It is less glamorous, less media attention-grabbing, but is the core of proper care of children.

The vision we have for our children in the twenty-first century, while new, has ancient antecedents as all the great religions had this same ideal of the child as the ultimate 'prophet' needing and meriting proper nurturing. As non-believers we remain impressed by the child-centred message of Jesus of Nazareth. He demanded that we forgive seventy times seven for wrongs against ourselves, but for those who abused children, he proposed that 'a millstone be hung around their neck and [they] be cast into the depths of the sea'.

Knowledge is power; it also brings responsibility, sometimes uncomfortably so. Hence the misuse of children in the times of Dickens might in part be forgiven as the Victorian middle-classes could claim they did not know it was happening. Not so today! We do know that a significant number of British children live in relative poverty, which until the expansion of the European Union last year was amongst the worst in the EU.

One of the underlying inspirations of these initiatives introduced by this government has been its unwillingness to accept that children in poverty must continue to lead 'blighted lives'. The failure of children is a parental, community, professional and societal failure to meet children's needs in time, as envisaged by the UN. This is no longer sustainable, not least because that individual, underdeveloped or wrecked life costs the community and society greatly as well as perpetuating the cycle of alienation. Morally, spiritually, politically and financially it is too expensive.

We now know that the vast majority of seriously anti-social adults come from families in which educational alienation has continued (Thornberry *et al.* 2003; Smith and Farrington 2004), and quite apart from the fractured and disrupted lives, as we showed, the early costs to the community are high (Pritchard 2001), while others have shown even greater fiscal and psychiatric costs as socially excluded young people move into later adulthood (Scot *et al.* 2001; Knapp *et al.* 2002). Yet this can be reduced if we engage the child to like school.

Despite the world's imperfections, the new century has the opportunity to be an age for the child and, under the new frameworks that are emerging, the old fiefdoms of education, health, housing, social services will disappear in the vision of having services for children which will include all these aspects of the child's life.

It is especially exciting for the new teacher at the dawn of a new social revolution, which aims to realise the vision of the fully developed child, and the teacher will have the excitement and the responsibility of being at the very centre of such aspirations, namely the school, the classroom. All this builds upon the individual teacher's relationship with the individual child as they seek to promote 'healthy minds'.

The teacher of the twenty-first century has the opportunity to share with parents in maximising their highest aspirations for their child and for those of you who share the vision, who reject half-measures, who tolerate only the giving of your best, then the joy, stimulus, excitement and privilege of moulding the mind of the new human being will lead us to say 'Oh Milton, thou should'st be here now.'

Our final vision for the teacher in the twenty-first century is that they have the responsibility and opportunity to mould the future, the lives of today's children, who so rapidly become tomorrow's parents. To paraphrase the great Quaker Charles Fox, the teacher can 'Seek the godhead in every child'. Yes, in every child because:

We speak of a race of real children
Not too good or too wise, but bounded up and down by love and
hate.

Oh may their early joys be nature and in books
And knowledge, rightly honoured by that word,
Not purchased by the loss of power.

(Wordsworth, *The Prelude*)

Bibliography: A Resource

ACE (Advisory Centre for Education) (2003) *Children Out of School.* London: ACE.

Adams, E.J., Charlett, A., Edmunds, W.J. and Hughes, G. (2004) Chlamydia trachomatis in the UK: a systematic review and analysis of prevalence studies, *Sexual Transmitted Infections,* 80: 331–3.

Ainsworth, J. (2002) Why does it take a village? The mediation of neighbourhood effects on educational achievement, *Social Forces,* 81: 117–52.

Akehurst, M., Brown, I. and Wesley, D.M. (1995) *Dying for Help: Offenders at Risk of Suicide.* Wakefield: ACPO.

Alcohol Concern (2002) *Young People's Drinking: Fact Sheet.* London: Alcohol Concern.

American Academy Paediatrics (2003) Out-of-school suspension and expulsion: AAP committee on school health, *Paediatrics,* 112: 1206–9.

Andersen, R. and Cheung, S.Y. (2003) Time to read: family resources and educational outcomes in Britain, *Journal of Comparative Family Studies,* 34: 413–33.

Andreasson, S., Allbeck, P. and Rydberg, U. (1990) Schizophrenia in users and non-users of cannabis: a longitudinal study in Stockholm, *Acta Psychaitrica Scandinavia,* 79: 505–10.

Apostopoulos,Y., Sonmez, S. and Yu, C.H. (2002) HIV risk behaviours of American spring-vacationers: a case of situational disinhibition, *International Journal of STD and AIDS,* 13: 733–43.

ARG (Assessment Reform Group) (2000) *Children's Behaviour: Beyond the Black Box.* London: ARG.

Arum, R. (1998) Invested dollars or diverted dreams: the effect of resources on vocational students' educational outcomes, *Sociology of Education,* 71: 130–51.

Atkins, M.S., McKay, M.M. Fazier, S.L. and Lambrecht, L. (2002) Suspensions and detentions in an urban low-income school: punishment or reward?, *Journal of Abnormal Psychology,* 30: 361–77.

Attwood, G., Crol, I.P. and Hamilton, A. (2003) Re-engaging with education, *Research Papers in Education,* 18: 75–95.

Audit Commission (1996) *Misspent Youth: The Cost of Juvenile Crime.* London: Audit Commission.

Audit Commission (1998) *Misspent Youth: Follow-up.* London: Audit Commission.

Audit Commission (2000) *Getting In On the Act: Provision for Pupils with Special Educational Needs.* London: Audit Commission.

Ayton, A., Rascool, H. and Cotrell, D. (2003) Deliberate self-harm in children and adolescents: association with deprivation, *European Child and Adolescent Psychiatry,* 12: 303–7.

Balding, J. (2004) Y*oung People in 2003. Health Related Behaviour Questionnaire.* Exeter: Schools Health Education Unit.

Barker, D. (2003) *The Best Start in Life.* London: Century Books.

Barnes, J. (2000a) *The Working Class and the Transformation of Learning. The Fraud of Educational Reform under Capitalism.* London: Pathfinder.

Barnes, M. (2000b) Users' views of mental health services, in D. Bailey (ed.) *At the Core of Mental Health.* London: Pavilion.

Barr, B. and Pearce, K. (1992) A place for every crime and every crime in its place, in D.J. Evens and N.R. Fyfe (eds) *Crime, Policing and Place.* London: Routledge.

Bates, R. (2003) Impact of educational research: alternative methodologies and conclusions, *Research Papers in Education,* 17: 403–8.

Battle, J.J. (1998) What beats having two parents? Educational outcomes for African–American students in single versus dual-parent families, *Journal of Black Studies,* 28: 783–801.

BBC (2005) Government initiatives to reduce truancy, *Today,* 4 February, BBC Radio 4.

Bellis, M.A., Hughes, K. and Lowey, H. (2002) Healthy night-clubs and recreational substance abuse: from harm-minimisation to a healthy setting approach, *Addictive Behaviour,* 27: 1025–35.

Bellis, M.A., Hughes, K. and Wyke, S. (2004) Assessing and communicating the health and judicial impact of alcohol, *Public Health,* 118: 253–61.

Bennett, N. (1998) Class size and the quality of educational outcomes, *Journal of Child Psychology and Psychiatry,* 39: 797–804.

Bennett, S., Farrington, D.P. and Huesmann, L.R. (2005) Explaining gender differences in crime and violence: the importance of social cognitive skills, *Aggression and Violent Behaviour,* 10: 263–88.

Birmingham City Council (2004) *Excellence in Cities Evaluation 2003.* Birmingham: School Effectiveness in Cities Unit.

Bjarnason, T. and Johnson, S.H. (2005) Contrasts effects in perceived risk of substance abuse, *Substance Use and Misuse,* 40: 1733–8.

Bjarnason, T. and Sigurdardotti, T.S. (2003) Psychological distress following unemployment and beyond: social support and material deprivation in youth across six Northern European countries, *Social Science and Medicine,* 56: 973–85.

Black, P. and William, D. (1998a) Assessment and classroom learning: assessment, *Education,* 7: 74–8.

Black, P. and William, D. (1998b) Inside the black box: raising standards through classroom assessment, *Education,* 7: 139–48.

Blakely, T.A., Collings, S.C. and Atkinson, J. (2003) Unemployment and suicide, *Journal of Epidemiology and Community Health,* 57: 2487–91.

Blatchford, P., Kutnick, P., Baines, E. and Galton, M. (2003) Toward a social pedagogy of classroom group work, *International Journal of Educational Research,* 39: 153–72.

Bloomfield, L., Kendall, S., Applin, E.E. and Newcombe, T. (2005) A qualitative study exploring the experiences and views of mothers, health visitors and family support workers on the challenges and difficulties of parenting, *Health and Social Care in the Community,* 13: 46–55.

Bonnell, C.P., Allen, E., Strange, V. and Johnson, A. (2005) The effect of dislike of school on risk of teenage pregnancy, *Journal of Epidemiological and Community Health,* 59: 223–30.

Bonnell, C.P., Strange, V., Stephenson, J. and Black, S. (2003) Effects of social exclusion on the risk of teenage pregnancy: development of hypothesis using long-term data from a randomised trial of sex education, *Journal of Epidemiological and Community Health,* 57: 871–6.

Booth, T., Ainsow, M.I. and Shaw, L. (2001) *Index for Inclusion.* London: CSIE.

Borg, M.G., Riding, R.J. and Falzon, J.M. (1991) Stress in teaching: a study of occupational stress and its determinants, job satisfaction and career commitments among primary school teachers, *International Journal of Educational Psychology,* 11: 59–75.

Breslin, R. and Evans, H. (2004) *Inform: key child protection statistics,* London: NSPCC.

Britain, A. and McPherson, K. (2001) Mortality in England and Wales attributable to current alcohol consumption, *Journal of Epidemiology and Community Health,* 55: 383–8.

Brook, R. (2004) 'My Mum would be as pleased as punch if I actually joined but my Dad seems a bit more particular': parental involvement in young people's higher education, *British Educational Research Journal,* 30: 496–514.

Brooks, L. (2005) The Guardian interview: Aynsley-Green, Children's Commissioner for England, *Guardian,* 28 July.

Brooks-Gunn, J. and Leventhal, T. (2004) Randomised study of neighbourhood effects on low-income children's educational outcome, *Developmental Psychology,* 40: 488–507.

Brugha, T., Jenkins, R., Bebbington, P., Meltzer, H. and Farrell, M. (2004) Risk factors and the prevalence of neurosis and psychosis in ethnic groups in Great Britain, *Social Psychiatry and Psychiatric Epidemiology,* 39: 939–46.

Buckland, L.G, Greaves, C. and Rose, J. (2005) New roles for nurses: preventing exclusion, *Community Practitioner,* 78: 16-19.

Bufkin, J.L. and Luttrell, V.R. (2005) Neuroimaging studies of aggressive and violent behaviour: current findings and implications for criminology and criminal justice, *Trauma, Violence and Abuse,* 6: 176–91.

Burns, B.J., Phillips, S.D., Wagner, H.R. and Landsverk, J. (2004) Mental health needs and access to mental health services by youths involved in child welfare: a national survey, *Journal of Academic Child and Adolescent Psychiatry,* 43: 960–70.

Cata, J.E. and Canetto, S.S. (2003) Young adults' reactions to gay and lesbian peers who become suicidal following 'coming out' to their parents, *Suicide and Life Threatening Behaviour,* 33: 201–10.

Clarke, R.V. (ed.) (1992) *Situational Crime Prevention: Successful Case Studies.* New York: Arrow and Heston.

Cole, P.M., Teti, L.O. and Zhan-Walker, C. (2004) Mutual emotional regulation and the stability of conduct problems between pre-school and early school age, *Developmental Psychopathology,* 15: 1–18.

Coniglario, J., Gordon, A.J. and Justice, A.C. (2003) How harmful is hazardous alcohol use and abuse in HIV infections?, *Journal of Acquired Immune Deficiency Syndrome,* 35: 521–5.

Cox, M. (2003) The locale of the offence and the offender. Unpublished PhD, University of Southampton.

Cox, M. and Pritchard, C. (1995) Troubles come not singly but in battalions: the pursuit of social justice in probation practice, in M. Lacy and D. Ward (eds) *Probation: Working for Justice.* London: Birch and Whiting.

Crawford, T., Geraghty, W. and Simonoff, E. (2003) Staff knowledge and attitudes towards deliberate self-harm in adolescents, *Journal of Adolescence,* 26: 623–33.

Crawford, T. and Simonoff, E. (2003) Parental views about services for children attending schools for emotionally and behaviourally disturbed: a qualitative analysis, *Child Care and Health Development,* 29: 481–91.

Daley, F.K. (2004) Update on Attention Deficit Hyperactivity Disorder, *Current Opinion in Psychiatry,* 16: 217–26.

Danckaerts, M., Heptinstall, E. and Taylor, E. (2000) A natural history of hyperactivity and conduct problems: self-reported outcome, *European Child and Adolescent Psychiatry,* 9: 26–38.

David, G.R. (2000) *Underclass, Children and Civil Society.* London: International Study of Civil Society.

DE (Department of Employment) (1990–2000) *Employment Gazette*, April/July, HMSO.

Del Rey, C.J. (2004) Poverty, social exclusion, social capital and health, *Annals Royele e Acadamia Nacion Medicale*, 121: 57–72.

DfE (Department for Education) (1992) *Exclusion: A Discussion Paper*. London: DfE.

DfEE (Department for Education and Employment) (1999) *Social Inclusion: Pupil Support*, Circular 11(99). London: Department for Education and Employment.

DfEE (2000) *Removing Barriers: Raising the Achievement Levels for Minority Ethnic Pupils*. London: Department for Education and Employment.

DfEE (2001) *National Statistics: Special Educational Needs in England*, SFR 21/2001. London: Department for Education and Employment.

DfEE (2002) *Drug Abuse: Guidelines for Schools*. London: Department for Education and Employment.

DfEE (2003) *Inclusion: Providing Effective Learning Opportunities for All Pupils*, www.nc.uk.net/inclusion.htm1

DfEE (2004) *Work Related Learning*, www.teachernet.gov.uk/teachinglearning/14to19/ks4/workrelaredlearning/1–2

DfES (Department for Education and Science) (1989) *The Elton Report: Discipline in Schools*. London: HMSO.

DfES (2003a) *Aiming High: Raising the Achievement of Minority Ethnic Pupils*, www.literacytrust.org.uk/Database/refugees.html 1-6

DfES (2003b) *Every Child Matters*, Green Paper. London: HMSO.

DfES (2003c) *The Skills for Life Survey: A National Needs and Impact Survey of Literacy, Numeracy and ICT Skills*. London: HMSO.

DfES (2004) Tackling homophobia, *Teachers Magazine*, Issue 33, www.teachernet.gov.uk/teachers/issue33/primary/features/TacklingHomophobia 1-4

DfES (2005) *14–19 Education Skills*: White Paper, www.literacytrust.org.uk, 1–3.

Diamond, I., Pritchard, C. and Fielding, M. (1988) Incidence of drug and solvent abuse in normal school children. A repeat study, 1985 and 1986, *Public Health*, 102: 107–14.

DoH (Department of Health) (1998) *Towards a Healthy Nation*. London: HMSO.

Dougan, S., Brown, A.E., Logan, L.E. and Gill, O.N. (2004) Epidemiology of HIV in young people in England, Wales and Northern Ireland, *Communicable Disease and Public Health*, 7: 15–23.

Eccles, J. and Popper, K. (1974) *The Self and Its Brain*. London: Macmillan.

Eisenberg, M.E., Neumark, D. and Storey, M. (2003) Associations of weight-based teasing and emotional well-being amongst adolescents, *Archive of Paediatric and Adolescent Medicine*, 157: 733–8.

Emery, R.E. (2005) Parental alienation syndrome: proponents bear the burden of proof, *Family Court Review*, 43: 8–13.

Extended School and Adult Learners, (2004) www.niace.org.uk/information/Briefing_sheets/53-extendedschools.htm, 1–6.

Eysenck, H. (1971) *Race, Intelligence and Education*. London: Smith MT.

Farrell, M. (2001) *Standards and Special Educational Needs: The Importance of Standards of Pupil Achievement*. London: Continuum.

Farrell, M. and Ainsow, M. (2002) Making special education inclusive: mapping the issues, in M. Farrell and M. Ainsow, *Special Educational Needs*. London: David Fulton.

Farrington, D.P. (1980) Truancy, delinquency, the home and school, in L. Hersov and I.B. Berg (eds) *Out of School: Modern Perspectives in Truancy and School Refusal*. Chichester: Wiley.

Farrington, D.P. (1992) Criminal career research in the United Kingdom, *British Journal of Criminology*, 3: 521–36.

Farrington, D.P. (1994) The influence of family on delinquent development, in C. Henricson (ed.) *Crime and the Family*, Paper 20. London: Family Policy Studies Centre.

Farrington, D.P. (1995) The development of offending and anti-social behaviour from childhood: key findings from the Cambridge Study in Delinquent Development, *Journal of Child Psychology and Psychiatry*, 36: 929–64.

Farrington, D.P. and Loeber, R. (2000) Epidemiology of juvenile violence, *Child and Adolescent Psychiatric Clinics of North America*, 9: 733–48.

Fergusson, D.M., Horwood, L.J. and Lynskey, M.T. (1993) The effects of conduct disorder and attention deficit in middle childhood on offending and scholastic ability at age 13, *Journal of Child Psychology and Psychiatry*, 34: 463–89.

Fitzpatrick, K.K., Euton, S.J., Jones, J.N. and Schmidt, N.B. (2005) Gender role, sexual orientation and suicide risk, *Journal of Affective Disorders*, 87: 35–42.

Flouri, E., and Buchanan, A. (2004) Early father's and mother's involvement and child's later educational outcome, *British Educational Psychology*, 74: 141–53.

Ford, P., Pritchard, C. and Cox, M. (1996) Consumer opinions of the probation service: advice, assistance, befriending and the reduction of crime, *Howard Journal*, 36: 41–62.

Foxcroft, D.R., Ireland, D. and Breen, R. (2002) Primary prevention of alcohol misuse in young people, *Cochrane Data Base Systematic Review*, CDO 003024.

Furman, K. and Thompson, J.K. (2002) Body image, teasing, and mood alterations: experimental study of exposure to negative verbal commentary, *International Journal of Eating Disorders*, 32: 449–57.

Gabriel, J. (2000) *Alcohol on the Mind: The Effect of Drinking on Adolescent Brains*. London: Routledge.

Gilbert, M. (1998) *The Holocaust*. London: HarperCollins.

Gilchrist, A., Green, J. and Rutter, M. (2005) Development and current findings on adolescents with Asperger's Syndrome, *Journal of Child Psychology and Psychiatry*, 42: 227–40.

Glasgow, K.L., Dornbusch, S.M. and Ritter, S.L. (1997) Parenting styles, adolescent attributions and educational outcomes in nine hetero-geneous high schools, *Child Development*, 68: 507–29.

Goffman, I. (1961) *Stigma*. Harmondsworth: Penguin.

Goleman, D. (1997) *Emotional Intelligence: Why It Can Matter More than IQ.* Harmondsworth: Penguin.

Graham, J. and Bowling, B. (1995) *Young People and Crime*. London: Research Statistics Department, Home Office.

Green, D. (ed.) (2001) *The Under Class 10+ and the Civil Society*. Institute of Study of Civil Society.

Gruber, A.J., Pope, H.G. and Yurgelun-Todd, D. (2003) Attributes of long-term heavy cannabis users: a case-control study, *Psychological Medicine*, 33: 1415–22.

Grunbaum, J.A., Kann, L., Kinchen, S. and Collins, J. (2004) Youth risk behaviour surveillance, United States 2003, *Surveillance Summary*, 53: 536–56.

Guttmacher Institute (2003) UK youth prefer peer-led sexuality educa-tion classes to teacher-led programs, *Perspectives on Sexual and Reproductive Health*, 35(2): 1–3.

Hall, P.W., Christie, P.M. and Crow, D. (2005) Cannabis and cancer: causation, remediation and palliation, *Lancet Oncology*, 6: 35–42.

Hawton, K., Hall, S., Simkin, S. and Stewart, A. (2003) Deliberate self-harm in adolescents: a study of characteristics and trends in Oxford 1990–2000, *Journal of Child Psychology and Psychiatry*, 44: 1191–8.

Hay, I. (2001) Gender self-concept profiles of adolescents suspended from high school, *Journal of Child Psychology and Psychiatry*, 41: 345–52.

Heyderman, R.S., Ben-Shlomo, Y., Brennan, C.A. and Somerset, M. (2004) The incidence and mortality for meningococcal disease associated with area deprivation: an ecological study of hospital episodes statistics, *Archives of Children's Diseases*, 89: 1064–8.

Hill, J. (2003) Early identification of individuals at risk of antisocial personality disorder, *British Journal of Psychiatry*, Supplement, 44, S11-4.

Hill, N.E. and Craft, S.A. (2003) Parent–school involvement and school performance mediated pathways amongst comparable African–American and Euro-Americans, *Journal of Educational Psychology*, 95: 74–83.

Hill-Smith, A.J., Hugo, P., Fongay, P. and Hartman, D. (2002) Adolescent murderers: abuse and adversity in childhood, *Journal of Adolescence,* 25: 221–30.

Hingson, R., Heeren, T., Winter, M.R. and Wechsler, H. (2003) Early age of first drunkenness as a factor in college students' unplanned and unprotected sex attributable to drinking, *Paediatrics,* 111: 34–41.

Hingson, R., Heeren, T., Winter, M.R. and Wechsler, H. (2005) Magnitude of alcohol-related mortality and morbidity amongst college students, *Annual Review of Public Health,* 26: 219–27.

HM Treasury Comprehensive Spending Review Aims and Objectives, http://archive.treasury.gov.uk/pub/html/csr/aims.html, 1–2.

Hoge, R.D., Andrews, D.A. and Lescheid, A.W. (1996) An investigation of risk and protective factors in a sample of youthful offenders, *Journal of Child Psychology and Psychiatry,* 37: 419–24.

Hogland, W.L. and Leadbeater, B.J. (2004) Effects of family, school and classroom ecologies on changes in children's social competence and emotional and behavioural problems in first grade, *Developmental Psychology,* 40: 533–44.

Holle, C. (2004) Male body image: self-perceived weight status and avoidance of body exposure, *Perceptual Motor Skills,* 99: 853–60.

Holmes, S.E., Slaughter, J.R. and Kashani, J. (2001) Risk factors in childhood that lead to the development of conduct disorder and anti-social personality disorder, *Child Psychiatry and Human Development,* 31: 183–93.

Home Office (1992) *Cost of the Criminal Justice System: Magistrates' Courts,* Volume 6, Section 95. London: Home Office.

Hunter, S.C., Boyle, T. and Warden, D. (2004) Help seeking amongst children and adolescents: victims of peer-aggression and bullying. Influence of school strategy, *British Journal of Educational Psychology,* 74: 375–90.

Ingoldsby, E.M. and Shaw, D.S. (2002) Neighbourhood contextual factors and early starting antisocial pathways, *Clinical Child and Family Psychological Review,* 5: 21–55.

Iyers, D.S. and Haslam, N. (2003) Body image and eating disturbance among south Asian–American women, *International Journal of Eating Disorders,* 34: 142–7.

Jackson, C. (2003) Motives for 'laddishiness' at school: fear of failure and fear of the 'feminine', *British Educational Research Journal,* 29: 23–31.

Jackson, E. (2002) Mental health in schools: what about the staff?, *Journal of Child Psychotherapy,* 28: 129–46.

Jozefowicz-Simbeni, D.M.H. and Allen-Meares, P. (2002) Poverty and schools: intervention and resource building through school-linked services, *Children and Schools,* 24: 123–36.

Kalant, H. (2004) Adverse affects of cannabis on health: an update of the literature, *Prognosis and Neuropsychopharmacology and Biological Science*, 28: 849–63.

Kelly, R. (2005) Persistent truants and delinquency, BBC report, *Today*, Radio 4, 16 June.

Kendler, K.S., Myers, J. and Crescott, H. (2000) Parenting and adult mood and substance abuse, *Psychological Medicine*, 30: 281–94.

Killen, M., Lee-Kim, J. and Stangor, C. (2002) How children and adolescents evaluate gender and racial exclusion, *Monographs in Social Research and Child Development*, 67: 1–19.

Knapp, M., McCrone, P., Fombonne, E. and Wostear, G. (2002) The Maudsley long-term follow-up of child and adolescent depression, 3: impact of co-morbid conduct disorder on service use and costs in adulthood, *British Journal of Psychiatry*, 180: 19–23.

Kristensen, S.M. and Smith, P.K. (2003) Use of coping strategies by Danish children classed as bullies, victims, bully/victims and not involved in different types of bullying, *Scandinavia Journal of Psychology*, 44: 479–88.

Kuntscher, E., Rehm, J. and Gemel, G. (2004) Characteristics of binge drinkers in Europe, *Social Science and Medicine*, 59: 113–27.

Laird, R.D., Jordan, K.V., Dodge, K.A. and Bates, J.E. (2001) Peer rejection in childhood, involvement with antisocial peers in early adolescence and development of externalising behaviour problems, *Development Psychopathology*, 13: 337–54.

La Montagne, D.D., Fenton, K.A., Pimenta, J.M and Tobin, J.M. (2005) Using chlamydia positively to estimate prevalence: evidence from the Chlamydia Screening Pilot in England, *International Journal of the Study of AIDS*, 16. 323–7.

Larzelere, R.E. and Patterson, G.R. (1990) Parental management: mediator of the effects of socio-economic status on early delinquency, *Criminology*, 28: 301–324.

Levacic, R. and Hammond, J. (1998) Competing for resources: the impact of social disadvantage, *Oxford Review of Education*, 24: 303–28.

Levi, F., Lucchini, F. and Le Vecchia, C. (2004) Suicide mortality in adolescents and young adults, *Review Epidemiologica et Sante Publique*, 52: 668–71.

Levitas, R. (1998) *The Inclusive Society? Social Exclusion and New Labour*. London: Macmillan.

Lindjord, D. (2001) Families of economically disadvantaged backgrounds and children's educational performance. Challenge and opportunities, *Journal of Early Education and Family Review*, 9: 4–5.

Llewellyn, G.D., Johnson, N.W. and Warnakulasuriya, K.A. (2004) Risk factors in oral cancer in newly diagnosed patients aged 45 and younger: a case-control study in the South of England, *Journal of Oral Pathology and Medicine*, 33: 525–32.

Loeber, R. and Farrington, D.P. (2001) Young children who commit crime: epidemiology, developmental origins, risk factors, early interventions and policy implications, *Developmental Psychopathology*, 12: 737–62.

Lundgren, J.D., Andersen, D.A., Thompson, J.K. and Paulosky, C.A. (2004) Perception of teasing in underweight persons, *Eating and Weight Disorders*, 9: 139–46.

MacCleod, J., Salisbury, C., Low, N. and Egger, M. (2005) Coverage and uptake of systematic postal screening for genital chlamydia trachomatis and prevalence of infection in the UK general population, *British Medical Journal*, 330: 940–1.

Macdonald, G. and Leary, M.R. (2005) Why does social exclusion hurt? The relationship between social and physical pain, *Psychological Bulletin*, 131: 202–23.

MacDonald, R. (ed.) (1997) *Youth, the Under Class and Social Exclusion*. London: Routledge.

MacGregor, S. (1988) *Drugs and British Society*. London: Routledge.

Marks, K. (2004) *Traveller Education: Changing Times, Changing Technologies*. London: Trentham Books.

Martin, J. and Webster, D. (1994) *Review of Motor Projects*. London: Home Office.

Maslow, A.H. (1998) *Towards a Psychology of Being*. New York: Wiley.

Mensah, G.A., Hanson, C.M., Richmond, J. and Satcher, D. (2005) Are health disparities on the public health agenda? Where?, *Ethnic Discourses*, 13: 6–8.

Merrell, C. and Tymms, P.B. (2001) Inattention, hyperactivity and impulsiveness: their impact upon academic achievement and progress, *British Journal of Educational Psychology*, 71: 43–56.

Mindle, J.S. (1995) Tobacco advertising, *Journal of the Royal Society of Health*, 115: 84–9.

Monoghan, F. (2004) *Practical Ways to Support New Arrivals in the Classroom*. London: National Centre for Language and Literacy/ACE.

Morgan, C. and Murgatroyd, S. (1994) *Total Quality Management Perspective in the Public Sector*. Buckingham: Open University Press.

Muir, J. and Boodram, A. (2002) *The Dilemma of Being African Caribbean in Britain's Schools*, www.caribvoice.org/Features/Africancarib.html, 1–4.

Muntaner, C., Lynch, J.W., Hillemeirer, L. and Borrell, C. (2002) Economic inequality, working-class power, social capital and cause-specific mortality in wealthy countries, *International Journal of Health Services*, 32: 629–56.

Muntz, R., Hutchings, J., Edwards, R.T. and O'Ceilleachair, A. (2004) Economic evaluation of treatments for children with severe behavioural problems, *Journal of Mental Health Policy and Economics,* 7: 177–89.

Murray, C. (ed.) (2000) *Charles Murray and the Under Class: The Developing Debate.* London: Institute of Study of Civil Society.

NASWE (National Association of Social Workers in Education) (1996) *The Educational Welfare Service Annual Year Book.* Southport: NASWE.

National Audit Office (2005) *Improving School Attendance in England. HC Report 212, 2004–05.* London: NAO.

National Centre for Social Research (2003) *Alcohol and Drugs amongst Pupils.* London: National Centre for Social Research and National Federation for Educational Research.

NLT (National Literacy Trust) (2004) *Immigrants, Refugees and Asylum Seekers.* London: NLT.

O'Brien, T. (ed.) (2001) *Special Educational Needs Leadership: Enabling Inclusion.* London: HMSO.

O'Donnell, D.A., Schwab-Stone, M.E. and Muyeed, A.Z. (2002) Multi-dimensional resilience in urban children exposed to community violence, *Child Development,* 73: 1265–82.

Ofsted (1993) *Education for Disaffected Pupils.* London: Ofsted.

Ofsted (1995) *Pupil Referral Unit: First 12 Inspections.* London: Ofsted.

Ofsted (1999) *Raising the Attainment of Ethnic Minority Pupils.* London: Ofsted.

Ofsted (2003) *The Education of Asylum-seeker Pupils,* www.ofsted.gov.uk.

Ofsted (2005) *Healthy Minds: Promoting Emotional Health and Well-being.* HMI 2457. London: Ofsted.

OHCHR (Office of the High Commission on Human Rights) (1989) *Convention on the Rights of the Child,* 20 November, www.unhcr.ch/html/menu3/b/k2crc.htm, 1-11.

O'Keefe, D. (1994) *Truancy in English Secondary Schools.* London: Department for Education.

Oliver, J. (1983) Dead children from problem families in North Wiltshire, *British Medical Journal,* 286: 113–17.

Oliver, J. (1985) Five generations of child maltreatment, social and medical disorders in parents, *British Journal of Psychiatry,* 147: 484–90.

Oliver, J. (1988) Successive generations of child maltreatment, *British Journal of Psychiatry,* 153: 543–53.

ONS (Office for National Statistics) (2003) *Social Trends 2003.* London: ONS.

ONS (2004) *Assessments and Children and Young People on Child Protection Registers: Year ending 31 March 2003.* London: ONS.

ONS (2005) *Annual Abstract of Statistics.* London: The Stationery Office.

Owen, G. (2003) Ofsted head deplores the lost generation of pupils, *The Times,* 11 June, *Timesonline.*

Pasteror, R.N. and Reuban, C.A. (2000) Attention Deficit Disorder and Learning Disability: United States 1997–98, *Vital Health Statistics,* 206: 1–12.

Patterson, G.R. (1994) Alternative to seven myths about treating families of antisocial children, in C. Henricson (ed.) *Crime and the Family,* Paper 20, London: Family Policy Studies Centre.

Pavey, S. and Visser, J. (2003) Primary exclusions – are they rising?, *British Journal of Special Education,* 30: 180–6.

Pawson, R. and Tilley, N. (1994) What works in evaluation research?, *British Journal of Criminology,* 35: 291–306.

Petersen, L., Andersen, P.K. and Sorensen, T.A. (2004) Premature death of adult adoptees: an analysis of a case-cohort, *Genetic Epidemiology,* 28: 376–82.

Phillips, S.D., Burns, B.J., Wanger, H.R. and Barth, R.P. (2004) Parental arrest and children involved with child welfare agencies, *American Journal of Orthopsychiatry,* 74: 174–86.

Pinker, S. (1997) *How the Mind Works.* London: Penguin Press.

Pitts, J. (2005) Re-evaluating beliefs and assumptions about youth justice, *Research Matters,* 19: 73–5.

Plomin, R. and Walker, O.S. (2003) Genetics and educational psychology, *British Journal of Educational Psychology,* 73: 3–14.

Pontius, A.A. (2005) Fastest fight/flight reaction via amygdalar visual pathways implicates simple face drawing as a marker, *Aggression and Violent Behaviour,* 10: 363–73.

Postlethwaite, K. and Haggarty, L. (2002) Towards the improvement of learning in secondary schools: students' views, their links to theories of motivation and issues of over- and under-achievement, *Research Papers in Education,* 17: 785–809.

Powell, C. (1995) *A Soldier's Way: An Autobiography.* New York: Random House.

Pritchard, C. (1995) An analysis of regional suicide by gender and age 1974–90 and regional unemployment 1990–93: indicators of future rises in suicide?, *British Journal of Social Work,* 25: 767–90.

Pritchard, C. (1999) *Suicide: The Ultimate Rejection.* Buckingham: Open University Press.

Pritchard, C. (2001) A child–family–teacher alliance to reduce truancy, delinquency and school exclusion. Occasional Paper No. 78. London: Research, Development and Statistics/Home Office.

Pritchard, C. (2004) *The Child Abuser: Research and Controversy.* Buckingham: Open University Press.

Pritchard, C. (2006) *Evidence-based Mental Health Social Work*. London: Routledge.

Pritchard, C, Baldwin, D.S. and Mayers, A. (2004) Changing patterns of adult neurological deaths in the major Western world countries 1979–97, *Public Health,* 118: 268–83.

Pritchard, C. and Butler, A. (2000a) Criminality, murder and the cost of crime in coterminous cohorts of 'excluded-from-school' and 'looked-after-children' adolescents as young adults, *International Journal of Adolescent Medicine and Health,* 12: 223–44.

Pritchard, C. and Butler, A. (2000b) Victims of crime, murder and suicide in coterminous cohorts of 'excluded-from-school' and 'looked-after-children' adolescents as young adults, *International Journal of Adolescent Medicine and Health,* 12: 275–94.

Pritchard, C. and Clooney, D. (1994) *Single Homelessness in Dorset: Fractured Lives and Fragmented Policies*. Bournemouth Churches Housing Association Report to Department of Environment. Bournemouth: BCHA.

Pritchard, C., Cotton, A. and Cox, M. (1992a) Truancy, drug abuse and knowledge of HIV infection in 926 normal adolescents, *Journal of Adolescence,* 15: 1–17.

Pritchard, C., Cotton, A. and Cox, M. (1993) Under-age drinking in 926 'ordinary' adolescent comprehensive school students, *Journal of Wine Research,* 4: 95–107.

Pritchard, C., Cotton, A., Godson, D., Cox, M. and Weeks, S. (1992b) Mental illness, drug and alcohol misuse and HIV risk behaviour in 214 young adult probation clients, *Social Work and Social Science Review,* 3(2): 150–62.

Pritchard, C. and Cox, M. (1990) Drug and solvent misuse and knowledge of Aids in 14- to 16-year-old comprehensive school students, *Public Health,* 104: 425–35.

Pritchard, C. and Cox, M. (1998) The criminality of former 'special educational provision' permanently 'excluded-from-school' adolescents as young adults (16–23): costs and practical implications, *Journal of Adolescence,* 21: 609–20.

Pritchard, C. and Cox, M. (2005) *Behaviour and Attitudes of 10th and 11th Year Secondary School Pupils*. Poole: Poole Drug Advisory Team.

Pritchard, C. and Cunliffe, A. (1983) GDP expenditure on health and education and mental health policy, *Social Policy and Administration,* 17: 32–45.

Pritchard, C., Dawson, A. and Cox, M. (1997) Suicide and violent death in a six-year cohort of male probationers compared with a general male population mortality: evidence of accumulative socio-psychiatric vulnerability, *Journal of the Royal Society of Health,* 117: 175–80.

Pritchard, C., Diamond, I., Fielding, M. and Choudry, N. (1986a) Incidence of drug and solvent abuse in 'normal' 4th- and 5th-year comprehensive school children, *British Journal of Social Work*, 16: 1–11.

Pritchard, C., Diamond, I., Fielding, M. and Cox, M. (1986b) Incidence of drug and solvent abuse in 'normal' 10th-and 11th-year comprehensive school children, *British Journal of Social Work*, 16: 17–39.

Pritchard, C. and Evans, B.T. (2000) Cancer survival rates and GDP expenditure on health: comparison of England and Wales and the USA, Denmark, Finland, France, Germany, Italy, Spain and Switzerland, *Public Health,* 114: 336–9.

Pritchard, C. and Galvin, K. (2006) Comparison of 'all-cause' and 'malignant neoplasm' deaths in England and Wales and the USA 1979-2000 and a review of GDP expenditure on health, *Public Health,* in press.

Pritchard, C. and Sunak, S. (2005) *Aetiology and Epidemiology of Amyotrophic Lateral Sclerosis. Report to Public Health Board, State of Massachusetts.* Boston, MA: ALS Treatment and Development Forum.

Pritchard, C. and Taylor, R.K.S. (1978) *Social Work: Reform or Revolution?* London: Routledge and Kegan Paul.

Pritchard, C. and Taylor, R.K.S. (1981) Violence in schools: some teacher and social work perspectives. Occasional Paper No. 3. Leeds: Department of Social Work and Applied Social Studies, University of Leeds.

Pritchard, C. and Wallace, S. (2006) Suicide and other violent deaths (homicide and roads) in the major Western countries compared with the toll of 11 September 2001, *Archives of Suicide Research,* in press.

Pritchard, C. and Williams, R. (2001) A three-year comparative longitudinal study of a school-based social work child–family service to reduce truancy, delinquency and school-exclusions, *Journal of Social Welfare and Family Law*, 23: 1–21.

Pritchard, C., Williams, R. and Bowen, D. (1998) A consumer's study of young people's view of their educational social worker's engagement and non-engagement as an indicator of effective intervention, *British Journal of Social Work,* 28: 915–38.

Pyle, D.J. and Deadman, D.F. (1994) Crime and the business cycle in post-war Britain, *British Journal of Criminology,* 34: 339–52.

Rey, J.M., Martin, A. and Krabman, P. (2004) Is the party over? Cannabis and juvenile psychiatric disorder over the past 10 years, *Journal of American Academic Child and Adolescent Psychiatry,* 43: 1194–205.

Rhodes, C., Nevill, A. and Allan, J. (2004) Satisfaction and dissatisfaction, morale and retention in an English local authority: a survey of valuing and supporting teachers, *Research in Education,* 71: 67–80.

Richardson, A.S. and Puri, B.K. (2000) The potential of fatty acids in ADHD, *Prostaglands and Essential Fatty Acids,* 63: 78–97.

Richman, J., Rosenfeld, M. and Lawrence, B. (2003) Social support and educational outcome for students in out-of-home care, *Children and Schools,* 25: 69–86.

Rigby, K. (2003) Consequences of bullying in schools, *Canadian Journal of Psychiatry,* 48: 131–9.

Rivers, L. (2004) Recollections of bullying at school and their long-term implications for lesbians, gay men and transsexuals, *Crisis,* 25: 169–75.

Rodham, K., Hawton, K. and Evens, K. (2000) Reasons for deliberate self-harm: comparison of self-poisoners and self-cutters in a community sample of adolescents, *Addiction,* 95: 1197–206.

Rossow, I. and Laurritzen, G. (2001) Shattered childhood: a key issue in suicidal behaviour amongst drug addicts?, *Addiction,* 96: 227–40.

Roye, C.F. and Balk, S.J. (1996) The relationship of partner support to outcome for teenage mothers and their children: a review, *Journal of Adolescent Health,* 19: 86–93.

Rustemier, S. (2002) Inclusive Education Guide, Studies for Inclusive Education, *Education,* 36: 1–12.

Rutter, M. (1985) Family and school influences on behavioural development, *Journal of Child Psychology and Psychiatry,* 26: 349–68.

Rutter, M. (2005) Incidence of autistic spectrum disorders: changes over time and their meaning, *Acta Paediatrica,* 94: 2–15.

Rutter, M., Maughan, S. and Smith, A. (1979) *15,000 Hours: Secondary Schools and their Impact upon Children.* London: Open Books.

Rutter, M. and O'Connar, T.G. (2004) Are there biological programming for psychological behaviour?, *Developmental Paediatrics,* 40: 81–94.

Rutter, M. and Quinton, D. (1984) *Parenting Breakdown.* Chichester: Wiley.

Rutter, M. and Smith, D.J. (eds) (1995) *Psychosocial Disorders in Young People: Time Trends and their Causes.* Chichester: Wiley.

Salovey, P., Bedell, B., Detweiler, J. and Mayer, J.D. (2000) Current direction in emotional intelligence research, in M. Lewis and J.M. Haviland-Jones (eds) *Handbook of Emotions,* 2nd ed. New York: Guildford Press.

Sampson, R.J. and Laub, J.H. (1993) *Crime in the Making: Pathways and Turnings Points through Life.* Cambridge, MA: Harvard University Press.

Savin-Williams, R.C. and Ream, G.L. (2003) Suicide attempts among sexual minority male youth, *Journal of Clinical Child and Adolescent Psychology,* 32: 509–22.

Scott, S., Knapp, M., Henderson, J. and Maughan, B. (2001) Financial cost of social exclusion: follow-up study of antisocial children into adulthood, *British Medical Journal,* 323: 191–203.

Scottish Office (1998) *Social Exclusion.* Edinburgh: Scottish Office.

Seeman, S., Lauby, J. and Cohen, A. (2003) Factors associated with perceptions and decisional balance of condom use with a new partner among women at risk of HIV infection, *Women's Health,* 37: 53–69.

Sherraden, M. and Zhan, M. (2003) Assets, expectations and children's educational achievement in female-headed households, *Social Service Review,* 77: 191–211.

Simonoff, E., Elander, J., Pickles, A. and Rutter, M. (2004) Predictors of antisocial personality. Continuities from childhood to adult life, *British Journal of Psychiatry,* 184: 118–27.

Smith, C.A. and Farrington, D.P. (2004) Continuities in antisocial behaviour and parenting across three generations, *Journal of Child Psychology and Psychiatry.* 45: 23–47.

Smith, P.K., Cowie, H., Olafsson, R.S. and Wenxin, Z. (2002) Definitions of bullying: a comparison of terms, uses, age and gender differences in a 14-country comparison, *Child Development,* 73: 1119–33.

Smith, P.K., Talamelli, L., Cowie, H., Naylor, P. and Chauhan, P. (2004) Profiles of non-victims, escaped victims, continuing victims and new victims of school bullying, *British Journal of Educational Psychology,* 74: 565–81.

Social Exclusion Unit (1998a) *Reducing Teenage Pregnancy.* London: HMSO.

Social Exclusion Unit (1998b) *Truancy and Social Exclusion.* London: HMSO.

Social Exclusion Unit (1998c) *Homelessness and Social Exclusion.* London: HMSO.

Stallard, P., Thomason, D. and Churchyard, S. (2003) The mental health of young people attending a Youth Offending Team: a descriptive study, *Journal of Adolescence,* 26: 33–43.

Stanistreet, D. and Jefffrey, V. (2003) Accident or suicide? Predictors of coroners' decisions in suicide and accident verdicts, *Medicine, Science and Law,* 41: 111–15.

Stephens, P., Kyriacou, C. and Tonnessen, F.E. (2005) Student teachers' views of pupils' misbehaviour in classrooms: a Norwegian and an English setting compared, *Scandinavian Journal of Educational Research,* 49: 203–16.

Stewart, J. and Rhoden, M. (2003) A review of social housing regeneration in the London Borough of Brent, *Journal of the Royal Society of Health,* 123: 23–32.

Storch, E.A., Roth, D.A., Coles, M.E. and Moser, J. (2004) The measurement and impact of childhood teasing in a sample of young adults, *Journal of Anxiety Disorder,* 18: 681–94.

Sutherland, I. and Shepherd, J.P. (2001) Social dimensions of adolescent substance abuse, *Addiction,* 96: 445–58.

Targosz, S., Bebbington, P., Lewis, G. and Meltzer, H. (2003) Lone mothers, social exclusion and depression, *Psychological Medicine,* 33: 715–22.

Taylor, A. (2004) Alarm bells ring in the staff-room; over drive to reduce exclusions, *Community Care,* 1526: 16–17.

Taylor, J., Iacono, W.G. and McGue, M. (2000) Evidence for genetic aetiology of early onset delinquency, *Journal of Abnormal Psychology,* 109: 634–43.

Thapar, A., Harrington, R. and McGuffin, P. (2001) Examining the comorbidity of ADHD-related behaviours and conduct problems using a twin study design, *British Journal of Psychiatry,* 179: 335–8.

Thompson, W. and Pritchard, C. (1987) *Public Attitudes towards People of Minority Groups.* Report to City of Southampton Equal Opportunities Sub-Committee.

Thornberry, T.P., Freeman-Gallant, A., Lizotte, A.J. and Smith, C.A. (2003) Linked lives: inter-generatational transmission of antisocial behaviour, *Journal of Abnormal Child Psychology,* 31: 171–84.

Tilley, N. (1993) *Understanding Car Park Crime and CCTV: Evaluation Lessons from Safer Cities,* Paper 42, Crime Prevention Unit, Home Office. London: HMSO.

UN (United Nations) (1948) *Declaration of Human Rights.* Geneva: United Nations Organisation.

UNHCR (United Nations High Commission for Refugees) (1968) *Convention Relating to the Status of Refugees: Augmented by the 1967 Article 1A(20).* New York: United Nations.

Van der Wal, M.F., de Wit, C.A. and Hirasing, R.A. (2003) Psychosocial health among young victims and offenders of direct and indirect bullying, *Paediatrics,* 111: 312–17.

Verdejo, A., Orozoc-Gimenez, C. and Perez-Garies, M. (2004) The impact exerted by the severity of recreational drug abuse on the different components of the executive function, *Review of Neurology,* 38: 1109–16.

Walker, O.S., Petrill, S.A., Spinath, F.M. and Plomin, R. (2004) Nature, nurture and academic achievement: a twin study of teacher assessments of 7-year-olds, *British Journal of Educational Psychology,* 74: 323–42.

Warner, J., McKeown, E. and King, M. (2004) Rates and predictors of mental illness in gay men: results from a survey based in England and Wales, *British Journal of Psychiatry,* 185: 479–85.

Watling, R. (2004) Helping them out: the role of teachers and health care professionals in the exclusion of pupils with special needs, *Emotional and Behavioural Difficulties*, 9: 8–27.

Webb, R. and Vulliamy, G. (2003) Bridging the cultural divide: the role of the home–school support worker, *British Educational Research Journal*, 29: 34–48.

Webber, M. and Huxley, P. (2004) Social exclusion and risk of emergency compulsory admission: a case-control study, *Social Psychiatry and Psychiatric Epidemiology*, 39: 1000–9.

West, D.J. and Farrington, D.P. (1973) *Who Becomes Delinquent?* London: Heinemann.

Weyts, A. (2004) The educational achievements of 'looked-after children'. Do welfare systems make a difference?, *Adoption and Fostering*, 28: 7–19.

WHO (World Health Organisation) (2005) *Mortality Data Base Table [1]*, www.who.whosis/mort/table1.cfm.

Wild, L.G., Fisher, A.J., Bhana, A. and Lombard, C. (2004) Associations among adolescent risk behaviours and self-esteem in six domains, *Journal of Child Psychology and Psychiatry*, 45: 1454–67.

Williams, J. (1990) An analysis of dysfunctional stress (Payne Model) in voluntary and statutory service agencies. Unpublished MPhil thesis, University of Southampton.

Williams, S., Hickman, M. and Avelyn, P. (2005) Hospital admissions for drug and alcohol use in people aged under 35, *British Medical Journal*, 330: 115–18.

Willoughby, M., Kuperscmidt, J. and Bryant, D. (2001) Overt and covert dimensions of antisocial behaviour in early childhood, *Journal of Abnormal Child Psychology*, 29: 177–87.

Wilson, E.O. (1998) *Consilence.* London: Little, Brown.

Zunz, O. (ed.) (2000) *Social Contracts under Stress: The Middle Classes of America, Europe and Japan at the Turn of the Century.* New York: Russell Sage.

Index

Locators shown in *italics* refer to tables.

Abbott, D., 98
abuse, child
  school staff responsibilities, 138–9
abuse, drugs
  adolescent behaviour, 25, 26, *25–6*
  school policies, 108–11
'accelerated learning', 155
accessibility, school
  strategies for disabled students,
    99–100
accountability, education alienation
  project, 43–4
adolescents *see* young adults
ADHD (Attention Deficit Hyperactivity
  Disorder), 19–20, 170–72
Aiming High (DfES, 2003), 99
Ainsow, M., 7
Ainsworth, J., 16
Alan, case study of, 42–3
Alcohol Concern, 109–10
alcohol consumption
  health effects on young adults, 31,
    32, *32*
  prevalence among young adults,
    23–6, *24, 25–6*, 31–2
  school policies, 108–11
Alice, case study of, 49–50
alienation, educational
  influences, 14–20, 46–8
  socio-economic impact, 3–6
  see also education alienation
    project; inclusion, educational
Alliance for Inclusive Education, 84
Andreasson, S., 30
Anti-Social Behaviour Act (2003), 119,
  120
Arum, R., 21

ASDs (Autistic Spectrum Disorders),
  162
Asperger Syndrome, 162–5
Assessment for Learning, 152–5
asylum seekers, educational inclusion,
  107–8
attendance, school
  case study, 121–2
  impact of individual tutoring,
    123–4
  student attitudes, 60–61, *61*
  targets, 120–21, *120*
  see also parents; truancy
Attention Deficit Hyperactivity
  Disorder (ADHD), 19–20, 170–72
attitudes, young adults

  alcohol consumption, 23–6, *24, 25–
    6, 31–2*
  drugs, 25, 26, *25–6*
  implications for school policies,
    108–113
  school, 58–61, *59, 61*
Attlee School
  alienation project cost savings, *75*
  educational outcomes, 61
  involvement in alienation project,
    35–45
  social profile of families, 46–8, *47,
    57*
  student attitudes and behaviour,
    57–8, *58,* 60–61, *61*
  student counselling, 48–51, *50–51*
Autistic Spectrum Disorders (ASDs),
  162
Aynsley-Green, A., 188
Ayton, A., 33

Baldwin, J., 44–5
behaviour, young adults
  implications for school policies, 113
  school, 58–61, *59, 61*
  socio-sexual, 23–9, *24, 25–6, 26–7,
    27–8*
  see also bullying; drugs, abuse;
    truancy
Behaviour and Attendance Strategy
  (DfES), 118
Behaviour Improvement Programme
  (BIP) (DfES), 118
Bennett, N., 21
Bevan School
  alienation project cost savings, *75*
  educational outcomes, 61
  involvement in alienation project,
    35–45
  social profile of families, 59
  student attitudes and behaviour,
    58–60, *59,* 60–61, *61*
  student counselling, 48–51, *50–51*
'binge drinking'
  health effects on young adults,
    31–2, *32*
  prevalence among young adults,
    25–6, *25–6*
BIP (Behaviour Improvement
  Programme) (DfES), 118
Blair, A. (Tony), 6
boys, Afro-Caribbean
  culture and educational inclusion,
    97–9
Brian, case study of, 50
Brighouse, T., 98
Britain, A., 31
Brooks-Gunn, J., 17
Buchanan, A., 14
bullying, 20–21, 40–41

CAF (Common Assessment
  Framework) (school attendance),
    123–4, 139
cannabis, impact on behaviour,
    30–31

Centre for Studies in Inclusive
  Education, 85, 86
children
  abuse of *see* abuse, child
  importance of social inclusion, 3
  media image, 117
  protection of *see* protection, child
  see also students; young adults
Children Act (1989), 43, 119, 142
Children Act (2004), 139
Children's Taskforce (Dept. of Health),
    188
*Choice for Parents, the Best Start for
  Children* (2004), 89
chronic fatigue syndrome, 20
Churchill, W., 8
Churchill School
  alienation project cost savings,
    73–7, *75*
  educational outcomes, 61
  involvement in alienation project,
    35–45
  social profile of families, 46–7, *47,*
    57
  student attitudes and behaviour,
    57–8, *58,* 60–61, *61*
  student counselling, 48–51, *50–51*
class, social
  influence on educational
    alienation, 15–16
classes, size of
  importance in educational
    inclusion, 21
Climbie, Victoria, case of, 138–9
Cole, P.M., 14
collaboration, inter-agency
  education alienation project, 43
Common Assessment Framework
  (CAF) (school attendance),
    123–4, 139
Connexions (careers service), 184
coordinator teams (education
  alienation project), 38
Council for Disabled Children, 85
counselling, child
  availability in schools, 139–40

education alienation project, 48–51, *50–51*
skills required, 168–70
crime, influence on educational alienation, 46–7
curricula, flexible
as aid to educational inclusion, 92–5

Dakar Framework for Action, 85
Danckaerts, M., 19
Davies, L., 141
death and disease, effect of binge drinking, 31–2, *32*
Deliberate Self Harm (DSH)
incidence among young adults, 33
development, sexual
implications for socio-educational inclusion, 111–12
see also orientation, sexual
Disability Discrimination Act (1995 & 2001), 99
disadvantage, educational
socio-economic impact, 3–6
disaffection, educational *see* alienation, educational
disease and death, effect of binge drinking, 31–2, *32*
Disraeli School
alienation project cost savings, 73–7, *75*
educational outcomes, 61
involvement in alienation project, 35–45
social profile of families, 59
student attitudes and behaviour, 58–60, *59*, 60–61, *61*
student counselling, 48–51, *50–51*
Donne, J., 17
drinking (alcohol) *see* alcohol consumption; 'binge drinking'
'dropouts', educational
socio-economic impact, 3–6
drugs
abuse *see* abuse, drugs
impact on behaviour, 30–31
Drugs Abuse: guidance for Schools (DfEE,

2002), 108–9
DSH (Deliberate Self Harm)
incidence among young adults, 33
dyscalculia, 172–7
dyslexia, 172–7
dyspraxia, 177–8

EAL (English as an Additional Language) students
and educational inclusion, 105–6
'ecstasy', effects of use, 31
education
academic outcomes, 61
socio-economic influences on achievement, 13–17
see also inclusion, educational; learning; schools; staff, school
education, health
programmes of, 41
education, vocational, 95
Education Act (1993), 84, 86
Education Act, (1996), 85, 86, 119
Education Act, (2002), 138
Education Act, (2005), viii
education alienation project
client views, 52–6
cost benefits, 73–7, *75*
evaluation, 44–5
organisation and action, 34–44, 48–51, *50–51*
see also names of participating schools eg Attlee School; Bevan School; Churchill School; Disraeli School
Education of Asylum-seeker Pupils, The (2003), 108
Education of Young People in Public Care (DfES), 143
'Education Other Than At School' (EOTAS), role of local authorities, 184–5
Education Social Workers (ESWs), 117
Education Supervision Order (ESO), 119
Education Welfare Officers (EWOs), 117

Emotional Intelligence (Goleman), 129
English as an Additional Language
  (EAL) students
  and educational inclusion, 105–6
EOTAS ('Education Other Than At
  School'), role of local authorities,
  184–5
ESO (Education Supervision Order),
  119
ESWs (Education Social Workers), 117
ethnicity, influence on educational
  alienation, 16
Every Child Matters (DfES, 2003), viii,
  13, 85–6, 116, 139, 180–81,
  186–7, 188
EWOs (Education Welfare Officers),
  117
Excellence in Cities Evaluation (2003), 98
exclusion, social
  categories at risk, 10–11
  definition and characteristics, 4
  philosophy and politics, 6–10
  socio-economic impact, 5–6
exclusions, school
  case study, 131–5
  characteristics, 131
  psycho-social implications, 22
'extended schools', 88–92
Eysenck, H., 8, 17–18

families
  changing structures, 14–15
  factors influencing educational
    alienation, 46–8
  see also parents
Farrell, M., 7
*Fast Track to Prosecution for School Non-
  Attendance*, 118–19
females, young
  drink patterns, 32
fixed-term school exclusions, 131–4
Flouri, E., 14
Forth, M., 117
Fox, C., 189
freedom, professional
  education alienation project, 43–4

genetics, role in educational
  alienation, 17–20
Glasgow, K.L., 14
Goleman, D., 129
gypsies, culture and educational
  inclusion, 96–7

Hackney, Borough of
  education achievement among
    Afro-Caribbeans, 98
Hawton, K., 33
headteachers
  role in education alienation project,
    38
  role in social inclusion, 11–12
health education, programmes of, 41
Healthy Alliance research project,
  81–2, 186
'Healthy Minds' initiative (2005), viii,
  85, 186
Heath, E., 8
home visits, method to enhance
  parental-school interest, 159
homelessness, and educational
  alienation, 17
homosexuality, implications for socio-
  educational inclusion, 112–13
housing, quality of
  influence on educational
    alienation, 16–17
Howard, M., 117

Immigration and Asylum Act (1999), 107
inclusion, educational
  and English as Additional
    Language, 105–6
  characteristics, 87–8
  disability policies, 99–105
  policy history, 84–7
  see also alienation, educational
  see also influences eg classes, size of;
    curricula, flexible; life chances;
    sexuality, student
inclusion, educational, *cont.*
  see also recipients eg asylum seekers;

boys, Afro-Caribbean; gypsies; refugees
inclusion, social
    definition and characteristics, 4
    ideologies and politics, 6–10
    socio-economic impact, 5–6
    see also influences eg homosexuality
    see also key players eg headteachers; schools
    see also exclusion, social
Inclusion Charter (Centre for Studies in Inclusive Education), 85, 86
Inclusive Education at Work (OECD), 85
Inclusive Education System, The (Alliance for Inclusive Education), 84
Inclusive Schooling (2002), 85, 86
Independent Race and Refugee News Network, 107
Index for Inclusion (Centre for Studies in Inclusive Education), 86
intelligence, types, 129–31, *156–9*

Jack, case study of, 175–6
job satisfaction (teacher), 64–6

Kelly, R., 118
Knapp, M., 14
Kristensen, S.M., 19–20

LACs (Looked-After Children)
    case studies of, 141–2, 144–51
    responsibilities of school staff, 140–41, 142–3
Lanning, P., 139
learning
    academic outcomes, 61
    styles, 155–9, *156–8*
    see *also* 'Assessment for Learning'; curricula, flexible; education; intelligence, types; schools; teachers
Learning Trust, The, 98
Leary, M.R., 18
Leventhal, T., 17
Levitas, R., 7–10
Lewis, I., 118

life chances, influence on educational inclusion, 15–16
literacy
    student assessment, 126–7
    teaching materials, 127–9
    see also dyslexia
local authorities, role in education provision, 181–4
Looked-After Children (LACs)
    case studies of, 141–2, 144–51
    responsibilities of school staff, 140–41, 142–3
Loyola, I. (Saint), 3

MacDonald, G., 18
McPherson, K., 31
males, young
    health effects of alcohol consumption, 32, *32*
Mary, case study of, 121–2
Maslow, A.H.
    triangle of human needs, 91–2
Meeting Special Educational Needs (DfEE, 1998), 85
men, young
    health effects of alcohol consumption, 32, *32*
Merrell, C., 19
Milliband, D., 118
misuse, substance
    school policies, 111
    see also abuse, drugs
monitoring, education
    role of local authorities, 182–3
    see also Ofsted
Moral Underclass Discourse (Murray), 7–8
morbidity and mortality, effect of binge drinking, 31–2, *32*
Moses, case study of, 93–5
mothers, teenage
    impact on offspring educational inclusion, 15
    implications for schools, 113–15
Murray, C., 7–8
Myung, case study of, 135–7

National Centre for Social Research (NatCen), 109
National Child Development Study, 14
National Foundation for Educational Research (NFER), 109
National Health Service (NHS)
    political consensus concerning, 7
neighbourhood, influence on educational alienation, 16–17
NFER (National Foundation for Educational Research), 109
NHS (National Health Service)
    political consensus concerning, 7

O'Donnell, D.A., 21
OECD (Organisation for Economic Cooperation and Development), 85
Ofsted (Office for Standards in Education)
    inspection criteria, 180–81
Oliver, J., 13, 14
Organisation for Economic Cooperation and Development (OECD), 85
orientation, sexual
    implications for student inclusion, 112–13
    see also development, sexual

Paddy, case study of, 141–2
Parenting Orders, 120
parents
    impact on educational inclusion, 14–15
    influence on school attendance, 135–7
    support in correction of educational alienation, 39
    views on alienation project, 52–4
Pasteror, R.N., 19
peers, child
    psycho-social importance, 20
Penalty Notices, (truancy), 119
permanent school exclusions, 134–5

personality, human
    role in educational alienation, 17–20
Plomin, R., 19
Policy Statement on Inclusive Education for Children with Disabilities (1996), 85
Popper, K., 18
Post Traumatic Stress Disorder (PTSD), 108
poverty, family
    impact on educational alienation, 15–16
Pritchard, R., 17
probation, influence on educational alienation, 46–7
Project Primary Teacher (PPT) (education alienation project), 36–9
Project Social Workers (PSWs) (education alienation project), 35–9, 43
protection, child
    importance in education alienation project, 40
    responsibilities of staff, 138–9
PTSD (Post Traumatic Stress Disorder), 108
pupils *see* students

Quinton, D., 17

reading
    student assessment, 126–7
    teaching materials, 127–9
    see also dyslexia
Redistributionism (Levitas), 7–10
refugees, educational inclusion, 107–8
resources, teaching
    for literacy, 127–9
    role of local authorities in supply, 182–3
Reuban, C.A., 19
Richman, J., 14
Rodham, K., 33
Romanies (WROM)

culture and educational inclusion, 96–7
Rutter, M., 17

Sajed, case study of, 100–105
Salamanca Statement (UNESCO, 1994), 84–5
Salovey, P., 129
SAOs (School Attendance Officers), 117
Sarah, case study of, 131–4
schizophrenia, and cannabis use, 30–31
School Attendance Officers (SAOs), 117
School Support Workers, 21
schools
    and student exclusion, 22, 131–5
    importance to children, 21–2
    role in social inclusion, 11–12
    transition adjustment of students, 40
    see also name eg Attlee School; Bevan School; Churchill School; Disraeli School
    see also types of school eg 'extended schools'
schools, special
    implication of inclusion policies, 87
Secondary Project Teacher (SPT) (education alienation project), 36–7
self harm, deliberate (DSH)
    incidence among young adults, 33
Semantic Pragmatic Disorder (SPD), 166–8
SENs (Special Educational Needs)
    categories of educational support, 159–60
    teaching strategies, 125–37, 178–9
    see also disorder eg Asperger Syndrome; Autistic Spectrum Disorders
sexuality, student
    implications for socio-educational inclusion, 111–13

Sexually Transmitted Diseases (STDs), 31–2
Shaw, G.B., 9, 15
Smith, P.K., 19–20
smoking, prevalence among young adults, 23–6, *24, 25–6,* 58
smoking, parental
    impact on child behaviour, 29–30
social capital, impact on educational alienation, 15–16
social exclusion see exclusion, social
Social Exclusion (Scottish Office, 1998), 4
social inclusion see inclusion, social
Social Inclusion: pupil support (DfES, 1999), 92
Social Inclusion Unit (Cabinet Office), 6, 10
Social Integration Discourse (Levitas), 7–9
social services departments (SSDs)
    and family contact, 46–7, *47*
social workers (education alienation project), 35–7
SPD (Semantic Pragmatic Disorder), 166–8
special educational needs (SENs)
    categories of support, 159–60
    teaching strategies, 125–37, 178–9
    see also disorder eg Asperger Syndrome; Autistic Spectrum Disorders
Special Educational Needs in England (DfES or DfEE, 2001), 87, 160
Specific Learning Difficulties (SpLD) (SEN category), **161**
    see also dyslexia; dyscalculia
Speech and Learning Difficulties (SEN category), 161
SPT (Secondary Project Teacher) (education alienation project), 36–7
SSDs (Social Services Departments)
    and family contact, 46–7, *47*
staff, school
    responsibilities regarding child

abuse, 138–9
see also headteachers; teachers
Statement of Special Educational
    Needs, 160
STDs (sexually transmitted diseases),
    31–2
Stephen, case study of, 176–7
stress, teacher, 66–73, *67*
students
    categories at risk of sex, 10–11
    school behaviour, 58–61, *59, 61*
    school excluded, 22, 131–5
    views on education alienation
      project, 54–6
students, disabled
    inclusion policies, 99–105
substance misuse
    school policies, 111
    see also abuse, drugs
suicide, incidence among young
    adults, 33

targets, education alienation project,
    34–5
Targosz, S., 16–17
Taylor, A., 18
teachers
    role in social inclusion, 11–12
    views of alienation project, 67–73,
      67–8
    views of teaching, 63–7, *63, 67*
teaching, individual
    impact on school attendance, 123–4
teams (education alienation project)
    activities, 41–3
    roles, 35–8
teenage mothers
    impact on offspring educational
      inclusion, 15
    implications for schools, 113–15
teenagers *see* young adults
temperament, human
    role in educational alienation, 17–20
Thapar, A., 19
Thatcher, M., 8
Thornberry, T.P., 14

Travellers (WIRT)
    culture and educational inclusion,
      96–7
truancy, 41, 57–8, 116–20
tutoring, individual
    impact on school attendance, 123–4
Tymms, P.B., 19

UN Convention on the Rights of the
    Child (1989), 84
UN Educational, Scientific and
    Cultural Organisation
    (UNESCO), 84–5
UN Standard Rules on the Equalisation
    of Opportunities for Persons
    with Disabilities (1993), 84
underachievers, educational
    socio-economic impact, 3–6
unemployment, influence on
    educational alienation, 46
United Nations *see* UN

Verbal Intelligence Test (Wechsler), 8
visits, home
    method to enhance parent-school
      interest, 159
volatile substance abuse (VSA)
    school policies, 111
Vulliamy, G., 21

Walker, O.S., 18–19
Warnock, M., 159
Webb, R., 21
welfare action
    education alienation project, 48–51,
      50–51
Whitby, M., 129–30
Wilson, E.O., 18
Winston, case study of, 144–51
WIRT (Travellers)
    culture and educational inclusion,
      96–7
women, young
    drink patterns, 32
Wordsworth, W., vii, 190
work, education for, 95

World Education Forum, 85
WROM (Romanies)
    culture and educational inclusion,
      96–7

young adults
    attitudes to health, 27–9, *27–8*
    educational influence of
      homelessness, 17
    health effects of binge drinking,
      31–2, *32*
    prevalence of suicide, 33

    school behaviour, 58–61, *59, 61*
    socio-sexual behaviour, 23–6, *24,
      25–6, 26–7*
    see also students; teenage mothers
Young People's Drinking Factsheet
    (Alcohol Concern), 109–10
Youth Inclusion Project, 185
Youth Justice Survey (MORI), 117

Zunz, O., 10

LEARNING WITHOUT LIMITS

Susan Hart, Annabelle Dixon, Mary Jane Drummond and Donald McIntyre

This book describes and explores the importance of using ways of teaching that are free from determinist beliefs about ability. It draws on a partnership research project, based at the Faculty of Education, University of Cambridge, which involved case studies of nine teachers' classroom practice.

From these case studies the authors have constructed a model of pedagogy based on the principle of transformability: the principle that children's futures as learners are not fixed or pre-determined, since teachers can act to remove the limits on learning created by ability-focused teaching. The authors show how transformability-based teaching could play a central and critical role in the construction of an alternative improvement agenda, offering a focus for school and curriculum development that is rooted in teachers' own values, commitments and aspirations.

The book will appeal to teachers, lecturers and policy makers, and to everyone who has a stake in how contemporary education and practice affect children's future lives and life chances.

Contents: Foreword by Clyde Chitty / Acknowledgements / **Part one: Beyond ability-based teaching and learning** / Ability, educability and the current improvement agenda / What's wrong with ability labelling? / The Learning Without Limits project: methods and approaches / **Part two: Accounts of the teachers' practices** / Introduction / Anne's approach: 'They all have their different ways to go' / Claire's approach: 'a thinking classroom' / Alison's approach: 'an open invitation' / Narinder's approach: 'the promise of tomorrow' / Patrick's approach: 'only connect' / Nicky's approach: 'Step back and look at the children' / Yahi's approach: 'raising the level of trust' / Julie's approach: 'access, security, success' / Non's approach: 'the bridge between values and practice' / **Part three: the core idea of transformability** / Transforming the capacity to learn / Purposes and principles in practice / Young people's perspectives on learning without limits / Framing learning without limits teaching: contexts and retrospectives / Towards an alternative improvement agenda / Bibliography

296pp   0 335 21259 X (EAN: 9 780335 212590) Paperback
        0 335 21260 3 (EAN: 9 780335 212606) Hardback

SES Awards 2005: Second Prize

TEACHERS AND ASSISTANTS WORKING TOGETHER

Karen Vincett, Hilary Cremin and Gary Thomas

"Few areas of education can equal the growth rate of that for teaching assistants over the past seven years, doubling to more than 133,000 in England between 1997 to 2004. TAs are vital in the development of inclusive education, yet their status, pay, conditions, qualifications and their relationship with classroom teachers are all of deep concern in the majority of cases. This excellent, practical book is a welcome and much-needed authoritative study of the all-important relationship between TA and teacher."

Mark Vaughan OBE, Founder and
Co-Director, Centre for Studies on Inclusive Education

This book is for teachers and teaching assistants seeking to improve the ways in which they work together to meet the needs of children in their classes. It outlines the thinking behind the employment of teaching assistants in the classroom and spells out some of the teamworking opportunities and problems that can arise. Drawing on research, it explores ways in which teachers and teaching assistants can work together to support children's learning and examines different models of working together.

This unique book provides:

- Highly effective models for working together, tried and tested in schools
- A practical section with activities, hand-outs and resources that teachers can use to develop these models in their own schools

This is a key text for classroom teachers, teaching assistants, trainee teachers and postgraduate education students, and those studying foundation degrees for teaching assistants. It is also of use to parents, headteachers, educational psychologists, and other support personnel.

Contents: Preface / Acknowledgements / **Part 1: Theory, Research and Practice on Teamwork in Classrooms** / Introduction / The rise of the teaching assistant / Teacher-TA partnership working / Meeting children's needs – reflective practice, reflective teamwork / Three models of teamwork in classrooms / Action research into the models – phase 1 / Themes from using the models in practice – phase 1 / Action research into the models Phase 2 – 'Working Together' / **Part 2: Implementation in Schools** / Introduction / Using the models / CPD activities / A Toolkit for classroom research / References / Index.

192pp   0 335 21695 1 (EAN: 9 780335 216956) Paperback
         0 335 21696 X (EAN: 9 780335 216963) Hardback

LADS AND LADETTES IN SCHOOL

Carolyn Jackson

This innovative book looks at how and why girls and boys adopt 'laddish' behaviours in schools. It examines the ways in which students negotiate pressures to be popular and 'cool' in school alongside pressures to perform academically. It also deals with the fears of academic and social failure that influence pupils' school lives and experiences.

Drawing extensively on the voices of students in secondary schools, it explores key questions about laddish behaviours, such as:

- Are girls becoming more laddish – and if so, which girls?
- Do boys and girls have distinctive versions of laddishness?
- Do laddish behaviours lead to the same outcomes?
- What are the implications for teachers and schools?

The author weaves together key contemporary theories and research on masculinities and femininities with social and psychological theories and research on academic motives and goals, in order to understand the complexities of girls' and boys' behaviours.

This topical book is key reading for students, academics and researchers in education, sociology and psychology, as well as school teachers and education policy makers.

Contents: Introduction - **Part 1: Theoretical frameworks: motives and behaviours** / Academic motives: achievement goal theory and self-worth protection / Social motives: constructing 'appropriate' masculinities and femininities / The interplay between academic and gender identities / **Part 2: From theory to practice and back again** / Testing times: pressures and fears at school / School work or 'cool' work: competing goals at school / Self-defence: techniques and strategies for protecting self-worth / Balancing acts: who can balance the books and a social life? / **Part 3: Implications and ways forward** / Implications for teachers today / Implications for the policy makers of tomorrow / Conclusions.

176pp   0 335 21770 2 (EAN: 9 780335 217700) Paperback
         0 335 21771 0 (EAN: 9 780335 217717) Hardback

RAISING BOYS' ACHIEVEMENT IN SECONDARY SCHOOLS
Issues, Dilemmas and Opportunities

Mike Younger and Molly Warrington with Ros McLellan

"Boys' achievement has attracted great attention in recent years in many countries. This comprehensive book based on sound research in schools provides practical insights into how the achievement of boys and girls can be raised. It reminds us that it is not all boys or no girls who underachieve. It demonstrates the respective roles of teaching and learning, school culture and social factors. No easy answers but excellent ideas backed by evidence from authoritative, thorough researchers with a firm basis in schools."

Judy Sebba, Professor of Education, University of Sussex

"Teachers will find this book invaluable. It is based on quality research which actually evaluates the impact of the various strategies suggested for raising boys' achievement. What is more, in contrast to many of the more 'quick-fix' works in this field, the authors' discussion and analysis is measured and nuanced, and supported by an in-depth understanding of the wealth of theory and research around gender and achievement. It provides a welcome and weighty contribution to an ever controversial debate."

Becky Francis, London Metropolitan University

In this important book, the authors evaluate different approaches and advocate practical, evidence-based strategies, which have the potential to promote boys' as well as girls' achievements. The approaches are discussed within the context of inclusivity, acknowledging the diverse needs and interests of different boys and the invisibility and continuing disadvantage of some girls. The book begins and ends with reflections from students of their own school experiences, and makes practical recommendations for the future.

This book draws upon empirical research and work initiated as part of the DfES project on Raising Boys' Achievement. It brings together theoretical and practical issues, and reflects upon the construction of the debate about boys' apparent under-achievement from the perspectives of girls as well as boys. The authors critically explore notions of under-achievement and 'value added', and consider how useful the concept of the 'gender gap' is in advancing the debates.

Raising Boys' Achievement in Secondary Schools is key reading for undergraduate and postgraduate Education students, PGCE students, headteachers, senior managers within schools and local education authorities, and policy makers.

192pp   0 335 21608 0 (EAN: 9 780335 216086) Paperback
        0 335 21609 9 (EAN: 9 780335 216093) Hardback